# STUDENT MANUAL FOR THEORY AND PRACTICE OF GROUP COUNSELING

D1449691

# SEVENTH EDITION

# STUDENT MANUAL FOR THEORY AND PRACTICE OF GROUP COUNSELING

## Gerald Corey

*California State University, Fullerton*
*Diplomate in Counseling Psychology,*
*American Board of Professional Psychology*

THOMSON

BROOKS/COLE

Australia • Brazil • Canada • Mexico • Singapore
Spain • United Kingdom • United States

© 2008 Thomson Brooks/Cole, a part of The Thomson Corporation. Thomson, the Star logo, and Brooks/Cole are trademarks used herein under license.

ALL RIGHTS RESERVED. No part of this work covered by the copyright hereon may be reproduced or used in any form or by any means—graphic, electronic, or mechanical, including photocopying, recording, taping, Web distribution, information storage and retrieval systems, or in any other manner—without the written permission of the publisher.

Printed in the United States of America

1  2  3  4  5  6  7   10  09  08  07

Printer: West Group

Library of Congress Control Number: to come

ISBN-13: 978-0-495-11523-6
ISBN-10: 0-495-11523-1

Cover Image: © Jim Brandenburg/Minden Pictures

**Thomson Higher Education**
**10 Davis Drive**
**Belmont, CA 94002-3098**
**USA**

For more information about our products,
contact us at:
**Thomson Learning Academic Resource Center**
**1-800-423-0563**

For permission to use material from this text or
product, submit a request online at
**http://www.thomsonrights.com.**
Any additional questions about permissions
can be submitted by email to
**thomsonrights@thomson.com.**

# Contents

# PART ONE

# BASIC ELEMENTS OF GROUP PROCESS: AN OVERVIEW

# CHAPTER ONE

# Introduction to Group Work

This student manual is designed to accompany *Theory and Practice of Group Counseling* (seventh edition), by Gerald Corey (Thomson–Brooks/Cole, 2008). It is intended to help you gain practical experience in the various theoretical approaches to group work and to stimulate you to think about ethical and practical issues that are typically encountered by group leaders.

The design of the manual is based on the assumption that you will learn best by becoming actively involved in the learning process and by actually experiencing group concepts and techniques. Reading about them provides a foundation, but this knowledge remains abstract unless you can see how these theories are actually part of the group process.

Much of this material consists of things you can think about, experiment with, and do on your own. There are also many exercises you can practice in small groups, both as a leader and as a member. You will be provided with opportunities to function in numerous role-playing situations. I encourage you to modify these exercises so that they will become personally meaningful. The material in the "Exercises and Activities" sections includes:

- Self-inventories to assess your attitudes about various theories
- Open-ended questions for you to explore
- Ideas and suggestions for role playing
- Techniques for group interaction
- Practical problems that occur in groups
- Group exercises for experiential practice
- Questions for reflection and discussion
- Suggestions of things you can do to apply what you are learning in the course to yourself as a person and as a group leader

There is more material in this manual than a given course can cover thoroughly. However, my preference is to provide a wide variety of activities so that you can select the ones you find most meaningful. This manual helps you focus as you read, personalize the material, and apply it to the practice of group counseling.

## About the Textbook

*Theory and Practice of Group Counseling* will introduce you to some basic issues of group leadership and group membership, and it will show you how groups function. Part One treats the basic elements of group process and practice that you will need to know regardless of the types of groups you may lead or the theoretical orientation you prefer. Chapter 2 deals with basic concerns of group leadership, such as the personal characteristics of effective leaders, the problems they face, the different styles of leadership, the range of specific skills required for effective leading, and the components of an effective multicultural group counselor. Chapter 3 addresses important ethical issues that you will inevitably encounter as you lead groups. The emphasis is on the rights of group members and the responsibilities of group leaders. In Chapters 4 and 5 you are introduced to the major developmental tasks confronting a group as it goes through its various stages from formation to termination, including evaluation and follow-up. The central characteristics of the stages that make up the life history of a group are examined, with special attention paid to the major functions of the group leader at each stage. These chapters also focus on the functions of the members of a group and the possible problems that are associated with each stage in the group's evolution.

Part Two of the text is designed to provide you with a good overview of a variety of theoretical models underlying group counseling so that you can see the connection between theory and practice. Eleven models have been selected to present a balanced perspective. Each of these theoretical orientations has something valid to offer you as a future group leader.

To provide a framework that will help you integrate the theoretical models, these 11 chapters follow a common outline. They present the key concepts of each theory and their implications for group practice, outline the role and functions of the group leader according to the particular theory, discuss how each theory is applied to group practice, and describe the major techniques employed under each theory. Illustrative examples make the use of these techniques more concrete. Each chapter contains my evaluation of the approach under discussion—an evaluation based on what I consider to be its major strengths and limitations—and a brief description of how the approach can be applied to group counseling in the schools and with diverse client populations.

You will learn some essential aspects of the therapies explored, but this book is not designed to make you an expert in any one group approach. My aim is to provide you with an understanding of some of the significant commonalities and differences among these theoretical models. My hope is that you will become sufficiently motivated to select some approaches and learn more about them by doing additional reading (there are suggestions after each chapter in Part Two) and by actually experiencing some of these group approaches as a participant. The ultimate goal is that you develop your own personal style of group leadership and that you begin thinking about how to translate theory into practice.

Part Three focuses on the practical application of the theories and principles covered in Parts One and Two, making these applications more vivid and concrete. Chapter 17 is designed to help you pull together the various methods and approaches, realizing commonalities and differences among them. In this chapter, I discuss the basic concepts and key techniques of various theories that can be used in many kinds of groups. Chapter 18 follows a group in action and presents Marianne Schneider Corey's and my version of an integrative model for group practice, drawing from various theoretical models as they apply to the different stages of a group that we facilitated together, which is a part of the first DVD program in *Groups in Action: Evolution and Challenges*.

I invite you to keep an open mind yet to read critically. By being an active learner and by raising questions, you will gain the necessary foundation for becoming an effective group leader. This *Student Manual for Theory and Practice of Group Counseling* has been designed as a supplement to the textbook. Your active involvement in the exercises and activities will give you actual experience with the techniques you are studying.

## How to Use the Manual and the Textbook

Here are some suggestions for getting the maximum value from the textbook and the manual. These suggestions are based on my experience in using the material in classes, and my students have found them helpful:

1. Look over the contents of the manual to get an overview of the course and the reading program.

2. Before you read and study a chapter in the textbook, read any summary material in the corresponding chapter of the manual, and then look over the questions and exercises, both in the manual and in the textbook. For the 11 chapters that deal with theories of group counseling (Part Two), complete the manual's corresponding prechapter self-inventory, which is based on the key concepts discussed in the textbook. Completing these self-inventories will help you determine the degree to which you agree or disagree with the concepts of a given theory. Spending a few minutes reviewing these inventories will give you a clearer focus on the chapter you are reading in the textbook.

3. After reading and studying the text chapter, return to the manual and do the following:
   a. If you have just finished a chapter on theory, retake or at least review the prechapter self-inventory to see if your views have changed.
   b. For the theoretical chapters, study the summary chart that briefly describes the theory's view of the developmental stages of a group.
   c. Look over the basic assumptions of the theory and the summary of key concepts.
   d. Select some exercises to do on your own and some that you would be willing to do in your group or class.

4. The manual is designed as a resource to help you eventually create your own theory and style of group leading. Toward this end, I recommend that as you read and study the textbook and manual you select specific aspects of each approach that appear to be suited to your personality. The manual's main purpose is to make these theories and issues come alive for you. To accomplish this aim, it is essential that you involve yourself actively by thinking critically, sharing your thoughts with others in class, and, if appropriate, investing yourself personally by bringing your own life experience into this course.

5. As you read and study, be alert for topics for class discussion and points that most interest you. Write down a few key questions and bring them to class. Look for concepts and techniques you can apply to the group you are leading or expect to be leading. As you work through the material, develop a capacity for critical evaluation by thinking about what you most like and least like about each of the theories. The charts dealing with the stages of development as applied to each theory are especially useful in this evaluation.

6. It is helpful to get some actual experience by working in small classroom groups with the concepts and techniques of the various counseling approaches. The more you are willing to become an active learner and participant in your class or group, the more you will be able to see the possibilities for actually using these techniques as a group leader. I encourage you to use your ingenuity with the exercises presented here or others you create. Think of ways to apply the concepts and techniques to groups in various settings. As part of my course, students meet in small experiential groups (which are supervised) to practice being a group member and co-leading a group. They work within the framework of the model

they are studying in class, and in this way they get a better idea of how the 11 therapy styles are actually applied.

7. The "Exercises and Activities" include a mixture of discussion questions and personal topics for self-exploration. Here are some cautions and recommendations about using these activities:

   a. The use of the exercises will depend largely on the format of your class. These exercises have been designed for use in a supervised group and for classes that include an experiential as well as a didactic component.

   b. Because many of the activities tap into personal material, you will need to decide what you are willing to disclose in your group. It is largely up to you. The purpose of the course is to learn about group process, not to experience group therapy. Yet it is possible to explore some of your personal concerns in a supervised group and at the same time learn how group process works by experiencing a group as a participant. Care should be taken, however, to avoid opening up deeply personal issues that cannot be adequately attended to in an academic environment.

   c. It is essential that certain ground rules be established from the outset, especially rules about level of participation, "right to pass," and matters of confidentiality. The purpose and goals of your class need to be clearly defined and understood. Both your expectations and your instructor's expectations and requirements should be discussed early in the course.

   d. As you study the manual by yourself, you can benefit from reflecting on your personal concerns and by attempting to relate your life experiences to each of the therapies you study. These approaches will have more meaning for you if you apply them to understanding yourself. The manual can help you in this personal application and self-exploration even if you do not have opportunities to participate in a group.

   e. If you take the exercises seriously, your personal problems may come into focus for you. Although this process can lead to growth, it can also involve some anxiety. I hope you will consider becoming a member of a group (besides any group that might be a part of your course). Through such participation you can explore areas you want to change, and the experience can provide you with increased empathy for the members of the groups you will lead. My students often mention that their own experience as a client in counseling, especially group counseling, has been the most useful component in actually learning how to facilitate a group.

   f. I present a wide range of exercises that are based on particular therapeutic models. Let me emphasize that practitioners that adhere to a given approach may not use these exercises in the way I describe them. My aim is to help you find ways to use the concepts of each therapeutic model and to create exercises that you can practice, modify, and adapt to fit your situation. Use these exercises as a basis for creating approaches that will work for your groups.

8. Many students find it helpful to keep a journal as a part of their group course. This journal helps students keep track of their experiences as both members and facilitators of groups, and it motivates them to do writing on some of the exercises contained in the manual.

9. Look for opportunities to attend professional workshops and courses that deal not only with group work but also with specialized populations with whom you might work. You will probably find that once you graduate you will need to keep involved in professional work-

shops as a way of updating your knowledge, refining your skills, and learning new therapeutic strategies.

10. As a student, consider joining the professional organization of your specialty field. There are many advantages in becoming involved in such organizations, including receiving journals and information about annual conferences and specialized workshops. I recommend that as a group worker you also join the Association for Specialists in Group Work (ASGW), a division of the American Counseling Association. You can get more information about ASGW through this website: www. asgw.org. As an ASGW student member, you qualify for a reduced fee and will receive the *Journal for Specialists in Group Work* four times a year.

## Ways of Getting the Most from Your Group Experience

I hope your program will include some kind of therapeutic group experience, which is invaluable in the training of group counselors. Learning to be an effective group leader entails much more than simply taking a course and reading about group process. Your level of self-awareness and sensitivity to others are crucial factors in determining your effectiveness. If you are open to experiencing the group process and to committing yourself to becoming an active group participant, you can do a great deal to increase your chances of helping your clients see the value of a group experience.

How can you get the most from a group experience and maximize your learning? You can apply the recommendations below to both yourself as a member and to teaching others about groups. For a more detailed discussion of these points, I refer you to *Group Techniques* (G. Corey, Corey, Callanan, & Russell, 2004) and *Groups: Process and Practice* (M. S. Corey & Corey, 2006); both books are available from Thomson Brooks/Cole.

1. Recognize that trust is not something that "just happens" in a group but that you have a role in creating it. If you are aware of anything getting in the way of a climate of safety, share your hesitations with the group.
2. Commit yourself to getting something from your group by focusing on your personal goals. Before each meeting, make the time to think about how you can get involved, what personal concerns you want to explore, and other ways to use the time in the group meaningfully.
3. Rather than waiting to be called on, bring yourself into the interactions at the beginning of each session by letting others know what you want from this particular meeting. Although it is useful to have a tentative agenda of what you want to discuss, don't cling inflexibly to your agenda if other issues surface spontaneously within the group. Be open to pursuing alternative paths if you are affected by what others are exploring.
4. Realize that if the work other members are doing is affecting you, it is crucial that you let them know how you are reacting. If you are able to identify with the struggles or pains of others, it generally helps both you and them to share your feelings and thoughts.
5. Decide for yourself what, how much, and when you will disclose personal facets of yourself. Others will not have a basis for knowing you unless you tell them about yourself. If you have difficulty sharing yourself personally in your group, begin by letting others know what makes it hard for you to self-disclose.

6. Don't confuse self-disclosure with storytelling. Avoid getting lost and overwhelming others with mere information about you or your history. Instead, express what is on your mind and in your heart presently. Reveal the struggles that are significant to you at this time in your life, especially as they pertain to what others in the group are exploring.

7. Express persistent feelings that relate to what is emerging in the group in the here-and-now. If you are feeling intimidated by other people in the group, for example, announce that you feel that way. If you feel somewhat isolated, share this emotion. If you do not want to be a part of the group, it is essential that you talk about it. Be willing to assume responsibility for what you feel rather than blaming others.

8. Although silence may sometimes be golden, don't become a silent member. Realize that others will not know you if you do not let them know what issues are important to you, nor will they know that you identify with them or feel close to them unless you tell them.

9. Practice your attending and listening skills. If you can give others the gift of your presence and understanding, you are contributing a great deal to the group process.

10. Try to challenge yourself if you sense that you are taking too much group time for yourself. If you become overly concerned about measuring how much you are taking and receiving, you will inhibit the spontaneity that can make a group exciting and productive.

11. Use your group as a place to experiment with new behaviors. Allow yourself to try out different ways of being to determine how you may want to change. Discover how to extend new ways of thinking, feeling, and acting into your outside life. Between sessions, practice the skills you are learning in your group. Give yourself homework assignments, and let others in your group know how you are applying group learning to your behavior with family, friends, and associates.

12. Understand that making changes will not be instantaneous. You can also expect some setbacks. Keep track of any progress you are making, and remember to give yourself credit for your efforts and the subtle changes you are achieving.

13. Avoid giving others advice, giving intellectualized interpretations of their behavior, or using questioning as your main style of interacting. If you are inclined to ask a question, let others know why you are interested in hearing their answer. Or if you want to give advice, reveal to others what your investment is in giving this advice. Learn to speak *for* yourself and *about* yourself.

14. Concentrate on making personal and direct statements to others in your group. Direct communication with a member is more effective than talking about that person through the leader.

15. In giving feedback to others, avoid categorizing or labeling them. Instead of telling others who or what they are, tell them what you are observing, and let them know how they are affecting you. Rather than judging them as persons, focus on how you respond to some of their specific behaviors in the group.

16. Pay attention to any consistent feedback you might receive. If you hear that others perceive you as being somewhat judgmental and critical, don't be too quick to argue and convince others that you are open and accepting. Instead, take in what you are hearing, and consider their input to determine the degree to which what they are saying might apply to you.

17. Respect your defenses, and understand that they have served a purpose for you. When you become aware of feeling or acting defensively in your group, however, challenge your

defenses by seeing what will happen if you strive to be less guarded. At least identify out loud that you are feeling defensive, and begin exploring what you might be resisting.

18. Provide support for others by expressing your care for them, but don't quickly intervene by trying to comfort others when they are experiencing feelings, such as expressing pain over an event. Realize that they need to experience, share, and work through certain feelings; they do not need reassurance that "all will turn out for the best." Let them know how their pain may be touching you, but don't attempt to "cure" them of their pain.

19. Take responsibility for what you are accomplishing in your group. Spend some time thinking about what is taking place in these meetings and evaluating the degree to which you are attaining your goals. If you are not satisfied with your group experience, look at what you can do to make the group a more meaningful experience.

20. Be aware of respecting and maintaining the confidentiality of what goes on inside your group. Even though you may not maliciously breach others' confidences, recognize how easy it might be to inappropriately talk to others who are not in the group about what members have revealed. How you handle confidentiality says a great deal about your professional character. If you have any concerns that what you are sharing is not staying within the group, be willing to bring this matter up in a session.

21. Be prepared if your friends and loved ones do not always understand or accept you, especially as you make changes. Some people may not support the new directions you choose to travel, and your changes may be threatening to them. It is a good idea to create a support system within your group. Ask selected members to help you remember the lessons you have learned in the group. Reporting to others in your group is an accountability procedure that will enable you to meet your personal goals.

22. Keep a personal journal in which you record impressions of your own explorations and learning in your group. The journal is a good place to enter your reactions to books you read for your personal development. A journal will be invaluable in keeping track of your progress and noting changes in your ways of thinking, feeling, and acting.

## Listen to Lectures on Each Chapter by the Author of Your Textbook

New to this Seventh Edition of *Theory and Practice of Group Counseling* is a Mobile Content Program, with lecturettes that I present as a way to introduce you to some key concepts and techniques from each of the chapters. This is an online feature that you can access with a pass code that instructors can give to students who are using this textbook. You can then download onto iTunes each of these chapters. The brief presentations are about 10 minutes for each of the theory chapters and are aimed at orienting you to key points of the chapter. My attempt was to share with you some of the key themes that I incorporate from each of the theories into my integrative approach to group counseling. This will, I hope, assist you in thinking about what aspects from each of the theories that you might want to incorporate into your own personal style of group leadership. The lecturettes can be listened to as away to introduce you to key themes of each chapter and they can also he used as a way to review the book as a preparation for the final examination.

## Professional Organizations of Interest to Group Workers

It is a good idea while a student to begin your identification with state, regional, and national professional associations. You might consider contacting the organization of your choice to find out what they can offer.

American Counseling Association (ACA)
Web site: www.counseling.org

Association for Specialists in Group Work (ASGW)
Web site: www.asgw.org

American Group Psychotherapy Association (AGPA)
Web site: www.groupsine.org

American Society for Group Psychotherapy and Psychodrama (ASGPP)
Web site: www.asgpp.org

American Psychological Association
Web site: www.apa.org

National Association of Social Workers (NASW)
Web site: www.sociaIworkers.org

American Association for Marriage and Family Therapy (AAMFT)
Web site: www.aamft.org

# CHAPTER TWO

# Group Leadership

Group leaders (both those who are beginning and those who are experienced) typically face several common problems. Assume that you are now leading or co-leading a group (even though you may not have done so), and give your reactions to each of the following situations. What do you imagine you'd think and feel in each of these cases? Think about your possible courses of action, and then discuss these situations in your class or group. Plenty of role-playing activities can be generated from this material.

1. Imagine yourself getting ready to co-lead your first group. What kind of anxiety would you experience? What would be your main concerns before you actually began the first session? Assume you are meeting your co-leader an hour before the group meets. What things do you think you would say? What would you do if you and your co-leader had different ideas about how to open the first session?

2. Many beginning group leaders are afraid to make mistakes, and out of their fear they may be inactive and may not try interventions or follow their intuition. How does this description apply to you? Can you think of some ways to challenge yourself to be active as a leader? Are you willing to risk making mistakes in doing this? (In small groups discuss how being afraid of making mistakes might result in passive leading and also ways in which you could become more active.)

3. Again in small groups, discuss your thoughts on the topic of leader self-disclosure. How do you decide *what, when,* and *how* to disclose to make self-disclosure facilitate rather than interfere with the group process? Tell others in your group what you are likely to disclose (or not disclose) in a group you are leading, and get their feedback. In your discussion groups work toward developing a brief list of guidelines for appropriate leader disclosure that you can agree on.

4. It is extremely important for group counselors to be aware of the personal traits and characteristics needed to become effective leaders. Select some of the following questions to discuss in your class or small group, and use them as a basis for self-reflection on effective leadership:
   a. Why do you want to lead groups?
   b. What do you have to offer as a group counselor?
   c. What experiences have you had that you think will contribute to your success?
   d. What shortcomings do you have that may limit your effectiveness as a leader?
   e. Do you feel a sense of personal power in your own right, or do you depend on a role or position to give you power?
   f. In what ways do you appreciate, value, respect, accept, and like yourself?
   g. Do you see yourself as having courage? In what ways is courage important for a group leader?

## Checklist and Self-Evaluation of Group Leadership Skills

Table 2–1 in the textbook lists 22 specific group leadership skills. The following form will help you review these skills and provide you with a self-inventory of your strengths as a group leader and specific areas that need improvement. Read the brief description of each skill, and then rate yourself. Next, think about the questions listed under each skill; these will help you determine your level of skill development and examine your behavior as a leader. Ask yourself which skills you most need to develop or improve.

    You can profit from this checklist by reviewing it before and after group sessions. If you are working with a co-leader, it could be very useful to have him or her also rate you on each of these skills. These questions can also provide a systematic framework for exploring your level of skill development with fellow students and with your supervisor or instructor.

    On these 22 skills, rate yourself on this five-point scale:

**5** = I do this most of the time with a very high degree of competence.
**4** = I do this much of the time with a high degree of competence.
**3** = I do this sometimes with an adequate degree of competence.
**2** = I do this occasionally with a relatively low level of competence.
**1** = I rarely demonstrate this or do it with an extremely low level of competence.

You are strongly encouraged to take this self-inventory at three points during the semester or quarter. The three blank spaces to the left of each number are for these ratings. I recommend that you cover your previous ratings with a piece of paper so that you are not influenced by them. It is ideal if you rate yourself (and have your co-leader and supervisor rate you) about every five weeks. This will give you a regular pattern of your progress in developing group leadership skills. Above all, strive for the maximum degree of honesty with yourself as you complete this rating scale and as you reflect on the questions concerning each of these skills.

    It is a good idea to circle the letter of the questions that are the most meaningful to you, as well as the questions that indicate a need for further skill development or special attention.

*To what degree does the group leader demonstrate the following?*

___4___ ___ ___ 1. *Active listening.* Hearing and understanding, and communicating that one is doing this.
    a. How well do you listen to members?
    b. How attentive are you to nonverbal language?
    c. Are you able to detect incongruity between members' words and their nonverbal cues?
    d. Are you able to hear both overt and subtle messages?
    e. Do you teach members how to listen and to respond?
    f. Do you focus on content to the extent that you miss how a message is delivered?

___3___ ___ ___ 2. *Restating.* Capturing the essence of what is said in different words with the effect of adding meaning or clarifying meaning.
    a. Can you repeat the essence of what others say without becoming mechanical?
    b. Do your restatements add meaning to what was said by a member?

   c. Do your restatements eliminate ambiguity and give sharper focus to what was said?

   d. Do you check with members to determine if they think your restatement was accurate?

*3*   3. *Clarifying.* Focusing on underlying issues and assisting others to get a clearer picture of what they are thinking or feeling.

   a. Do your clarifying remarks help members sort out conflicting feelings?

   b. Are you able to focus on underlying issues?

   c. Do members get a clearer focus on what they are thinking and feeling?

   d. Does your clarification lead to a deeper level of member self-exploration?

*2*   4. *Summarizing.* Tying together loose ends, identifying common themes, and providing a picture of the directional trends of a group session.

   a. Do you use summarizing as a way to give more direction to a session?

   b. Do you tie together various themes in a group?

   c. Are you able to identify key elements of a session and present them as a summary of the proceedings at the end of a session?

*2*   5. *Questioning.* Using questions to stimulate thought and action and avoiding a question/answer pattern of interaction between leader and member.

   a. Do you avoid overusing questioning as a leadership style?

   b. Do you use open-ended questions to encourage deeper exploration of issues?

   c. Do your questions lead clients in a definite direction? Do you have a hidden agenda? Do you have an expected answer?

   d. Do you avoid bombarding members with questions that set up a question/answer format?

   e. Do you ask "what" and "how" questions, or "why" questions?

   f. Do you keep yourself hidden as a counselor through questioning instead of making statements?

*2*   6. *Interpreting.* Explaining the meaning of behavior patterns within the framework of a theoretical system.

   a. Can you present your interpretations in a tentative way, as a hunch or a hypothesis?

   b. Are your interpretations dogmatic and authoritarian? Do you have a need to convince members of what you see as "truth"?

   c. Do you have a tendency to rescue members from difficult feelings too quickly through the use of interpretations?

   d. Are you conscious of appropriateness and timing in making interpretations?

   e. Do you encourage members to provide their own meaning of their behavior?

   f. Do you invite other members to make interpretations?

*3*   7. *Confronting.* Challenging members in a direct way on discrepancies and in such a manner that they will tend to react nondefensively.

   a. How do you confront members? What are the effects of your confrontations, generally?

b. What kind of model do you provide for confronting others with care and respect?

c. As a result of your confrontations, are members encouraged to look at discrepancies in a nondefensive manner?

d. Do you confront people about their unused strengths?

e. Are you sensitive to the timing and appropriateness of your confrontations?

f. Are your confrontations related to specific behavior rather than being judgmental?

3 ___ ___ 8. *Reflecting feelings.* Mirroring what others appear to be feeling without being mechanical.

a. Do you reflect feelings accurately?

b. Do your reflections foster increased contact and involvement?

c. Do your reflections help members clarify what they are feeling?

4 ___ ___ 9. *Supporting.* Offering some form of positive reinforcement at appropriate times in such a way that it has a facilitating effect.

a. Do you recognize the progress that members make?

b. Do you build on the strengths and gains made by members?

c. Do you make use of positive reinforcement and encouragement?

d. Does your support allow and encourage members to both express and explore their feelings? Or does your support tend to bolster members and aid them in avoiding intense feelings?

4 ___ ___ 10. *Empathizing.* Intuitively sensing the subjective world of others in a group, being able to adopt the frame of reference of others, and communicating this understanding to clients so that they feel understood.

a. Are your life experiences diverse enough to provide a basis for understanding the subjective world of a range of clients?

b. Are you able to demonstrate the ability to adopt the internal frame of reference of the client and communicate to that person that you do keenly understand?

c. Are you able to maintain your separate identity at the same time as you empathize with others?

3 ___ ___ 11. *Facilitating.* Helping members clarify their own goals and take steps to reach them.

a. How much do you encourage member interaction?

b. Do you foster autonomy among the members by helping them accept an increasing degree of responsibility for directing their group?

c. Are you successful in teaching members how to focus on themselves?

d. Do you foster the spirit in members to identify and express whatever they are feeling as it relates to the here-and-now process of group interaction?

2 ___ ___ 12. *Initiating.* Demonstrating an active stance in intervening in a group at appropriate times.

a. Do you have the skills to get group sessions started in an effective manner?

b. Are you able to initiate new work with others once a given member's work is concluded?

c. Do you take active steps to prevent the group from floundering in unproductive ways?

d. Are you able to get interaction going among members or between yourself and members?

e. Do you avoid initiating to the degree that members assume an active stance?

_2_ ___ ___ 13. *Setting goals.* Being able to work cooperatively with members so that there is an alignment between member goals and leader goals, and being able to assist members in establishing concrete goals.

a. Do you help members establish clear and specific goals?

b. Are you able to help members clarify their goals?

c. Do you encourage members to develop contracts and homework assignments as ways of reaching their goals?

d. Do you impose your goals on the members without making them partners in the goal-selection process?

_3_ ___ ___ 14. *Evaluating.* Appraising the ongoing group process and the individual and group dynamics.

a. What criteria do you use to assess the progress of your groups?

b. What kinds of questions do you pose to members to help them evaluate their own gains as well as their contributions to the group?

c. Do you make a concerted effort to assist members in assessing their progress as a group?

d. What kind of evaluation instruments, if any, do you think are helpful in assessing the group process?

_4_ ___ ___ 15. *Giving feedback.* Providing information to members in such a way that they can use it to make constructive behavior changes.

a. Do you continually give concrete and useful feedback to members, and do you encourage members to do this for one another?

b. Is your feedback both honest and personal?

c. Do you teach members to sift through feedback and ultimately decide what they will do with this information?

d. Do you offer feedback that relates to both the strengths and weaknesses of members?

e. How do members typically react when you give them feedback?

_4_ ___ ___ 16. *Suggesting.* Offering information or possibilities for action that can be used by members in making independent decisions.

a. Can you differentiate between suggesting and prescribing?

b. Do you give too many suggestions, and are they just ways of providing quick solutions for every problem a member presents?

c. Do you rush in too quickly to give advice or information, or do you encourage group members to provide themselves with possible courses of action?

d. Do you invite others in the group to offer suggestions for members to consider?

e. Do your directions and suggestions actually restrict members from becoming autonomous?

*3* ___ ___ 17. *Protecting.* Actively intervening to ensure that members will be safeguarded from unnecessary psychological risks.

a. Do you take measures to safeguard members from unnecessary risks?

b. Do you show good judgment in risky situations?

c. Do you intervene when members are being treated unfairly or are being pressured by others?

d. Do you talk with members about the possible psychological risks involved in group participation?

*4* ___ ___ 18. *Disclosing oneself.* Willingly sharing with members any persistent personal reactions that relate to the here-and-now occurrences in the group.

a. What is your style of self-disclosure? Are you aloof? Do you remain hidden behind a role? Do you model appropriate self-disclosure?

b. What impact do your self-disclosures tend to have on the group?

c. Are you willing to reveal your present feelings and thoughts to members when it is appropriate?

*3* ___ ___ 19. *Modeling.* Demonstrating to members desired behaviors that can be practiced both during and between group sessions.

a. What kind of model are you for your clients?

b. What specific behaviors and attitudes do you model?

c. Are you doing in your own life what you ask the members in your group to do?

d. What might the members of your group know about you by observing your actions in the group?

*3* ___ ___ 20. *Linking.* Promoting member-to-member interaction and facilitating exploration of common themes in a group.

a. What interventions do you make that enhance interactions between members?

b. In what ways do you attempt to foster a norm of member-to-member interactions rather than leader-to-member interactions?

c. What are some specific instances when you would be most inclined to link the work of one member with that of other members?

*2* ___ ___ 21. *Blocking.* Being able to intervene effectively, without attacking anyone, when members engage in counterproductive behaviors.

a. Do you take active steps to intervene when there are counterproductive forces within a group?

b. Do you generally block the following behaviors when you are aware of them: scapegoating? group pressure? questioning? storytelling? gossiping?

c. Do you block counterproductive behavior in a firm yet sensitive manner?

*3*
_____ _____ _____ 22. *Terminating.* Creating a climate that encourages members to continue
working after sessions.
   a. Do you attempt to get members to transfer what they are learning in the group to their everyday lives?
   b. Do you assist members in reviewing and integrating their experiences?
   c. Do you create a climate in which members are encouraged to continue to think and act after sessions?

## Suggestions for Using the Checklist

Obviously, all of the preceding 22 items are not merely skills to learn. Many of them represent attitudes related to your leadership effectiveness; some represent personal characteristics that many writers think are ideal qualities of group leaders. Again, you are encouraged to complete this self-evaluation three times during the course and to use it when you actually lead groups.

Finally, I recommend again that you look over the list and circle the numbers of those items that are most important to you. Then use the following guide to summarize your major strengths, the areas you most need to improve, and the areas that you would like to explore more fully in class. Also, it could be valuable to make comparisons of these ratings; for example, how does your self-rating compare with ratings by your supervisor, your co-leader, and the members of your group?

1. Some areas where I feel particularly strong are: ___Empathy and listening___

_____

_____

_____

_____

2. Areas that need improvement most are: ___Blocking   Initiating___
___Questioning    Blocking_____

_____

_____

_____

3. Some specific steps I can take now to work toward improving these skills, attitudes, behaviors, and personal characteristics are: _____
___Read more; more education_____

_____

_____

_____

# Checklist for Becoming a Diversity-Competent Group Counselor

The ASGW's (1999) "Principles for Diversity-Competent Group Workers" can be retrieved online: http://www.asgw.org/diversity.htm. I recommend you download this document and take some time to think about how these principles might apply to your group work. After reading ASGW's "Principles for Diversity-Competent Group Workers" and the sections in the textbook that deal with becoming a diversity-competent group counselor, reflect on the areas of competence you now possess as well as areas in which you need to acquire knowledge and skills. The checklist below can help you to assess your current level of skill development in the multicultural competencies. Strive to identify your strengths and limitations in working with groups from a multicultural perspective.

## Beliefs and Attitudes of Diversity-Competent Group Leaders

Put a check mark in the blank space before each of the beliefs and attitudes you think you already hold or that represents an area of awareness you already possess.

*With respect to beliefs and attitudes, diversity-competent group leaders . . .*

   ✓   recognize and understand the stereotypes and preconceived notions they may hold toward other racial and ethnic minority groups.

   ✓   do not allow their personal biases, values, or problems to interfere with their ability to work with a diverse range of clients.

   ✓   believe cultural self-awareness and sensitivity to one's own cultural heritage are essential for any form of helping.

       are aware of their negative and positive emotional reactions toward other racial and ethnic groups that may prove detrimental to establishing collaborative helping relationships.

       are aware of how their own cultural background and experiences have influenced attitudes, values, and biases about what constitutes psychologically healthy individuals.

       have moved from being culturally unaware to knowing their cultural heritage.

   ✓   are able to recognize the limits of their competence with diverse client populations.

       seek to examine and understand the world from the vantage point of their clients.

   ✓   respect clients' religious and spiritual beliefs and values.

       recognize their sources of discomfort with differences that exist between themselves and others in terms of race, ethnicity, culture, age, gender, sexual orientation, and beliefs.

       welcome diverse value orientations and diverse assumptions about human behavior, and thus, they have a basis for sharing the worldview of their clients as opposed to being culturally encapsulated.

   ✓   rather than maintaining that their cultural heritage is superior, they are able to accept and value cultural diversity.

       are able to identify and understand the central cultural constructs of their clients, and they avoid applying their own cultural constructs inappropriately to people with whom they work.

       respect indigenous helping practices and respect help-giving networks within the community.

_____ monitor their functioning through consultation, supervision, and further training or education.

✓ realize that traditional concepts and helping strategies may not be appropriate for all clients or for all problems.

## Knowledge of Diversity-Competent Group Leaders

Put a check mark in the blank space before each of the knowledge areas in this section that you think you already possess.

_With respect to knowledge areas, diversity-competent group leaders . . ._

✓ possess knowledge about their own racial and cultural heritage and how it affects them personally and in their work.

✓ possess knowledge and understanding about how oppression, racism, discrimination, and stereotyping affect them personally and professionally.

✓ acknowledge their own racist attitudes, beliefs, and feelings.

_____ do not impose their values and expectations on their clients from differing cultural backgrounds and avoid stereotyping clients.

✓ understand the worldview of their clients, and they learn about their clients' cultural backgrounds.

_____ understand the basic values underlying the helping process and attempt to learn about their clients' cultural backgrounds.

✓ are aware of the institutional barriers that prevent minorities from utilizing the mental health services available in their communities.

_____ have knowledge of the potential bias in assessment instruments and use procedures and interpret findings keeping in mind the cultural and linguistic characteristics of clients.

_____ possess specific knowledge and information about the particular individuals with whom they are working.

_____ are aware of the values, life experiences, cultural heritage, and historical background of their culturally diverse clients.

_____ possess knowledge about their social impact on others.

_____ are knowledgeable about communication style differences and how their style may clash with or foster the helping process with persons from different cultural groups.

_____ are knowledgeable about the community characteristics and the resources in the community as well as those in the family.

✓ have knowledge about sociopolitical influences that impinge on the life of ethnic and racial minorities, including immigration issues, poverty, racism, stereotyping, and powerlessness.

✓ view diversity in a positive light, which allows them to meet and resolve the challenges that arise in their work with a wide range of client populations.

_____ know how to help clients make use of indigenous support systems. In areas where they are lacking in knowledge, they seek resources to assist them.

## Skills and Intervention Strategies of Diversity-Competent Group Leaders

Put a check mark in the blank space before each of the skill areas in this section that you think you already possess.

*With respect to specific skills, diversity-competent group leaders . . .*

_____ take responsibility for educating their clients to the way the helping process works, including matters such as goals, expectations, legal rights, and the helper's orientation.

✓ familiarize themselves with relevant research and the latest findings regarding mental health and mental disorders that affect diverse client populations.

_____ are willing to seek out educational, consultative, and training experiences to enhance their ability to work with diverse client populations.

✓ are open to seeking consultation with traditional healers or religious and spiritual leaders to better serve diverse client groups, when appropriate.

_____ use methods and strategies and define goals consistent with the life experiences and cultural values of their clients and modify and adapt their interventions to accommodate cultural differences.

✓ are not limited to only one approach in helping but recognize that helping strategies may be culture bound.

_____ are able to send and receive both verbal and nonverbal messages accurately and appropriately.

_____ are able to exercise institutional intervention skills on behalf of their clients.

_____ become actively involved with minority individuals outside of the office (community events, celebrations, and neighborhood groups) to the extent possible.

_____ are committed to understanding themselves as racial and cultural beings and are actively seeking a nonracist identity.

_____ actively pursue and engage in professional and personal growth activities to address their limitations.

Once you've completed this checklist, take a few minutes to decide how you can develop or strengthen specific competencies that will enhance your ability to work more effectively with cultural diversity in your groups.

1. *Assessing Your Beliefs and Attitudes*

a. What is your main strength in the area of beliefs and attitudes? _____

   *I feel very open minded to different cultures*

   _____

b. What specific kind of belief or attitude would you most want to change? _____

   *Tension I feel w/ dominant males who have been culturally taught to look down on women.*

c. What steps can you take to bring about this change?_____

_____Work to understand why people of this_____

_____culture feel this way (ie Religion)_____

2. *Assessing Your Knowledge*

   a. What is your main strength in the area of knowledge?_____

_____Deep understanding of own culture_____

_____

   b. What specific kind of knowledge would you most want to acquire?_____

_____More info about other cultures_____

_____

   c. What steps can you take to gain this knowledge?_____

_____Read Research_____

_____

3. *Assessing Your Skills*

   a. What is your main strength in the area of skills?_____

_____Open for outside help_____

_____

   b. What specific skill would you most want to acquire or refine?_____

_____Professional growth_____

_____

   c. What steps can you take to acquire or refine this skill?_____

_____Prof. development classes; experience_____

_____

Now that you have completed this checklist, you will have a good sense of your strengths and weaknesses in the area of multicultural counseling competencies. This assessment will be of major importance if it leads you to take action to enhance your awareness, knowledge, and skills.

## Skills in Opening and Closing Group Sessions

Leaders in training are frequently ineffective in opening and closing group meetings. At times leaders quickly focus on one group member at the beginning of a session with no mention of the previous session. Members should at least be given a brief opportunity to share what they did in the way of practice outside of the group since the previous session. Additionally, it is useful to have each member briefly state what he or she wants from the upcoming session. Closing a group session should entail more than an abrupt announcement of the end of the meeting. Group leader tasks include summarizing, integrating, and helping one another find ways of applying what they've learned to outside situations.

The phrases, statements, and questions in the next two sections will give you some concrete tools for opening and closing group sessions. Review these lists frequently, and experiment with parts of them at different times. Add your own opening and closing statements to help you get sessions moving well and to end each of your meetings most effectively. Do not employ these phrases mechanically; rather, find ways to introduce them in a timely and appropriate fashion. Eventually, some of these catalytic statements may become a natural part of your own leadership style.

## Guidelines for Opening Group Sessions

- What would you be willing to talk about in this session?
- Last week we left off with _____.
- Did anyone have any afterthoughts about our last meeting?
- I'd like to share some of my thoughts regarding our last session.
- My expectations and hopes for this session are _____.
- What did you do this week with what you learned in the last session?
- I'd like to go around the group and have each person complete the sentence "Right now I'm feeling _____."
- How would each of you like to be different today from the way you were in the last session?
- Let's go around the group and have each person briefly say what your issues or agendas are for this session. What does each of you want from the group today?
- If you don't participate in the group today, how will that be for you?
- How is each of you feeling about being here today?
- What are you willing to do to make this session productive?
- If you're not here by choice, are you still willing to keep yourself open to getting something from the session?
- Today marks the halfway point for our group. We have 10 weeks remaining, and I'd like to discuss whether there is anything you'd like to change during that time. How would each of you like to be different?
- Is there any unfinished business from the last session that anyone wants to pursue?
- I'd like to go around the group and have each person finish the sentence "Today I could be actively involved in the group by _____."

## Guidelines for Closing Group Sessions

- Before we end for today, does anyone want to say something to anyone else in here?
- What, if anything, did you learn in today's session?
- What did you hear yourself or someone else say that seemed especially significant to you?
- If you were to summarize the key themes that we explored today, what would they be?
- Are there any issues that anyone wants to work on at the next session?
- Let's spend the last 10 minutes talking about your plans for the coming week.

- A homework assignment I'd like you to consider is _____.
- Are there any changes you'd like to make in the group?
- How is the group going for you so far?
- How would you evaluate your participation in this session?
- We had a very intense session today. Would you like to say how you're feeling now?
- Before we close, I'd like to share my own reactions to this session.
- I noticed that you were very quiet during the session. Are you willing to say how this meeting was for you?
- You opened up some pretty scary feelings. You made important steps, and I hope you continue in future sessions with what you're finding out about yourself.

## Guidelines for Meeting with Your Co-Leader

In the textbook, I make frequent reference to learning to work effectively with a co-leader. If you are working with a co-leader, I cannot overemphasize the value of making the time to meet regularly before and after group sessions. In addition to talking about the progress of members in the group and the progress of the group as a whole, you will find it helpful to talk about your relationship with your co-leader. To provide you with some framework for assessing how well you and your co-leader are functioning as a team, I've prepared the following questions. Look over this list in meetings with your co-leader, and select those issues that pertain to your relationship at various times. You can identify the areas in which you see yourself functioning especially well and those areas that both of you need to work on improving.

1. Did you select your co-leader, or were the two of you assigned to each other? To what degree is there a trusting relationship between you? Do you respect each other? Are your differences complementary, or do they present problems in your functioning as a therapeutic team?
2. Did the two of you make plans and preparations together as the group was being organized? Are both of you actively involved and interested in the group now?
3. Are you making the time to meet between group sessions on a regular basis? How productive are your meetings? Do you focus exclusively on your group and the members? Or are you also willing to talk about your reactions to the group, to the members, and to each other?
4. Are your theoretical orientations compatible? How do your theoretical views affect the goals and procedures of your group?
5. Do you and your co-leader agree on the division of responsibility between the leaders and the members? Are the two of you sharing leadership responsibility to the satisfaction of each of you?
6. Are the two of you together in your expectations for the group?
7. How are the members reacting to each of you as a leader? How are you and your co-leader reacting to each member? Is either of you having particular difficulty with any member?
8. Do both of you feel free to initiate suggestions and techniques in the group? Is either of you "holding back" and hoping that the other will do most of the leading?
9. Are both of you paying attention to how you open the group sessions and how you bring each session to a close?

10. Does each of you think of ways to continually evaluate the progress of individual members and the group as a whole? Do you have some systematic feedback from the members about how they respond to your leadership?

11. Are you in agreement with your co-leader about self-disclosure? Do both of you reveal to the members your reactions to what is going on in the group? If you see things differently from your co-leader, are you open about this in the group? How do you handle problems between the two of you? Are you competitive with each other? Can you talk openly with the members about your relationship and the way you lead together?

12. What is the balance between confrontation and support in your group? Does one of the team typically support the members and the other challenge them? Are both of you able to be appropriately supportive and confrontive?

13. How do your two styles of leadership blend, and what effect does your co-leadership have on the group?

14. Do both of you spend time talking about how it is for each of you to lead with the other? Are you able to tell your co-leader what you like and do not like about working as a team?

15. Are the two of you reviewing each session and paying attention to any changes in the direction of the group? Can you profit from any mistakes that you have made? What are you learning about yourselves and about groups by co-leading? Are you devoting some time to making plans for upcoming sessions? And are you able to change your plans if it is called for in a particular session?

# CHAPTER THREE

# Ethical and Professional Issues in Group Practice

## A Self-Inventory of Your Views on Ethical Practice in Group Work

This inventory is designed to stimulate your thinking about what constitutes ethical practice when leading groups. There are also exercises and activities, consisting of case vignettes for you to evaluate, as well as a self-evaluation of your level of training. These activities provide material for reflection and lively discussion in class.

In taking this first self-inventory, decide for each item the degree to which you think the leader's behavior is proper or improper, using the following code:

**1** = This behavior is unethical.
**2** = This behavior is somewhat unethical.
**3** = I am uncertain about this behavior.
**4** = This behavior is somewhat ethical.
**5** = This behavior is ethical.

You may have your own reaction to an item besides one of the five listed here. Bring any of your reactions to class to compare with others' ideas.

___1___ 1. A leader has no formal training or courses in group work but maintains that the best way to learn how to conduct groups is to do them.

___1___ 2. A leader does not screen prospective members, mainly on the ground that members will screen themselves out of a group if they find it is not appropriate for them.

___2___ 3. A counselor continues to lead groups even though claiming to be extremely tired of group work (and not really believing it to be of therapeutic value).

___1___ 4. A leader makes tapes of the group sessions without the knowledge and consent of the members, based on the rationale that telling them would inhibit their free participation.

___1___ 5. A leader refuses to see members between sessions, even if they request such a private session, and instead asks them to bring up the issue at the next group meeting.

___4___ 6. A leader makes it a practice to avoid socializing with members of the group.

___1___ 7. A group counselor says that she sees nothing wrong in dating a *former* group member.

___5___ 8. A leader intervenes when several members focus on another member and pressure that person to make a decision.

___1___ 9. A leader does not modify his techniques, even though many of the culturally different members in his group seem to have difficulty with his style.

_____1___ 10. A leader does not discuss with members any personal risks associated with joining a group, on the ground that he should not give members any fears that they might not already have.

_____5___ 11. A group counselor who works with ethnic groups different from her own obtains specialized knowledge to better work with these members.

_____3___ 12. A group leader assumes that a given individual will be hesitant to share emotional material because of his cultural background.

_____1___ 13. A group leader does not mention confidentiality, thinking that if this topic is important the members will eventually bring it up.

_____1___ 14. A leader consciously attempts to impose her values on group members, based on the assumption that people who attend a group need clear direction from her.

_____5___ 15. A group counselor is willing to engage in a bartering arrangement with certain group members who say they cannot afford to pay the regular fee.

_____1___ 16. A leader sees nothing wrong in influencing the group in a subtle manner to accept his values.

_____1___ 17. A leader conducts groups to get her personal needs met through this work.

_____1___ 18. A leader regularly uses the group as a place for working out his personal problems, stating that this is good modeling for the other members.

_____1___ 19. A group counselor asserts that it is acceptable for him to develop sexual relationships with a former group member, so long as they wait at least six months after the termination of the group.

_____2___ 20. A leader allows one member to dominate the group and does not intervene when this member rambles on and monopolizes the group's time.

_____1___ 21. A counselor pressures a culturally different group member to "open up" and share details about her family, maintaining that her silence is causing others in the group to mistrust her.

_____1___ 22. Without getting her permission, a leader contacts the parents of an adolescent girl who has disclosed her conflict over whether to have an abortion or keep her child.

_____2___ 23. A group leader is conducting research that involves the group, but she does not disclose this fact to the members.

_____2___ 24. A leader is uncomfortable when members explore a conflict, and thus he pushes clients to make decisions too soon.

_____2___ 25. A group counselor excludes a gay man from his group, contending that since he does not approve of homosexuality it would be difficult for him to be objective or compassionate with his struggles.

_____1___ 26. A leader says to the members in her group that everyone shares the same struggles, regardless of his or her cultural background, and that everyone in the group therefore needs to be treated equally and in the same fashion.

_____1___ 27. A leader does not state what services will be provided within the structure of the group.

_____1___ 28. A leader allows the expression of pent-up rage in group sessions but does not take precautions to see that members are not physically injured in these exercises.

_____1___ 29. A leader coerces members to participate in nonverbal touching exercises, thinking that this type of pressure is needed if they are to challenge their inhibitions.

_____1___ 30. A leader presses members to experience intense emotions and pushes for a catharsis—even if they say they do not want to explore a struggle—out of the conviction that they need to experience their emotions to become free.

_____31. A leader encourages certain ethnic members to give up their collectivist values in favor of thinking more of their own individual welfare.

_____32. A leader does not explain a technique the group will be using and does not give members a choice whether to participate.

_____33. When confidentiality is broken in a group of high school students, the leader ignores the situation, assuming that to discuss the matter or to take action will make things worse.

_____34. A leader forms a group with elementary schoolchildren without getting parental permission.

_____35. A group leader discusses in some detail his involvement with drugs, thinking that this will promote openness and trust among a group of adolescents.

## Association for Specialists in Group Work: Best Practice Guidelines (1998)

This section presents the Association for Specialists in Group Work (ASGW) "Best Practice Guidelines." These guidelines were prepared by Lynn Rapin and Linda Keel (the co-chairs of the ASGW Ethics Committee) and were approved by the Executive Board on March 29, 1998. The "Best Practice Guidelines" address group workers' responsibilities in planning, performing, and processing group work. These guidelines are placed early in this manual with the expectation that you will want to refer to them often during the course.

The Association for Specialists in Group Work is a division of the American Counseling Association, which means that members of ASGW are bound to practice within the framework of the *Code of Ethics* (as revised in 2005) of the parent organization, the American Counseling Association (ACA). The ASGW "Best Practice Guidelines" are meant to clarify and supplement the ACA's *Code of Ethics and Standards of Practice,* not to replace them. The "Best Practice Guidelines" define group workers' responsibilities and scope of practice consistent with current ethical and community standards.

*Note:* The following ASGW guidelines fit well with the chapter on ethical issues in group work. I recommend carefully reading these guidelines and addressing the questions following the guidelines. You can also access the Best Practice Guidelines online: www.asgw.org. You will also find a wide range of information about ASGW from the main Web site.

**Section A: Best Practice in Planning**
**A.1. Professional Context and Regulatory Requirements**
  Group Workers actively know, understand, and apply the ACA Code of Ethics and Standards of Best Practice, the ASGW Professional Standards for the Training of Group Workers, these ASGW Best Practice Guidelines, the ASGW diversity competencies, the ACA Multicultural Guidelines, relevant state laws, accreditation requirements, relevant National Board for Certified Counselors Codes and Standards, their organization's standards, and insurance requirements affecting the practice of group work.
**A.2. Scope of Practice and Conceptual Framework**
  Group Workers define the scope of practice related to the core and specialization competencies defined in the ASGW Training Standards. Group Workers are aware of personal strengths and weaknesses in leading groups. Group Workers develop and are able to articulate a general conceptual framework to

Source: L. Rapin and L. Keel, "Association for Specialists in Group Work: Best Practice Guidelines," *The Group Worker,* 28 (3), Spring 2000, pp. 1–5. [Special insert]. Reprinted with permission of ASGW.

guide practice and a rationale for use of techniques that are to be used. Group Workers limit their practice to those areas for which they meet the training criteria established by the ASGW Training Standards.

### A.3. Assessment

  a. *Assessment of self.* Group Workers actively assess their knowledge and skills related to the specific group(s) offered. Group Workers assess their values, beliefs, and theoretical orientation and how these affect the group, particularly when working with a diverse and multicultural population.
  b. *Ecological assessment.* Group Workers assess community needs, agency or organization resources, sponsoring organization mission, staff competency, attitudes regarding group work, professional training levels of potential group leaders regarding group work, client attitudes regarding group work, and multicultural and diversity considerations. Group Workers use this information as the basis for making decisions related to their group practice or for implementing groups for which they have supervisory, evaluation, or oversight responsibilities.

### A.4. Program Development and Evaluation

  a. *Group Workers identify the type(s) of group(s) to be offered and how they relate to community needs.*
  b. *Group Workers concisely state in writing the purpose and goals of the group.* Group Workers also identify the role of the group members in influencing or determining the group goals.
  c. *Group Workers set fees consistent with the organization's fee schedule, taking into consideration the financial status and locality of prospective group members.*
  d. *Group Workers choose techniques and a leadership style appropriate to the type(s) of group(s) being offered.*
  e. *Group Workers have an evaluation plan consistent with regulatory, organization, and insurance requirements, where appropriate.*
  f. Group Workers take into consideration current professional guidelines when using technology, including but not limited to Internet communication.

### A.5. Resources

Group Workers coordinate resources related to the kind of group(s) and group activities to be provided, such as: adequate funding, the appropriateness and availability of a trained coleader, space and privacy requirements for the type(s) of group(s) being offered, marketing and recruiting, and appropriate collaboration with other community agencies and organizations.

### A.6. Professional Disclosure Statement

Group Workers have a professional disclosure statement that includes information on confidentiality and exceptions to confidentiality; theoretical orientation; information on the nature, purpose(s), and goals of the group; the group services that can be provided; the role and responsibility of group members and leaders; Group Workers' qualifications to conduct the specific group(s); specific licenses, certifications, and professional affiliations; and address of licensing/credentialing body.

### A.7. Group and Member Preparation

  a. *Group Workers screen prospective group members if appropriate to the type of group being offered.* When selection of group members is appropriate, Group Workers identify group members whose needs and goals are compatible with the goals of the group.
  b. *Group Workers facilitate informed consent.* Group Workers provide in oral and written form to prospective members (when appropriate to group type): the professional disclosure statement, group purpose and goals, group participation expectations including voluntary and involuntary membership, role expectations of members and leader(s), policies related to entering and exiting the group, policies governing substance use, policies and procedures governing mandated groups (where relevant), documentation requirements, disclosure of information to others, implications of out-of-group contact or involvement among members, procedures for consultation between group leader(s) and group member(s), fees and time parameters, and potential impacts of group participation.
  c. *Group Workers obtain the appropriate consent forms for work with minors and other dependent group members.*
  d. *Group Workers define confidentiality and its limits (for example, legal and ethical exceptions and expectations; waivers implicit with treatment plans, documentation, and insurance usage).* Group Workers have the responsibility to inform all group participants of the need for confidentiality and potential consequences of breaching confidentiality; they must explain that legal privilege does not apply to group discussions (unless provided by state statute).

### A.8. Professional Development

Group Workers recognize that professional growth is a continuous, ongoing, developmental process throughout their career.

a. *Group Workers remain current and increase knowledge and skill competencies through activities such as continuing education, professional supervision, and participation in personal and professional development activities.*

b. *Group Workers seek consultation and/or supervision regarding ethical concerns that interfere with effective functioning as a group leader.* Supervisors have the responsibility to keep abreast of consultation, group theory, and process and to adhere to related ethical guidelines.

c. *Group Workers seek appropriate professional assistance for their own personal problems or conflicts that are likely to impair their professional judgment or work performance.*

d. *Group Workers seek consultation and supervision to ensure appropriate practice whenever working with a group for which all knowledge and skill competencies have not been achieved.*

e. Group Workers keep abreast of group research and development.

### A.9. Trends and Technological Changes

Group Workers are aware of and responsive to technological changes as they affect society and the profession. These include but are not limited to changes in mental health delivery systems, legislative and insurance industry reforms, shifting population demographics and client needs, and technological advances in Internet and other communication and delivery systems. Group Workers adhere to ethical guidelines related to the use of developing technologies.

## Section B: Best Practice in Performing

### B.1. Self-Knowledge

Group Workers are aware of and monitor their strengths and weaknesses and the effects these have on group members.

### B.2. Group Competencies

Group Workers have a basic knowledge of groups and the principles of group dynamics and are able to perform the core group competencies, as described in the ASGW Professional Standards for the Training of Group Workers. In addition, Group Workers have adequate understanding and skill in any group specialty area chosen for practice (psychotherapy, counseling, task, psychoeducation, as described in the ASGW Training Standards).

### B.3. Group Plan Adaptation

a. *Group Workers apply and modify knowledge, skills, and techniques appropriate to group type and stage and to the unique needs of various cultural and ethnic groups.*

b. *Group Workers monitor the group's progress toward the group goals and plan.*

c. *Group Workers clearly define and maintain ethical, professional, and social relationship boundaries with group members as appropriate to their role in the organization and the type of group being offered.*

### B.4. Therapeutic Conditions and Dynamics

Group Workers understand and are able to implement appropriate models of group development, process observation, and therapeutic conditions.

### B.5. Meaning

Group Workers assist members in generating meaning from the group experience.

### B.6. Collaboration

Group Workers assist members in developing individual goals and respect group members as coequal partners in the group experience.

### B.7. Evaluation

Group Workers include evaluation (both formal and informal) between sessions and at the conclusion of the group.

### B.8. Diversity

Group Workers practice with broad sensitivity to client differences including but not limited to ethnic, gender, religious, sexual, psychological maturity, economic class, family history, physical characteristics or limitations, and geographic location. Group Workers continuously seek information regarding the cultural issues of the diverse population with whom they are working, both by interaction with participants and by using outside resources.

### B.9. Ethical Surveillance

Group Workers employ an appropriate ethical decision-making model in responding to ethical challenges and issues and in determining courses of action and behavior for self and group members. In addition, Group Workers employ applicable standards as promulgated by ACA, ASGW, or other appropriate professional organizations.

**Section C: Best Practice in Group Processing**

**C.1. Processing Schedule**

Group Workers process the workings of the group with themselves, group members, supervisors, or other colleagues, as appropriate. This may include assessing progress on group and member goals, leader behaviors and techniques, group dynamics and interventions, as well as developing understanding and acceptance of meaning. Processing may occur both within sessions and before and after each session, at time of termination, and later follow-up, as appropriate.

**C.2. Reflective Practice**

Group Workers attend to opportunities to synthesize theory and practice and to incorporate learning outcomes into ongoing groups. Group Workers attend to session dynamics of members and their interactions and also attend to the relationship between session dynamics and leader values, cognition, and affect.

**C.3. Evaluation and Follow-Up**

a. *Group Workers evaluate process and outcomes.* Results are used for ongoing program planning, improvement and revisions of current group, and/or for professional research literature. Group Workers follow all applicable policies and standards in using group material for research and reports.

b. *Group Workers conduct follow-up contact with group members, as appropriate, to assess outcomes or when requested by a group member(s).*

**C.4. Consultation and Training with Other Organizations**

Group Workers provide consultation and training to organizations in and out of their setting, when appropriate. Group Workers seek out consultation as needed with competent professional persons knowledgeable about group work.

---

# Questions to Consider in Examining the "Best Practice Guidelines"

As you work through these questions, pay particular attention to ways you might apply the "Best Practice Guidelines" to group practice. I hope these questions will raise further questions in your mind and begin the process of developing your own ethical guidelines. Ask yourself what additional guidelines might be included, or consider guidelines you want to challenge. If you were a member of the ASGW Ethics Committee charged with the task of revising these guidelines, which ones would you most want to modify, and why? Do you think the guidelines are complete and comprehensive? Do you see any bias in these guidelines? Are there any specific areas that need to be addressed in more detail for group counselors? Take the time to thoroughly review each of these guidelines in a critical way, and discuss the issues raised by them in small groups in class.

1. Scope of Practice and Conceptual Framework
   a. To what extent are you committed to limiting your practice to those areas for which you have met the training criteria established by the ASGW Training Standards?
   b. How well are you able to articulate a general conceptual framework to guide your practice? Can you provide a rationale for the techniques you use?

2. Assessment of Self
   a. To what degree are you able to assess your knowledge and skills against those required to effectively lead a specific group?
   b. How well are you able to assess your values, beliefs, and theoretical orientation? How do these factors influence your work with groups?
   c. To what extent are you aware of your own values, biases, assumptions, and beliefs that most apply to working with culturally different clients?
   d. How do you make decisions about which techniques and leadership styles are appropriate to the specific groups you offer?

3. Professional Disclosure Statement
   a. As a group worker, what kind of professional disclosure statement do you believe is appropriate and useful?
   b. What would you most want to include in this document?

4. Group and Member Preparation
   a. What kind of minimal information would you provide to a person wanting to join one of your groups?
   b. How do you think informed consent can best be accomplished in both voluntary and mandatory groups?
   c. What are some legal and ethical issues pertaining to informed consent?

5. Screening Members
   a. Is it unethical to fail to screen?
   b. What are some alternatives when screening is not practical?
   c. How can screening and orientation be handled in mandatory groups?

6. Confidentiality
   a. How would you explain what confidentiality is and its purpose to members of your groups?
   b. Under what circumstances are you ethically or legally required to breach confidentiality?
   c. How can confidentiality best be taught to group members and maintained?
   d. How are you likely to explain to members of your groups that legal privilege does not apply to group work unless it is provided by state statute?

7. Professional Development
   a. What steps might you take to remain current and to increase your knowledge and skill competencies?
   b. As a group worker, when would you seek consultation or supervision?
   c. If you were encountering difficulties leading a group, what steps might you take in getting supervision or consultation?
   d. Can you think of any areas of unresolved personal problems that could impair your professional judgment or inhibit your effectiveness as a group leader?
   e. If you became aware of countertransference issues or personal problems that affected your performance as a group worker, what would you do?

8. Goal Development
   a. What are some ways in which you can help members continually assess the degree to which they are meeting their own goals?
   b. How would you monitor the group's progress toward the group goals and purpose of the group?

9. Diversity
   a. As a group practitioner, what ethical issues might you expect to confront with respect to working with diverse client populations?
   b. To what degree are you willing to seek information regarding the cultural issues of the diverse populations in your groups?

10. Evaluation and Follow-Up
    a. What are some ideas you have for evaluating the process and outcomes of your groups?
    b. Is it unethical to fail to arrange for follow-up meetings?
    c. What are some alternatives to follow-up meetings on either an individual or a group basis?

# Exercises and Activities

## Case Vignettes: Practice with Ethical Decision Making

*Directions:* The following situations in groups are presented for your analysis and for class discussion. What do you see as the ethical issues in each situation? To what degree do you think the group leader in each situation acted in an ethical or an unethical manner? What do you think you would have done differently? How might the situation in each case be remedied? Do you have any thoughts about how an unethical practice might have been avoided?

The object of these exercises is to give you practice in ethical decision making and an opportunity to discuss ethical issues involved in the practice of group work. Read each of the case situations presented, and respond by placing the number in the blank that best represents your professional ethical opinion regarding the *group leader's behavior.* Use this code:

**1** = unethical
**2** = somewhat unethical
**3** = uncertain
**4** = somewhat ethical
**5** = ethical

*[handwritten: 1. Read   2. Ethical / Unethical]*

___ *[handwritten: 1]* (1) *Orientation and providing information.* The group leader assumes that the more information about group process she provides, the more the members will attempt to please her. She is opposed to giving prior information, either in writing or orally. If members flounder in defining goals, she believes this is part of the group process; therefore, she does not emphasize goal definition. She does not discuss the procedures she will use because she believes procedures are not possible without specified goals. Thus, procedures will be dictated by the eventual goals members define. This leader is convinced that informed consent is not really possible and thinks members should follow their own spontaneous paths rather than learning about group norms and other expected group behavior.

___ *[handwritten: 1]* (2) *Screening members.* The case involves a busy mental health clinic that is understaffed. Counselors are under some pressure to do group work as a way of dealing with more clients in a given time. A counselor decides to organize a group by putting a notice on the bulletin board in the clinic and by sending colleagues a memorandum asking for candidates. There are no provisions for individual screening of potential members, no written announcement informing the members of the goals and purposes of the group, and no preparation for incoming members. No information is given to the members about the leader's background, possible techniques to be used, expectations, and so forth. No consideration is given to the leader's qualifications to work with special populations. The receptionist is asked to admit the first 12 people who come to sign up. The receptionist puts people into the group as they inquire, irrespective of the nature of their problems, and they are simply told to show up at the first meeting.

___ *[handwritten: 5]* (3) *Confidentiality.* A group leader discusses the legal aspects of confidentiality, the reasons for it, and the impact on the group of a lack of it. He summarizes member responsibility in keeping confidentiality by saying, "Anything that happens here, stays here." In discussing the importance of confidentiality in the group, he also points out how confidentiality can be violated in subtle ways and how confidences are often divulged without malice.

**4** **(4)** *Voluntary/involuntary participation.* A group leader agrees to accept court-ordered members into her group. In spite of her attempts to get these members involved, they consistently make it clear that they are there only as a condition of their probation and that they have no intention of getting personally involved. After the 10 required sessions, the group leader reports back to the probation officer that these individuals made satisfactory progress, mainly because they attended the sessions and she was convinced they must have learned something simply by listening to others even though they didn't share or participate.

**1** 5. *Leaving a group.* A leader says: "Because this is a voluntary group, your attendance cannot be required. If at any time you don't want to attend, use your judgment and stay away. If for any reason you find that this group is not meeting your needs, you're perfectly free to leave. We want you in this group only if you're choosing to be a member." Several members simply drop out of the group without telling the leader or the other members that this is their intention. The leader continues the group, making no references to the missing members.

**5** 6. *Coercion and pressure.* Joan is having difficulties with her husband, and she discusses her struggles with him in her group. Before she has really explored this issue and before she has had a chance to express the full range of her feelings and her own part in the conflict, many members intervene with advice, such as "Leave the guy," "You're better off without him," "Don't waste any more of your life—you deserve better," and "If someone did that to me, I sure wouldn't hang around." The leader intervenes and redirects the group discussion to Joan's feelings.

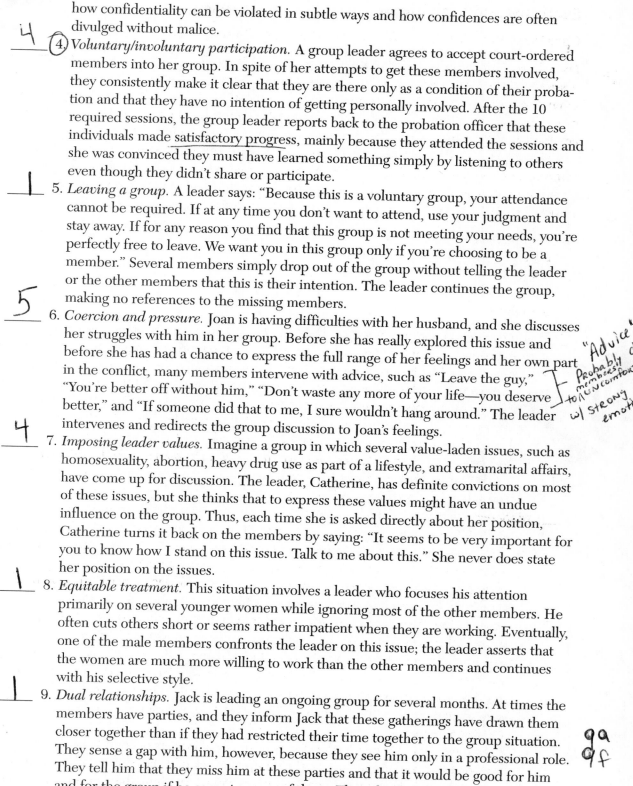

*"Advice"*
*Probably due*
*members uncomfortable*
*to w/ strong*
*emotion*

**4** 7. *Imposing leader values.* Imagine a group in which several value-laden issues, such as homosexuality, abortion, heavy drug use as part of a lifestyle, and extramarital affairs, have come up for discussion. The leader, Catherine, has definite convictions on most of these issues, but she thinks that to express these values might have an undue influence on the group. Thus, each time she is asked directly about her position, Catherine turns it back on the members by saying: "It seems to be very important for you to know how I stand on this issue. Talk to me about this." She never does state her position on the issues.

**1** 8. *Equitable treatment.* This situation involves a leader who focuses his attention primarily on several younger women while ignoring most of the other members. He often cuts others short or seems rather impatient when they are working. Eventually, one of the male members confronts the leader on this issue; the leader asserts that the women are much more willing to work than the other members and continues with his selective style.

**1** 9. *Dual relationships.* Jack is leading an ongoing group for several months. At times the members have parties, and they inform Jack that these gatherings have drawn them closer together than if they had restricted their time together to the group situation. They sense a gap with him, however, because they see him only in a professional role. They tell him that they miss him at these parties and that it would be good for him and for the group if he came to some of them. They clearly express their desire for more personal contact with him because they want to get to know him in a more

*9a*
*9f*

informal situation. He decides to attend, hoping to increase the cohesion in the group.

*Know technique well enough that you can explain to client*

_____ 10. *Use of techniques.* Steve, a relatively inexperienced group leader, attends a weekend workshop designed to "open your feelings" through the use of body-oriented techniques. He is impressed with the power of this therapy and is eager to try out these techniques in his group. In a later session, one member, Tom, says, "I feel choked up with pain and anger, and I don't know how to deal with my feelings." Steve intervenes by having Tom lie down while Steve pushes on his abdomen and encourages him to scream, kick, shout, and release all the feelings he has been keeping pent up.

"Rolfing" en vogue in 70's

*ignored 1st 2 stages (went right to working stage)*

_____ 11. *Goal development.* Phil begins a group session with this statement: "We are all here, and I assume that you all want something from this group, so let's get down to business right away. Who wants to work?" Because of Phil's skills in working with members, there is rarely a dull session, and things seem to keep moving. He is active in using role-playing techniques, in suggesting homework assignments, in taking members on guided fantasies, and in providing structured exercises. He does not spend group time talking about the members' personal goals or how they might best accomplish what they came to the group to attain.

(Best Practices)
A 4 b
A 6
B 3 b

2/4 12. *Consultation.* Fran is conducting a short-term group in an elementary school aimed at helping children of divorce. At the beginning of the group, she lets the children know that for the most part, what they explore in the group will stay there. She becomes concerned about one of the children, Brad, thinking that he might be suicidal. She seeks consultation from the school psychologist and discusses her concerns about Brad with his teachers. She does not tell him that she is seeking outside consultation because she does not want to alarm him, nor does she want to convey the impression that she is sharing information from the group with other school personnel. *She needs to let Brad know she is consulting others*

12 c, f

*You need to spell out confid. exceptions + give examples*

4 13. *Termination from the group.* Ken is just finishing a group that he has led weekly for a year. The group members express a unanimous desire to continue. They feel good about themselves and one another and are sad to leave these weekly sessions, which they believe have been very productive for them. They express anxiety about continuing to make it without group support and without Ken's direction. This is the final session, and now they ask him to keep the group going. He decides not to continue the group.    *Ethical if did all he could do*

13a
5c

*Need constant awareness of progress + promote independence*

_____ 14. *Evaluation and follow-up.* Bart comes to the West Coast from the East to offer an intensive personal growth workshop. During the workshop, many personal conflicts emerge and much emotion is expressed. There is no letup in the intensity because Bart assumes that the way to achieve breakthroughs is to "keep at it constantly" so that defenses are broken down. This leader believes people develop tough defenses and that the best way to crack them is through a sustained period of confrontations. No follow-up is planned, and Bart asserts, "Group members are responsible for themselves and will go only as far as they choose." After the residential workshop ends, Bart leaves the state the next morning to conduct another group, providing no information on where the members can turn for further assistance.

ethics
#14

B5
B7
C1
C3

*intense*
*No follow up*

_____ 15. *Referrals.* Paula is employed as a counselor at a community mental health agency where no groups are available. She believes in the value of group counseling after her

*dual Relationships          9g          A2  A3a*

clients have completed a number of individual sessions with her. In spite of her best efforts to begin a group at her agency, the director does not give her permission. Paula then suggests to some of her individual clients that she would be pleased to accept them into a group through her private practice. Since she knows they are financially strapped, she is willing to have them join her group at a reduced fee.

*Refer to someone else* [handwritten]

___ 16. *Professional development.* Because of the demand, Rhonda agrees to organize and lead a group for battered women at the agency where she is employed. She is hesitant to lead the group because she did not have a course in group counseling in her graduate program, has not been in a group as a member, and has not had any supervision or training in group work. She finally agrees to set up the group because she thinks she can use her techniques and skills in individual counseling in a group situation. She convinces herself that since it is not realistic for her to obtain group training quickly the pressing demand for this group makes it acceptable for her to lead it.

*No experience No training* [handwritten]

## Self-Evaluation of Your Level of Training as a Group Worker

*Note:* You can access the ASGW (2000) Professional Standards for the Training of Group Workers online: www.asgw.org. You will also find a wide range of information about ASGW from the main Web site.

The following activity allows you to assess your current level of knowledge and skills as a group counselor. It is based on "Professional Standards for the Training of Group Workers," which were expanded, revised, and adopted by the ASGW's Executive Board in 2000* [Download this document by linking to the Web site given above.] These standards contain both knowledge competencies and skill competencies that the ASGW considers as core training in group work for all counselors. The ASGW also specifies 10 hours of observation of and participation in a group experience as the minimum level of supervised practice (with a recommended 20 hours of such experience). There should be a minimum of one course in basic group work that deals with knowledge and skills. Besides the core group competencies, advanced competencies are specified for group work specialists in these four areas of group work: (1) task facilitation groups, (2) psychoeducation groups, (3) counseling groups, and (4) psychotherapy groups.

*Directions:* Rate yourself on the following competencies, using this scale:

**5** = I am especially strong in this area.
**4** = I am very good to good in this area.
**3** = I am just adequate and could surely improve.
**2** = I am deficient and need much improvement.
**1** = I am especially weak in this competency.

---

*The sections dealing with knowledge competencies and skill competencies are adapted by permission of the ASGW. The rating scale is an adaptation of the standards for the purposes of this manual.

Source: "Association for Specialists in Group Work: Professional Standards for the Training of Group Workers," *Group Worker,* 28(3), Spring 2000, pp. 1–10. [Special insert]. Reprinted with permission of ASGW.

## Core Knowledge Competencies for Group Workers

*To the following degree, I am able to:*

___2___ 1. state the four major group work specializations, the distinguishing characteristics of each, the commonalities shared by all, and the appropriate instances in which each is to be used.

___2___ 2. identify the basic principles of group dynamics.

___2___ 3. discuss the basic therapeutic ingredients of groups.

___3___ 4. identify the personal characteristics of group workers that have an impact on members and know my personal strengths, weaknesses, biases, and values and their effect on others.

___4___ 5. describe the specific ethical issues that are unique to group work.

___2___ 6. discuss the body of research on group work and how it relates to my academic preparation.

___2___ 7. define the process components involved in the typical stages of a group's development.

___2___ 8. describe the major facilitative and debilitative roles that group members may play.

___4___ 9. state the advantages and disadvantages of group work and the circumstances for which it is indicated or contraindicated.

___3___ 10. identify therapeutic factors of group work.

___4___ 11. identify principles and strategies for recruiting and screening prospective group members.

___4___ 12. explain the importance of group and member evaluation.

___3___ 13. deliver a clear, concise, and complete definition of group work.

___4___ 14. explain and clarify the purpose of a particular form of group work.

## Core Skill Competencies for Group Workers

*To the following degree, I am able to effectively:*

___4___ 1. encourage the participation of group members.

___4___ 2. observe and identify group process events.

___3___ 3. attend to and acknowledge group members' behavior.

___4___ 4. clarify and summarize group members' statements.

___2___ 5. open and close group sessions.

___3___ 6. impart information in the group when necessary.

___4___ 7. model effective group leader behavior.

___3___ 8. engage in appropriate self-disclosure.

___3___ 9. give and receive feedback in the group.

___3___ 10. ask open-ended questions in the group.

___5___ 11. empathize with group members.

___3___ 12. confront group members' behavior.

___3___ 13. help group members attribute meaning to their experience.

___3___ 14. help group members integrate and apply their learning.

___5___ 15. demonstrate the ASGW ethical and professional standards in group practice.

___3___ 16. keep the group on course in accomplishing its goals.

## Evaluating Group Leadership Competencies

1. Look over your knowledge and skill ratings to get a sense of your current level of proficiency. What do you think you can do to develop those areas that need strengthening? Form small groups in class to discuss your self-assessments. As a group, what ideas can you come up with to develop and maintain each of the knowledge and skill competencies?

2. Carefully look at the ASGW's recommendations for practice as a part of the core training in group work. What training experiences have you received to date? What supervised group experiences have you had? What experiences do you expect to have had by the time you complete your program?

3. Review the four group work specializations (described in Chapter 3 of the textbook) with respect to the knowledge, skills, and supervised practice required. Which of the four areas is of most interest to you? What are some practical ways to acquire experience in the area of specialization that most interests you? Again, form small groups in class and discuss the ASGW's suggestions and the types of supervised experiences that you deem essential. You might also discuss ways in which you can continue to develop group leadership skills once you complete your program of studies.

4. In Chapter 2 of this manual there is a checklist of group leader skills. I suggest that you review and complete it several times during the course. These are concrete skills that are needed for effective group leadership. One way to improve your level of skill development is to periodically assess your areas of strength and specific areas needing improvement.

# CHAPTER FOUR

# Early Stages in the Development of a Group

## Guidelines for Writing a Proposal for a Group

A clear and convincing proposal is often essential for translating a good idea for a group into actual practice. If you are going to create a group under the auspices of your supervisors or an agency, you will probably have to explain your rationale and proposed methods. It is useful to write out your proposal, for doing so can help you conceptualize your goals, procedures, and strategies for evaluation.

The following guidelines provide some direction in designing a group. To gain practice in developing, writing, and presenting a proposal, think of a group that you would eventually like to organize. Once you have decided on a particular type of group (for example, a group for parents who want to learn better child-rearing skills, a group for children in an elementary school, or a group for adolescents who are having problems in school), consider the following questions in drafting your proposal. Later, spend some time in class discussing the various members' proposals and getting feedback from others on how to improve your proposal.

1. What type of group will you create? Will it be a counseling group? A therapy group? A psychoeducation group? A task group? Will it be long term or short term? Will it have a remedial (treatment) or a developmental (enhancement) focus?
2. Who is the group for? Is it for a particular population, such as children in an elementary school? For outpatients in a community mental health center? For substance abusers in a residential setting? for parents who are having major problems relating to their children? For couples who hope to learn better communication skills?
3. What are your goals for this group; that is, what will members gain from participating in the group? What are the short-term goals? Are the goals and objectives specific? How will these goals be accomplished in a group setting? How will the long-range goals be evaluated during the course of the group and once it comes to an end?
4. Why is there a need for such a group? In what ways would a group provide definite advantages over individual counseling?
5. What are your basic assumptions underlying this project? Do you have a clear and convincing rationale for your group? Are you able to answer questions that might be raised?
6. What are your qualifications for leading the group? What have you learned from doing previous groups that you could apply to the proposed group?
7. How will you announce your group and recruit members for it? Where will you get members? What will you want to convey in any written announcements?
8. What kind of screening and selection procedures will be used? What is the rationale for using these particular procedures? Whom will you include, and whom might you exclude?

9. How many members will be in the group? Where will the group meet? How often will it meet? How long will each meeting last? Will new people be allowed to join the group once it has started?

10. What structure will the group have? Will it be designed around special topics and issues? If so, what topics are likely to be the focus of the group?

11. How will members be prepared to derive the maximum benefit from the group? What ground rules will the group have?

12. Will you ask members to formulate contracts as a basis for structuring the sessions? What are some advantages and disadvantages of using contracts for your particular group?

13. How will you handle the fact that people will be taking some risks by participating in the group? What will you tell them about these risks, and what will you do to safeguard them from unnecessary risks? Will you take any special precautions with minors?

14. Will your group be voluntary or mandatory? If the members are required to attend, what measures are you taking to increase the chances of gaining their cooperation? How might you deal with the resistance of members who do not want to participate?

15. What ethical considerations need to be addressed? Does your proposal reflect an awareness of ethical practice? What ethical guidelines will you follow?

16. What do you expect to be the characteristics of the various stages of the group? What do you see as your function at each of these stages? What expectations do you have for the members at each phase?

17. What techniques and procedures might you employ in the group? Will there be structured exercises? Will you emphasize role playing? Will members be expected to practice new skills outside of the group sessions? What techniques might you use to get members to support one another in their efforts to change, both in the sessions and between meetings?

18. To what extent will you be available for individual consultation with group members? If the members are having difficulties resulting from the group, are you willing to meet with them privately, or do you expect them to bring up these problems in the group? When might you suggest a referral for a particular member?

19. What evaluation procedures do you plan? Will you evaluate each session? If so, how? Once the group ends, what methods might you use to assess the overall effectiveness of the group?

20. What follow-up procedures might you use? Will you meet each member privately to discuss the degree to which he or she has met personal goals? Will you meet with the group as a whole one or more times for evaluation purposes?

## Exercises and Activities

Your knowledge of the stages in the development of a group can help you carry out the specific functions of a group leader at these various phases. You can provide needed structure, make appropriate interventions, and predict certain blocks to the group process.

### Practicing Leadership Skills

These exercises and activities will give you practice in your class or group in developing the leadership skills needed at each stage. As you read through these activities, select the ones that have the most meaning for you and bring them up in the class/group. You can use some of them on your own as a way of learning techniques for organizing groups, establishing and maintaining a working climate, terminating groups, and opening or closing group sessions.

1. Imagine talking to potential group members. Explain to them what your group is for and how you expect to lead it. Assume that these people have never been in a group before. What would you stress regarding its purposes and procedures?

2. *Screening interview exercise.* Assume the role of a leader conducting a screening interview for members of a certain kind of group. Conduct a pregroup interview with a prospective member for about 10 minutes. Then the one who was interviewed can report on how he or she felt during the interview. What is your interviewing style like? What were some of the most effective questions or interventions? How could the interview have been improved? Next, interview another prospective member so you can gain from the feedback and try new ideas.

3. *Group member interviews the leader.* Prospective members may want to talk with the leader before they commit themselves to a group. In this exercise the same format can be used as in Exercise 2, except group members (several people in class can volunteer for this role) ask questions of the group leader. This exercise can be done in subgroups so that everyone has a chance to be both the member and the leader. Everyone can be invited to make observations and suggestions.

4. Draw up a list of specific questions that you as a leader might ask at a screening interview. What would you look for? On what basis would you include or exclude members?

5. How would you turn away a person if you thought either that he or she was not appropriate for the group or that the group was not appropriate for him or her? You might set this up as a group/class exercise. Are you able to exclude a person from a group without conveying rejection?

6. What screening methods, if any, can you apply to involuntary group members? Do you believe they can benefit? Why or why not? How would you deal with the situation if the agency you worked for insisted that all of the clients attend the group, whether they wanted to or not? Assume that all the mental health workers there had to use group therapy as the primary treatment method.

7. Discuss some of the problems you might encounter in an open group that you would not be so likely to have in a closed group. How do you expect to deal with the problems that arise in an open group (one with changing membership)?

8. What value, if any, do you see in arranging an initial private interview with each group member to explore matters such as goals, fears, expectations, questions, and concerns? How would you prepare members of your group?

9. *Initial stages of a group.* Try to recall what it was like for you when you first entered a counseling group or *any* group of strangers. Consider the possibility that your prospective group members feel the same way. Discuss with others in your class/group how you might be a more compassionate leader if you could keep these memories fresh.

10. *Trust building.* What are the most crucial tasks during the early stages of a group? Think of the ways in which you would attempt to create trust within the group. Also, think about how you would introduce yourself to your group and how you would take care of introductions of group members. What are some specific ways you might work on building trust at the initial meetings?

11. Most writers describe conflict, confrontations, competition, and rivalry as a basic part of a group's evolution. What could you do as a leader to ignore these dynamics? What effect would this choice have on subsequent group development?

12. Assume that you are leading your first group and several members are questioning your level of expertise. How would you deal with this challenge?

13. Imagine that group members are telling you they see you strictly as "the leader." They ask you to become more like them and to share more of yourself with them. How would you handle this situation? Explain to the group your understanding of the role of group leader.

14. Examine your own patterns of resistance as a group member. List some ways in which you may have found yourself reluctant in this class/group. Imagine that you are leading a group of people who have many of the same defenses and resistances that you have. How would this be for you?

15. In your own experience as a group member, what has helped you recognize and work through certain resistances? What has hindered you? What might have led you to deeper entrenchment in certain resistances and defensive styles of behaving in a group?

16. Can you respect a member's hesitations? Assume that a member says that she doesn't want to press onward with an issue on which she has been working. What courses of action would you be inclined to take? Do you see a difference between pressuring members to talk about a given issue and encouraging them to talk about possible fears that keep them from working on the issue?

17. What can a leader do, in general, to effectively handle defensive behaviors that occur in a group? What are helpful leader behaviors in a group whose members exhibit problem behaviors?

18. Discuss the differences between reducing a person to a label (such as "the monopolist," "the help-rejecting complainer," "the bore," and so on) and describing a specific behavior such as monopolizing. As a group leader, how can you encourage a member to recognize and deal with specific behaviors that are counterproductive to the progress of both the individual and the group?

19. There is a danger of pushing people too soon to give up a defense. Ask yourself if you are able to handle the reaction of a person who relinquishes a defense. For example, if you encourage a member to feel his anger instead of intellectualizing it, could you handle the possible explosive expression of his anger should he experience it fully? How can you determine whether you are competent to deal with what lies under a defense?

20. Your own objectivity can become distorted as a result of countertransference feelings that are aroused in you toward certain clients and that tend to be based on unrecognized and unresolved personal issues. Put yourself into each of the following eight common countertransference situations. How would you fit into each of these situations? What are you aware of in yourself that might prevent you from focusing on the needs and best interests of group members?

    a. You have an inordinate need for reassurance and constant reinforcement; this includes the need to please all the members, to win their respect, to get them to approve of you, and to have them confirm you as a "superb leader."

    b. You see yourself in certain clients; you overidentify with some members to the extent that you take on their problems.

c. You develop sexual and romantic feelings toward certain members; you engage in seductive behavior and allow your sexual attraction to become a central focus in the group.

d. You give people advice in such a way that you tell others what to do based on your own needs and values.

e. You develop social relationships with some members outside of the group and find that you challenge them less during group sessions than you do other members.

f. You use power over members to prove your adequacy; you gain power through the use of certain highly directive techniques.

g. You attempt to persuade members to accept the values you hold; you are more interested in having members subscribe to your idea of the right way to live than in letting members decide on their own values.

h. You see clearly the faults of members and use what they do or don't do to justify poor results in a group; at the same time you are blind to your own shortcomings or your part in the group process.

## Helpful Intervention Phrases for the Initial Stage of a Group

A few well-chosen and well-timed words can give group members the guidance that will enable them to explore personal issues in a significant way. Here is a list of sentences and phrases leaders can use during the early stage of a group. I hope you will not simply memorize these phrases but will modify them to fit your personal style as well as your specific group population. Although I use many of these phrases during the initial stage of a group, not all of them are used in a particular group.

- Whom in the group are you most aware of right now?
- How does it feel to be in the room right now?
- Are you here because you want to be?
- What do you most want to get from this group?
- What are you willing to do to get what you say you want?
- To what degree are you willing to try out new things in this group?
- What are three things you want us to know about you?
- What do you know about groups? What expectations are you bringing with you to this group?
- If a friend of yours introduced you to this group, what might he or she say about you?
- What was going on in your life that led you to join this group?
- I hope you challenge yourself early to get involved. The longer you wait, the more difficult it will get.
- What fears or doubts do you have about this group, if any?
- What do you fear most? What do you hope for most?
- Why would you want to change anything in your life now?
- What would you most like to say you have learned or decided when you leave the group?
- What you will learn about yourself is largely dependent on your willingness to participate in this group.
- It is important that you express persistent thoughts and feelings.
- If you are in the group now because someone sent you here, how do you feel about that?

## Helpful Intervention Phrases for the Transition Stage of a Group

The transition stage is an especially challenging time in a group's evolution. Defenses are typically high, and a leader's interventions need to be carefully made so that reluctance or resistance is not entrenched. The manner and tone in which a leader phrases his or her interventions is largely responsible for a member's willingness to take risks and to respond to challenges. My coleaders and I find the following statements and questions to be generally facilitative:

- I notice that you have been very quiet during many of these sessions. I would be interested in knowing what it has been like for you to be here and any reactions you may have had.
- I am aware how quiet the group as a whole is. I wonder what is not being said in here that needs to be expressed.
- Are you willing to continue now?
- You say that you are unwilling to continue. What stops you?
- Are you willing to explore the reasons for your reluctance to pursue this topic further?
- What is the worst thing that you can imagine happening if you continue now?
- Whom in this group were you thinking about last week, and what were you thinking?
- If you are experiencing difficulties in this group, I hope you will be willing to express them.
- Imagine that this is the last chance you have to change your life.
- Rather than questioning people, would you say what is prompting you to ask your questions?
- Rather than telling others your solutions to problems, consider saying more about the problems you are struggling with.
- With whom do you have unfinished business?
- If this were the end of the group, would that be all right?
- How would it be for you if you continued the rest of your life the way you are now?
- What are you willing to do with the tension you feel?
- I am aware that several of you are hesitant to become involved. Do you have any reactions to my observation?
- I feel as though I am working too hard at leading and that I am taking too much responsibility for the outcome of this session. I would like to explore the balance of responsibility in here.
- So, some of you say you are bored. What is not happening for you in here? What are you willing to do to change it?
- Take a moment to center yourself. If you had to pick just one problem right now, which one would it be?
- You are very willing to talk. I am concerned that I have not yet heard from several people, and I would like to check in with them.
- I am aware that you are very quiet in this group. Although you say you learn a great deal by observing others, I would like to know what it is that you have been observing and how you have been affected by it.
- I know this conflict is difficult and uncomfortable. I hope you don't give up. We have a better chance to find clarity and understanding if we continue talking.

## *Groups in Action: Evolution and Challenges* [DVD and Workbook]

### Getting the Most from the DVD and Workbook Program

We have developed a self-study student DVD and workbook combination titled *Groups in Action: Evolution and Challenges* that can be used as an integrated learning package with *Theory and Practice of Group Counseling*. *Groups in Action* consists of two separate programs. The first program, *Evolution of a Group* (2 hours) depicts central features that illustrate the development of the group process and how the co-leaders facilitated that process as the group moved through the various stages: initial, transition, working, and ending. The second program, *Challenges for Group Leaders* (90 minutes) demonstrates ways to work therapeutically with a variety of difficult behaviors in groups and approaches to addressing diversity issues in group counseling. The DVD and workbook are sold as a package only, and the workbook, which utilizes an interactive format, requires that students become active learners as they study the group process in action. The *Groups in Action* program is published by Thomson Brooks/Cole.

The aim of this interactive program is to raise questions and issues—and to help you understand the art of facilitating a group. The first DVD program (*Evolution of a Group*) shows significant incidents that emerged from the group process during a three-day residential group therapy session. You will see how the co-leaders (Marianne and Jerry Corey) facilitated that process as the group moved through the four group stages: initial, transition, working, and ending.

I hope you use the workbook that accompanies the DVD as your "interpreter" of the group process. The workbook provides a rationale for the interventions made, frequently discusses how an individual's work moved beyond what is shown in the video, and encourages you to interact with what you are observing. By completing the activities in the workbook, you will be actively experiencing how theory can be translated into practice.

---

*Note:* The page numbers shown in parentheses refer to pages in the textbook *Theory and Practice of Group Counseling* (7th ed.) where further information on these topics can be found.

---

### Stage 1: Pregroup Issues—Formation of the Group (pages 67-77)

Before making the decision to be a part of this group, the potential group members met together with the co-leaders (Marianne and Jerry Corey) to get acquainted with one another and to determine whether they wanted to participate in this type of special group experience. Of course, all the participants knew in advance that the purpose of this workshop was to produce an educational program.

During the formation of this group, we employed many of the procedures described in Chapter 4. For instance, we screened members, and we arranged for a pregroup meeting to prepare them for the group. We addressed topics such as confidentiality, dealing with genuine personal concerns, safeguards to protect members, and preparation for the actual weekend group that would be videotaped.

If you are using the DVD and workbook along with this text, you will see the detailed information that was provided when forming this special kind of group. Notice in the DVD how we asked members to begin by sharing any reactions they had about the pregroup meeting.

## Stage 2: Initial Stage—Orientation and Exploration (pages 77-84)

1. *Characteristics of the initial stage.* Think about how the characteristics described in the text are evident in the initial stage of the group depicted in the DVD. For instance, in the DVD what are some expectations and concerns of the members? Did all the members feel a sense of inclusion in the group?

2. *Establishing trust.* Trust is the foundation of a group. As you view the DVD, answer these questions: What early concerns did the members voice? What were some of the fears of members? For this kind of group, how could the fact that it was being videotaped become a hidden agenda if the topic had not been thoroughly discussed from the outset? How did the co-leaders steer the members of this group into a here-and-now focus from the beginning? What process was used to help the members get acquainted? How much trust seemed evident as you observed the initial session? What would it take for you to feel a sense of trust in a group? What did you learn about some ways to create trust in a group through viewing the early phase of the group?

3. *Role of the group leader.* What kind of roles did you see the co-leaders assuming in the DVD group? What behaviors did the co-leaders model? What did you notice about the way we worked together as co-leaders? If you were leading this group, would you have a clear sense of what the members wanted to get from the group experience? What did you notice about the way the co-leaders intervened to assist members in defining specific personal goals?

4. *Structuring and forming norms.* Structuring is an important process during the early stages of a group. What kind of structuring did you observe the co-leaders providing? How might you provide a different kind of structuring? How did the co-leaders deal with the issue of cultural diversity that emerged early in the life of the group? What specific norms are the co-leaders attempting to shape early in the group?

## Stage 3: Transition Stage—Dealing with Resistance (pages 84-93)

1. *Characteristics of the transition stage.* In the text I state: "Before a group can begin doing a deeper level of work, it typically goes through a somewhat challenging transition phase" (page 84). As you view the DVD, what evidence do you see of the members dealing with anxiety, resistance, and conflict? What were some specific manifestations of resistance during the early stages? What characteristics unfold in this group during the transition stage? What lessons can you learn from this about dealing therapeutically with resistance?

2. *Anxiety among group members.* Some common anxieties typical during the transition stage include fears of rejection, of not being understood, of being judged harshly, or of losing control. What anxieties are voiced by members in this group? What did you learn about what is helpful in exploring these fears? What fears might you have if you were a member of this kind of group?

   A member may say, "I'm being very careful in this group because I am afraid of being judged." As co-leaders, we ask members to talk more about the fears or reservations they may be experiencing so we can intervene in a way that makes the room safer and provides a climate whereby members can talk about their hesitations. This comes about by exploring fears, not simply by being reassured. After viewing the DVD, what is the importance of carefully working with whatever members bring to a group regarding their fears and reservations? How is this transitional work essential if you hope to help a group move to a deeper level of interpersonal interaction? From reading this chapter and viewing the transition stage segment of the DVD, what are you learning about the leader's task during this crucial stage in a group?

3. *Conflict.* Although conflict often occurs during the transition stage, it can erupt during the initial group session. In the video group, conflict occurs during both the initial and the ending stages. What are the possible consequences of ignoring conflict or dealing with it ineffectively? Did you learn anything about how to deal with conflict from viewing the sessions, regardless of when it occurs?

4. *Resistance.* Resistance is an inevitable phenomenon in groups that must be recognized and explored. You will notice that members in the DVD group are asked to share some of the ways they are likely to resist when they become anxious. What value do you see in asking members to identify and express what might get in their way of participating effectively in this group?

5. *Leader functions at early stages.* In viewing the DVD, did you notice the use of the go-around technique? What are some techniques you would want to use as a way to open a session in a group you are leading? From the DVD, what did you learn about leader functions in getting members to check in and state how they would like to use time for a session? What specific techniques for closing a session did you read about and also observe in this group?

# CHAPTER FIVE

# Later Stages in the Development of a Group

## Questions for Discussion

1. What characteristics distinguish a group in the working stage from a group in transition?
2. How is group cohesion a central variable at the working stage? What factors contribute to this cohesion? If a group you were leading seemed fragmented and lacked any sense of community, what might you say or do? Can you think of some reasons to explain the absence of cohesion?
3. Review the therapeutic factors of a group. What factors do you think are especially important?
4. Refer to the section of the textbook that deals with the characteristics of an effective working group. What factors do you think are most significant? Discuss your reasons.
5. How would you explain to a group member the nature and purpose of self-disclosure? What specific guidelines are useful in teaching participants the skills involved in appropriate self-disclosure?
6. What is the purpose of confrontation? What would you tell members about confronting in a constructive way?

## Assessment Devices for Group Sessions

I present two forms here on which members can assess group sessions. Look over these evaluation forms as examples of assessment devices you might create for your own groups. As you consider the purpose of your groups, take what you consider to be the best elements of each of these forms and develop a form that will tap the information you are looking for. Complete the self-evaluation form now to help you answer the question, "What kind of group member am I?" The second form consists of 11 items that can be administered in a few minutes at the end of each group session. Tally the results, and if any problems are apparent, bring the matter up for discussion in your group. This form helps chart the results on a weekly basis so that you can see trends in the groups you are leading.

### Self-Assessment Scale: What Kind of Group Member Am I?

One of the best ways of preparing for effective group leadership is to first become an effective group member. This self-inventory is geared to help you determine your strengths and weaknesses as a group member. I hope you have already had some form of experience as a member of a group. If not, you can rate yourself on the inventory in terms of your behavior in the class you are in now.

After this inventory is completed, the class can break up into small groups; the groups can be composed of people who know one another best. Members of these groups should then assess the self-ratings and discuss how to become a better group member.

Rate yourself on a scale of 1 to 5, with 1 being "almost never true of me" and 5 being "almost always true of me" as a *group member.*

_3_   1. I am an active and contributing group member.

_2_   2. I am willing to raise personal concerns and explore them in the group.

_5_   3. I listen attentively to others, and I respond to them.

_3_   4. I confront others with care, yet I do so directly.

_3_   5. As a group participant, I not only give direct feedback to others but also am open to feedback from them.

_3_   6. I am willing to formulate specific goals and contracts.

_3_   7. I am willing to openly express my feelings about and reactions to what is occurring within the group.

_4_   8. I serve as a positive model to others in the group.

_4_   9. I am active in taking steps to create and maintain trust in the group.

_3_ 10. I show that I am willing to put insights into action by practicing what I learn in the group in my life between sessions.

_3_ 11. I prepare myself for the group by thinking about what I want from the sessions.

_1_ 12. I am willing to get involved in role-playing activities.

_3_ 13. I am able to provide support to others in the group at appropriate times.

## Member's Weekly Evaluation of a Group

*Directions:* This evaluation exercise can be given to members at the end of each group session you may be leading to give you a quick index of the level of satisfaction of the members. You can summarize the results and begin a session with the trends you are noticing from the evaluation sheets. Have the members circle the appropriate number for each item, using the following scale:

**1 or 2** = very weak
**3 or 4** = moderately weak
**5 or 6** = adequate
**7 or 8** = moderately strong
**9 or 10** = very strong

1. What degree of preparation (reacting, thinking about the topic, reading, and writing) did you do for this week?

   1  2      3  4      5  6      7  8      9  10

2. How would you rate your involvement in the group today?

   1  2      3  4      5  6      7  8      9  10

3. How would you rate the group's level of involvement?

   1  2      3  4      5  6      7  8      9  10

4. Rate yourself on the degree to which you saw yourself today as willing to take risks, to share with other members what you thought and felt, and to be an active participant.

   1  2          3  4          5  6          7  8          9  10

5. To what degree do you feel satisfied with your experience in the group?

   1  2          3  4          5  6          7  8          9  10

6. To what degree do you feel that the group dealt with issues in a personal and meaningful way (sharing feelings as opposed to intellectual discussion)?

   1  2          3  4          5  6          7  8          9  10

7. To what degree do you experience trust within the group?

   1  2          3  4          5  6          7  8          9  10

8. How would you rate the group leader's level of involvement and investment in today's session?

   1  2          3  4          5  6          7  8          9  10

9. Rate your leader on the dimensions of his or her ability today to create a good working climate as characterized by warmth, respect, support, empathy, and trust.

   1  2          3  4          5  6          7  8          9  10

Members can also evaluate the group by filling in these blanks:

1. A new behavior I tried was _____

   _____

2. What I would like to do differently at the next meeting is _____

   _____

## Exercises and Activities

### Helpful Intervention Phrases for the Working Stage of a Group

You might find the following sentences and phrases helpful once your group gets under way and people are working. Again, these are not to be used mechanically; rather, they are specific statements that can serve as constructive interventions if you use them in context, with a sense of timing. If you sense that a member is leaving something out, for example, you might intervene with "What are you not saying that needs to be said now?" If these brief interventions are done appropriately, members can be given a gentle impetus to continue. As you lead groups, think of the phrases that are useful to you. Here are some that my co-leaders and I use:

- What would you like to do?
- Do any of you have any thoughts about our last session that you would like to share?

- What else needs to be said?
- How were you affected by _____?
- How does this issue relate to you? How are you affected by Sharon's work?
- I would like each person in the group to finish the sentence "_____."
- Could you say what you are experiencing right now?
- I like it when you _____.
- Right now I am aware of _____.
- Would you be willing to try this experiment to see how it works for you?
- You can cry and talk at the same time. Keep talking.
- Imagine that your mother were here now. What would you want to say to her?
- Instead of asking her questions, you could tell her what you are experiencing at this time.
- I notice that _____.
- You say that you are embarrassed by what you revealed. Look around the room and notice some of the people you are most aware of. What do you imagine they are thinking about you now?
- I am interested in _____.
- I hope you will consider _____.
- My hunch is _____.
- There are tears in your eyes. What are you reacting to?
- What will help you remember what is being said to you?
- You rehearse a lot before you speak. Could you rehearse out loud?
- You experienced a lot of emotions during this session. What did you learn about yourself?
- What decision did you make about yourself in that situation when you were a child?
- Become each part of your dream. Give each part a voice.
- Instead of talking about this situation, live it as though it were happening now.
- Instead of saying "I can't," say "I won't."
- What can you do between this session and the next to practice what you just learned?
- I think it is important that each of you ask if you are getting what you want from this group and whether there are any changes you would like to see.
- I would like to review our contracts to determine if any of them need to be revised or updated.

## Helpful Intervention Phrases for the Final Stage of a Group

During the consolidation stage of a group, it is important for members to think of ways to apply what they have learned in the group to everyday life, to take care of unfinished business, to express their feelings regarding separation, and to make sense of the total group experience. I frequently use the following phrases and sentences during the ending stage of a group. As you review this list, think of additional statements and questions that would help members accomplish the tasks at this stage:

- What are some of the most important things you have learned about yourself in this group?
- Are there any things you want to say to anyone here?
- How do you feel about saying good-bye?
- I am aware of the tendency to forget what we learn in a group, so I would like to talk about how you can remember what you have learned.
- How can you practice what you have learned here?

- With whom do you need to talk outside of the group? What is the essence of what you want them to hear?
- As a result of being in this group, what decisions have you made?
- If we were to meet a year from now as a group, what would you want to say that you had accomplished?
- If you had to say your message in one sentence, what would it be?
- Where can you go from here, now that the group is ending?
- How might you discount what you have learned in here?
- What steps will you take to translate your insight into actions?
- I hope each of you will find at least one person in this group to contact if you discover you are not putting your plans into action.
- I would like to spend some time exploring where each of you can go from here now that our group is ending.
- Let's practice and role-play some of the situations each of you expects to encounter after you leave the group.
- To what degree did you attain your goals?
- What did it take, and what steps did you go through to get what you wanted out of this group?
- If you could repeat this experience, what might you do differently?
- What kept you from becoming closer to others in this group?
- What did you learn about yourself in this group? What did you do to bring this learning about?
- What do you most want to take from this group and apply to your everyday life?
- Don't expect and insist that others in your life be different. If you are different with them, they are more likely to be different with you. Don't tell them, show them.
- When you talk with significant people in your life, remember that the focus needs to be on you.
- The trust and closeness you are experiencing in this group did not simply happen. You took steps to create this atmosphere. Let's look at what each of you did to help create this mood.

## Evolution of a Group: Getting the Most from the DVD Program

This is a continuation of the guide to using the first program in the DVD and workbook, *Evolution of a Group*, with this book. The specific topics covered in this section are in Chapter 5 of the textbook.

*Note:* The page numbers shown in parentheses refer to pages in the textbook *Theory and Practice of Group Counseling* (7th ed.) where further information on these topics can be found.

### Stage 4: Working Stage—Cohesion and Productivity (pages 94–107)

1. *Characteristics of an effective working stage.* Identify the key characteristics of a group in a working stage. How do these characteristics apply to the group shown in the DVD? How does the group seem different at this stage from the earlier stages?
2. *Therapeutic factors of a group.* Therapeutic factors such as intimacy, hope, catharsis, cognitive restructuring, self-disclosure, cohesion and universality, and feedback are

discussed in the textbook. As you view the working stage of this group, look for specific illustrations of these therapeutic factors in the various members' work.

Can you see how one member's disclosure and exploration of a personal issue can tap common issues in many other members (cohesion and universality)? As you view the working stage of this group, look for interventions used by the co-leaders, such as dealing with relationships, talking to parents in symbolic ways, expressing pain that one has been carrying around for many years, and dealing with loss. What is the value of allowing members to express their feelings over painful issues?

You will notice in this group that the co-leaders attempt to link members by role playing. Instead of having members merely report events, the co-leaders ask them to live out in a symbolic way painful events from their past. How does staying in the here-and-now enhance the depth of self-exploration? How does one member's work become a catalyst that brings others into the interactions? What are the values of linking members together with common themes and pursuing work with several members at the same time? How does role playing enhance the interactions within a group?

## Stage 5: Final Stage—Consolidation and Termination (pages 107–111)

1. *Effective ways of terminating a group.* A number of tasks need to be accomplished during the final stage of a group. Many of these tasks are illustrated briefly in the group shown in the DVD. As you observe the program, ask yourself these questions: How are members in this particular group prepared for the termination of the group? How do the members conceptualize their learnings? How does the group seem different at this stage from earlier phases of its development?
2. *Characteristics of the final stage.* What characteristics are common during the final stage of a group? What would you most want to teach members at this time in a group?

## Stage 6: Postgroup Issues—Follow-Up and Evaluation (pages 111–114)

1. *Follow-up sessions.* If you were going to arrange a follow-up meeting with the members in the DVD group, what topics would you be most interested in exploring with them? How would you go about evaluating the results of this group experience on these members?
2. *Reviewing key points in the text and the video group.* After reading Chapters 4 and 5 in the textbook, assess what you have learned about how groups function most effectively. I hope the DVD group brought to life some of the ideas presented in *Theory and Practice of Group Counseling* and gave you some ideas of interventions that can enhance member exploration.

Review what you have learned from studying the DVD program (and participating in the workbook). After viewing the entire video, it is a good idea to study the video in segments, making full use of the workbook. Consider these questions as you consolidate your learnings.

- How was trust created and maintained in this group?
- How did the co-leader interventions during the initial and transition stages facilitate movement into a working stage? What risks did you observe members taking that resulted in deeper self-explorations? How did the self-disclosure of one member lead to disclosure by others in the group?

- How is working with resistances and hesitations of members a critical factor in preparing members to delve more deeply into personal issues?
- What did you learn about the importance of addressing conflict when it occurs in a group session?
- What specific therapeutic factors did you see operating during the working stage?
- What value did you see in role enactments and asking members to stay in the here-and-now? How did linking members promote personal exploration?
- What value do you see in encouraging members to express their feelings in a group setting? How did the emotional work of the members affect you?
- What did you learn about co-leading a group as you studied this program? What did you learn about how groups either function or malfunction?
- What kind of personal work do you think you need to do as a group member to better enable you to meet the challenges of facilitating a group?
- What are the most significant turning points you observed in this group?

# THEORETICAL APPROACHES TO GROUP COUNSELING

# CHAPTER SIX

# The Psychoanalytic Approach to Groups

## Prechapter Self-Inventories: General Directions

The purpose of the self-inventories is to identify and clarify your attitudes and beliefs about the different theoretical approaches to group therapy. Each of the statements on these inventories is *true* from the perspective of the particular theory in question. You decide the degree to which you agree or disagree with these statements. Complete each self-inventory before you read the corresponding textbook chapter. Respond to each statement, giving the initial response that most clearly identifies how you think or feel. Then, after reading the chapter, look over your responses to see whether you want to modify them in any way. These self-inventories will help you express your views and will prepare you to actively read and think about the ideas you'll encounter in each of the chapters on theory.

I suggest that you go over your completed inventories and mark those items that you would like to discuss; then bring your inventories to class, and compare your positions with the views of others. Such comparisons can stimulate debate and help get the class involved in the topics to be discussed.

Using the following code, write next to each statement the number of the response that most closely reflects your viewpoint:

**5** = I *strongly agree* with this statement.

**4** = I *agree,* in most respects, with this statement.

**3** = I am *undecided* in my opinion about this statement.

**2** = I *disagree,* in most respects, with this statement.

**1** = I *strongly disagree* with this statement.

## Prechapter Self-Inventory for the Psychoanalytic Approach

_____ 1. The key to understanding human behavior is understanding the unconscious.

_____ 2. In group work it is particularly important to focus on experiences from the first six years of life because the roots of present conflicts usually lie there.

_____ 3. Group work encourages participants to relive significant relationships, and the group ideally functions as a symbolic family so that members can work through these early relationships.

_____ 4. Insight, understanding, and working through repressed material should be given a primary focus in group therapy.

_____ 5. Free association, dream work, analysis, and interpretation are essential components of effective group work.

_____  6. Transference should be encouraged in a group because it is through this process that members come to an understanding of unresolved conflicts in certain relationships.

_____  7. Because of the reconstructive element of analytic group work, it is best that the process be long term.

_____  8. It is essential for the group leader to understand the forms that resistance takes.

_____  9. Group leaders need to be continuously aware of ways in which their own feelings (countertransference) can affect the group.

_____ 10. The group serves as a mirror for members to see themselves as they are and to get a perspective on how they cope with anxiety in situations outside of the group.

## Summary of Basic Assumptions and Key Concepts of the Psychoanalytic Approach to Groups

1. Psychoanalytic therapists pay particular attention to the unconscious and to early childhood as crucial determinants of personality and behavior. Normal personality development is based on a successful resolution of conflicts at various stages of psychosexual development.

2. Psychoanalytic group work focuses on the influence of the past as a determinant of current personality functioning. Experiences during the first six years of life are seen as the roots of one's conflicts in the present. Analytic group work focuses on the historical basis of current behavior for the purpose of resolving its persistence in the present. Because it is necessary for clients to relive and reconstruct their past and work through repressed conflicts to understand how the unconscious is affecting them now, psychoanalytic group therapy is intensive and generally involves a long-term commitment.

3. The group provides a context for the re-creation of the original family so that members can work through their unresolved problems. The reaction of members to one another and to the leader are assumed to reveal symbolic clues to the dynamics of their relationships with significant figures from their family of origin. The present reactions of members are traced back and analyzed in terms of past influences.

4. The group context provides opportunities to observe defensive behaviors that were used in childhood. Through feedback, individuals can gain awareness of their defensive styles of interaction, and with this awareness they can eventually choose constructive forms of dealing with anxiety.

5. A major portion of group work consists of dealing with resistance, working through transference, experiencing catharsis, developing insight and self-understanding, and learning the connection between past experiences and their effect on current development.

6. Some analytically oriented group practitioners tend to remain relatively anonymous and encourage group members to project onto them the feelings that they have had toward the significant people in their lives. The analysis and interpretation of transference leads to insight and personality change. Increasingly, however, modern analytically-oriented practitioners are leaving behind the "detached-observer" model of classical analysis in favor of a more intersubjective style, called relational analysis, which puts more emphasis on therapist self-disclosure, responsiveness, reciprocity, and mutuality.

7. Some of the unique advantages of analytic group therapy are as follows: members re-experience relationships that are similar to their own early family relationships; there are opportunities for multiple transferences; members can gain insight into their defenses and

resistances more dramatically than they can in individual therapy; and dependency on the authority of the therapist is lessened because members get feedback from other members.

## Glossary of Key Terms for Psychoanalytic Theory

**Anal stage** The second stage of psychosexual development, when pleasure is derived from retaining and expelling feces.

**Anxiety** A feeling of impending doom that results from repressed feelings, memories, desires, and experiences emerging to the surface of awareness.

**Borderline personality disorder** A pattern characterized by instability, irritability, self-destructive acts, impulsivity, and extreme mood shifts. Such people lack a sense of their own identity and do not have a deep understanding of others.

**Brief psychodynamic therapy (BPT)** Applies the principles of psychoanalytic theory and therapy to treating selective disorders within a preestablished time limit of generally 10 to 25 sessions.

**Countertransference** The therapist's unconscious emotional responses to a client, resulting in a distorted perception of the client's behavior; unresolved conflicts of the therapist that are projected onto the client.

**Denial** In denial there is an effort to suppress unpleasant reality. It consists of coping with anxiety by "closing our eyes" to the existence of anxiety-producing reality.

**Dialectical behavior therapy (DBT)** A blend of cognitive behavioral and psychoanalytic techniques that generally involves a minimum of one year of treatment.

**Displacement** An ego-defense mechanism that entails redirection of some emotion from a real source to a substitute person or object.

**Ego-defense mechanism** A device protecting the ego from threatening thoughts and feelings.

**Ego psychology** The psychological approach of Erik Erikson, emphasizing the development of the ego or self at various stages of life.

**Electra complex** Unconscious sexual desire of the daughter for her father, along with feelings of hostility toward her mother.

**Fixation** The condition of being arrested, or "stuck," at one level of psychosexual development.

**Free association** A basic technique for uncovering repressed or unconscious material by communicating whatever comes to mind, with as little censoring as possible.

**Genital stage** The final stage of psychosexual development, usually attained at adolescence, in which heterosexual interests and activities are generally predominant.

**Identity crisis** A development challenge, occurring during adolescence, whereby the person seeks to establish a stable view of self and to define a place in life.

**Insight** A cognitive and emotional awareness of the connection of past experiences to present problems.

**Interpretation** A technique used to explore the meanings of free association, dreams, resistances, and transference feelings.

**Latency stage** A period of psychosexual development, following the phallic stage, that is relatively calm before the storm of adolescence.

*(Glossary continues on page 62)*

**STAGES OF DEVELOPMENT OF THE PSYCHOANALYTIC GROUP***

| Dimension | Initial Stage | Working Stage | Final Stage |
|---|---|---|---|
| Key developmental tasks and goals | Key task is uncovering and exploring unconscious material. Focus is on historical causes of present behavior. Unconscious processes are made conscious by promoting freedom to express any thought, fantasy, and feeling. Focus is on re-creating, analyzing, discussing, and interpreting past experiences and on working through defenses and resistances. | The group resembles the original family, allowing members to relive their childhood and get to the roots of their conflicts. Key tasks include recalling early childhood experiences and reworking past traumas. The basic work entails recognizing and working through resistances and transferences. Multiple transferences occur in the group; members become aware of past relationships that are brought into the group. The group present situation in the group. The group of today becomes the family of yesterday. | Key task is the development of insight into causes of problems. Analysis and interpretation of transference continues. Focus is on the conscious personal action that members can take and on social integration. Main goals are for members to analyze and resolve their own transferences toward other members and the group leader and to work through the repetition of behavior from early years. Personal autonomy is the goal of the final stage of group. |
| Role and tasks of group leader | Leader offers support and creates an accepting and nonstructured climate. Leader's tasks include setting limits, interpreting, and getting a sense of the members' character structures and patterns of defense. | Leader makes timely interpretations that lead to insight; helps members deal with anxiety constructively; is aware of countertransference; and helps members deal effectively with resistances and transferences in the group. | Leader relinquishes much of the leadership functions to allow the members a greater degree of independence; guides the members to fuller awareness and social integration. |
| Role of group members | Members build rapport by reporting dreams and fantasies. They are expected to free-associate with one another's dreams. They are expected to work through resistances that prevent unconscious material from becoming conscious. Members encourage one another to examine their projections. Through mutual sharing and exploration, members gradually give up some defenses. Members need to identify ways in which they experience resistance in a group, and they need to challenge themselves. | Members produce material in a free-floating manner; they ventilate and express feelings over past traumas. Emphasis is on working through transferences with leader and members. Members function as adjunct therapists by saying whatever comes to their mind; they may suggest interpretations for others. From observing the work of others in a group, the members learn that it is acceptable to have and express intense feelings that they may have kept out of awareness. Members become open and expressive as they discover their universal struggles. | Unfinished business and transferences are worked through, and the focus is on self-interpretation and reality testing. Members become able to identify their own transference figures and relationships; they also contribute to the interpretation of the transference of others. Members gain increased awareness of how they dealt with competition as children and how their earlier experiences now affect their present relationships with others. Members have a clear sense of how their defenses and resistances work. |

| | | |
|---|---|---|
| Techniques | Individual sessions are used to create readiness for a group. "Go-around" technique is used as a free-association device, where members respond spontaneously to one another. Initial resistances, anxieties, and expectations are identified. | Main techniques include free association, interpretation, analysis of resistance and transference, interpretation and analysis of dreams, and use of pregroup and postgroup sessions. Emphasis is given to the quality of the relationships between leaders and members. | Attempts are made to help members integrate what they've learned in the group, and they apply new learning to daily life. Members review insights gained. Members focus on putting a new perspective on their problems and past experiences. |
| Questions to consider | At the first group meeting, how can resistances to joining the group best be dealt with?<br><br>What are some ways to use here-and-now material in the group to understand a member's past? How can one's past provide a framework for understanding current behavior?<br><br>What are some ways to encourage members to give unrehearsed reactions to one another?<br><br>What are some values of simply reporting and sharing dreams in a group?<br><br>How can free association be promoted by the go-around technique?<br><br>Are members looking to the leader for direction and cues?<br><br>How can a trusting environment best be created? What are ways that members can be both supported and challenged? | How are members relating to others in the group in ways that are similar to relations in their original family?<br><br>How can the group be formed so that it can best work with the recalling of early childhood experiences?<br><br>What are some advantages and disadvantages of the leader's encouraging transference? How can this transference toward the leader be worked with therapeutically?<br><br>As a leader, how can you utilize the projections of group members? What techniques can you develop to work with projections?<br><br>What are some ways to make interpretations of individuals in a group without promoting their dependency on you? How can your interpretations stimulate their searching? How can you deliver interpretations in a tentative and respectful manner? | During the final stage, how can members be encouraged to take action based on their insight?<br><br>What are some ways of helping members understand and resolve their transferences to the leader and others in the group?<br><br>What are some ways of letting go of the leadership of the group so that the members are encouraged to become increasingly independent?<br><br>What are some signs that a member is ready to terminate a group?<br><br>How can the group be structured to promote a degree of independence in the members?<br><br>What are some dangers of continuing the group for an indefinite period of time? What are the values of long-term group therapy?<br><br>How can termination best take place in an analytic group? |

*The transition stage has been omitted because there are no clear demarcations between the initial and working stages. The intent of this table is to give you an idea of the early, middle, and ending stages of a group.

Reactions: Summarize your reactions to the psychoanalytic perspective of group developmental stages. What do you like *most? Least?* What aspects of this approach would you incorporate in your style of leadership?

**Narcissistic personality disorder** A pervasive pattern of grandiosity, hypersensitivity to the evaluations of others, and lack of empathy.

**Multiple transferences** A process whereby members develop intense feelings for certain others in a group; an individual may "see" in others some significant figure such as a parent, life-partner, ex-lover, or boss.

**Object relations theory** A contemporary trend in psychoanalytic thinking, focusing on predictable developmental sequences in which early experiences of self shift in relation to an expanding awareness of others. It holds that individuals go through phases of autism, normal symbiosis, and separation and individuation, culminating in a state of integration.

**Oedipus complex** Unconscious sexual desire of the son for his mother, along with feelings of hostility and fear toward his father.

**Oral stage** The initial phase of psychosexual development, during which the mouth is the primary source of gratification; a time when the infant is learning to trust or mistrust the world.

**Phallic stage** The third phase of psychosexual development, during which the child gains maximum gratification through direct experience with the genitals.

**Projection** An ego-defense mechanism that involves attributing our own unacceptable thoughts, feelings, behaviors, and motives to others.

**Psychodynamics** The interplay of opposing forces and intrapsychic conflicts, providing a basic understanding of human motivation.

**Psychosexual stages** The Freudian chronological phases of development, beginning in infancy. Each is characterized by a primary way of gaining sensual and sexual pleasure.

**Psychosocial stages** Erikson's turning points, from infancy through old age. Each presents psychological and social tasks that must be mastered if maturation is to proceed in a healthy fashion.

**Rationalization** An ego-defense mechanism whereby we try to justify our behavior by imputing logical and admirable motives to it.

**Reaction formation** A defense against a threatening impulse, involving the expression of the opposite impulse.

**Regression** An ego-defense mechanism whereby an individual reverts to a less mature form of behavior as a way of coping with extreme stress.

**Regressive-reconstructive approach** A regression into each group member's past to achieve the therapeutic goal of a reconstructed personality that is characterized by social awareness and the ability to be involved creatively in life.

**Relational analysis** A contemporary form of psychoanalytic therapy that places emphasis on both the client's and the therapist's reactions and experiences within the therapeutic relationship. Transference is regarded as an interactive process between therapist and client.

**Repression** An ego-defense mechanism whereby threatening or painful thoughts and desires are excluded from awareness.

**Resistance** Reluctance to bring into conscious awareness threatening unconscious material that has been repressed or denied; anything that prevents members from dealing with unconscious material.

**Therapeutic alliance**  A term that refers to a working relationship whereby the therapist "communicates commitment, caring, interest, respect, and human concern for the group member.

**Therapeutic regression**  A process that involves reexperiencing primitive patterns associated with earlier developmental stages and is a necessary element of the analytic group process.

**Transference**  The client's unconscious shifting to the therapist of feelings, attitudes, and fantasies that stem from reactions to significant individuals from the past.

**Unconscious**  The thoughts, feelings, impulses, motivations, and events that are kept out of awareness of the conscious ego as a protection against anxiety.

**Working through**  The final phase of the analytic group, consisting of a resolution of basic conflicts that are manifested in the client's relationship to the group therapist and to other members.

## Exercises and Activities for the Psychoanalytic Approach

### Rationale

For the exercises in this section I've selected several group techniques based on psychoanalytic concepts and procedures and modified them considerably in the hope that you will be able to apply some of them in your group work. The following exercises are geared to stimulate your thinking on issues such as the value of *working with the past,* being open to what you can learn from the *unconscious,* experimenting with techniques like *free association,* and understanding *dream work,* and increasing your appreciation of the importance of central concepts such as *resistance, transference,* and *countertransference.* Regardless of their theoretical orientation, group practitioners must understand these concepts. As you work through these exercises in your class or group, remain open to how you can incorporate some of them into your style of leading groups.

Some of these exercises can tap emotional material; therefore, it is best to restrict them to a supervised group situation. Some of these exercises may not be appropriate for the format and purpose of your class.

### Exercises

1. *Working with your past.* The analytic approach is based on the assumption that past experiences play a vital role in shaping one's current personality. The following short exercises and questions are designed to assist you in remembering and exploring in your group selected dimensions of your past.

   a. Recall and reconstruct some childhood experiences. Examining pictures of yourself as a child, interviewing people who knew you well, looking over diaries, and so on can be useful means of stimulating recall. Share in your group what you consider to be some significant influences from your past. How have these factors contributed to the person you are now?

   b. Write an outline (such as you might find in the table of contents) of a book that you could write about your life. Pay attention mainly to chapter headings. Examples might include: "The child who was never allowed to be a child"; "A time of abandonment"; "My most joyous memories"; "Dreams I had as a child"; "The things I wanted to be as a child." You could also write the preface to this book about your life and include an acknowledgment section. Who are the people you'd most want to acknowledge as having a significant impact on your life? In what ways have they made a difference?

   c. In the outline for the book on your life, include a chapter in which you rewrite your past the way you would have wanted it to be. Share your ideas for this chapter with your group.

   d. Make a list of your current struggles, and see if you can trace the origins of these conflicts to childhood events.

2. *Free association.* A key method of unlocking the unconscious is free association; the therapist asks clients to clear their mind of day-to-day thoughts and simply report in a spontaneous way whatever comes to mind. There are several ways to use free association in a group:

   a. Members can be encouraged to say whatever comes to them. Participants often censor their contributions; they rehearse what they will say for fear that "it won't come out right." Some members agonize over what to bring up in a group and exactly how to present a personal issue.

   b. It might also be a productive exercise in your group to make up incomplete sentences, finish them, and then find ways to free-associate with what seems to be significant material. For example, you might work with sentences such as these:

      When I'm in this group, I feel _____.

      One way I attempt to avoid things in this group is by _____.

      One fear I have in this group is _____.

3. *Dream work.* Report the key elements of one of your dreams to your group. You might try the following suggestions as a way of learning something about yourself through your dreams.

   a. Select any part of your dream and free-associate with that part. Say as many words as fast as you can without censoring them. After you've done this, see what your free-association work tells you.

   b. Give an initial interpretation of your dream. What themes or patterns do you see?

   c. Next, ask group members to give their interpretations of your dream. What do they think your dream means?

   d. If they want to, other group members can free-associate with any parts of your dream.

   e. You might want to begin keeping a dream journal. Write down your dreams. Record what you remember. Then look at the patterns of your dreams and interpret their meaning.

4. *Resistance.* Brainstorm all the possible ways in which you might resist in a group. What resistances have you experienced to simply getting into a group? List some avoidance patterns that you have seen in yourself in a group. How can you help group members recognize and work through resistances that could prevent them from effectively working in a group? What are some uses of resistances? What purposes do these member resistances serve?

5. *Transference.* To get some idea of this process, try some of these exercises in your group:

   a. Think of the people in your group. Does anyone remind you of a significant person in your life? Discuss the similarities.

   b. You can explore possible transferences that occur outside of the group. Have you ever experienced strong, immediate, and even irrational reactions to a person you hardly knew? Discuss what you can learn about unfinished business from your past by focusing on such occurrences.

    c. Be aware of transference onto the leader as an authority figure. Discuss the ways in which you might work with this therapeutically. How might such transferences block growth?

6. *Countertransference.*

    a. What kind of client do you think you'd have the most difficulty working with in a group? Why? How do you imagine you'd handle a client who had very strong negative feelings toward you, especially if you felt that these feelings were inappropriate and a function of transference?

    b. Select a client who you think is a difficult group member and who you anticipate will cause you problems. Become this client. Take on this person's characteristics as fully as you can. Others in the group can function as members, and one person can be the group leader and attempt to work with you. After you've had a chance to take on the role of this "problem member" for a while, explore what this experience was like for you. How did the other members respond to you? How did the group leader respond to you?

    c. Identify a specific problem of yours that could interfere with your effectiveness in leading groups. For example, you may have an extreme need to be appreciated, which could determine your leadership style. Discuss this problem with your group. Although it may be unrealistic to expect a solution, you can talk about steps you could take to work on this problem.

7. *Being a group member.* What do you imagine it would be like for you to be a member of an ongoing analytic group? What issues do you think you'd want to pursue in such a group? What kind of member do you think you'd be?

8. *Role of group leader.* Review the section in the textbook on the role of the analytic group leader. What would it be like for you to work within the framework of this model? Could you function within this model if it were your primary orientation? Why or why not?

9. *Personal critique.* Devote some time to a personal evaluation of the strengths and weaknesses of the analytic approach to group therapy. What specific techniques do you think are valuable? Why? What concepts could you draw on from this model in your work with groups, regardless of your orientation? What are the major contributions of the analytic model? What are the major limitations? With what kind of population do you think this model would be most appropriate? Least appropriate? Discuss how the psychoanalytic theory forms the basis on which most of the other theories have developed, either as extensions of the model or as reactions against it.

*Reminder:* If you've not yet read the last two chapters in the textbook (Chapters 17 and 18), I suggest that you do so at this point. The comparison of theories and the case of a group in action will help you get an overall picture of how these theories are related. As you read and study the theory chapters, the last two chapters will give you an increased appreciation of how diverse theories can be applied to the different stages of a group's development.

## Questions for Reflection and Discussion

1. To what extent are psychoanalytic groups appropriate for all sociocultural and socioeconomic groups? For what populations do you think they are best suited? In what cases do you think they are not suitable?

2. Compare and contrast psychoanalysis in groups with one-to-one therapy. What are some advantages of group analysis over the dyadic situation? What are some limitations and disadvantages?

3. How important do you see exploring of members' past experiences as being in a group? How would you work with present concerns if they seemed rooted in the past?

4. In general, psychoanalytic groups focus on the intrapsychic dynamics of the individual and emphasize relating everything that occurs in the group to historical determinants. What do you think of this focus on individual dynamics? What are some advantages and disadvantages of such a focus?

5. How do you imagine you would deal with members' transferences toward you as a group leader?

6. The psychoanalytic group in some ways replicates the original family of the members. Emphasis is put on recognizing and exploring multiple transferences in a group as a way of dealing with early familial issues. What are the possibilities of such a focus? To what degree do you think doing this can be an emotionally corrective experience?

7. Review the psychosexual and psychosocial stages of human development, which consist of an integration of Freud's and Erikson's ideas. How do these stages apply to you? Were there any critical turning points in your life that had an impact on who you are today? What applications of this developmental framework are useful for group counseling?

8. What concepts and techniques from the psychoanalytic approach would you be most interested in incorporating in your style of group leadership?

9. From an analytic perspective, therapists are not totally free of countertransference reactions. What kind of members do you think you'd have the greatest difficulty working with therapeutically? How do you see your reactions to certain types of members as related to your own unresolved personal issues?

10. The more traditional psychoanalytic group therapists maintain a stance characterized by objectivity, warm detachment, and relative anonymity. More contemporary psychoanalytic group therapists (relational or interpersonal therapists) have a style that involves psychological presence, self-disclosure, mutuality, and reciprocity. What advantages do you see with each style? Which style do you prefer and why?

## Quiz on Psychoanalytic Approach to Groups: A Comprehension Check                                  Score ____%

*Note:* Please refer to Appendix I for the scoring key for these quizzes. Count 5 points for each error, and subtract the total from 100 to get your percentage score. I recommend that you review these comprehension checks for the tests in your class. I also suggest that you bring to class questions that you would like clarified. If you get a wrong answer that you believe is right, bring it up for discussion.

*True/false items:* Decide if the following statements are "more true" or "more false" as they apply to the psychoanalytic approach to groups.

T    F    1. Most interpretations in a psychoanalytic group are made by the individual client and other members; the group therapist infrequently makes interpretations.

T  F  2. In an analytic group, dealing with transference and resistance constitutes the bulk of the work.

T  F  3. Countertransference refers to the irrational feelings that the members project onto the group therapist.

T  F  4. Insight is not deemed to be either useful or necessary in the psychoanalytic group.

T  F  5. In analytic group work, resistance is viewed as the result of ineptness and lack of therapeutic skill on the part of the leader.

T  F  6. Members of an analytic group also function as adjunct therapists, for they are expected to make interpretations for other members.

T  F  7. Ego integrity involves feeling optimistic about what one is planning to do with one's life.

T  F  8. Establishing an identity is an ongoing process during most of the life cycle.

T  F  9. Object relations are interpersonal relationships that shape the individual's current interactions with people.

T  F  10. The contemporary theoretical trends in psychoanalytic thinking center on predictable developmental sequences in which the early experiences of the self shift in relation to an expanding awareness of others.

*Multiple-choice items:* Select the *one best answer* among the alternatives given. Consider each question within the framework of psychoanalytic theory and practice.

_____11. Resistance in the psychoanalytic approach is viewed
　　　　a. as an unconscious dynamic.
　　　　b. as a conscious refusal of a member to explore a threatening topic.
　　　　c. as a result of lack of skill on the leader's part.
　　　　d. as a sign that the group is a failure.
　　　　e. generally as a way to avoid intimacy.

_____12. The primary goal of analytic group work is to work toward
　　　　a. adequate social adjustment.
　　　　b. uncovering early experiences.
　　　　c. helping members develop social interest.
　　　　d. formulating a concrete plan for changing specific behaviors.
　　　　e. teaching members problem-solving strategies.

_____13. In a group setting, free association could be used for
　　　　a. uncovering repressed material.
　　　　b. helping members develop more spontaneity.
　　　　c. working on dreams.
　　　　d. promoting meaningful interactions within the group.
　　　　e. all of the above.

_____14. Psychoanalytic dream work consists of
　　　　a. asking the member to act out all parts of the dream.
　　　　b. having the member analyze and interpret his or her own dream.
　　　　c. interpreting the latent meaning of the dream.
　　　　d. the leader avoiding suggesting any meanings the dream might have.
　　　　e. looking for universal and spiritual symbols in the dream.

_____15. An advantage of using groups with the psychoanalytic approach is that
     a. members can benefit from one another's work.
     b. multiple transferences can be formed.
     c. members can learn to identify their own transferences.
     d. the group can become the family of yesterday.
     e. all of the above.

_____16. Modern analytic practitioners are leaving behind the "detached-observer" model of classical analysis for
     a. a more intersubjective style.
     b. a form of relational analysis.
     c. both (a) and (b).
     d. a short-term therapy based on empirical findings.
     e. a model based on friendship.

_____17. Dialectical behavior therapy (DBT)
     a. is a group format that can be used in treating borderline clients.
     b. includes psychodynamic concepts in a cognitive behavioral framework.
     c. involves skills training in groups.
     d. ideally is practiced in conjunction with individual therapy.
     e. all of the above.

_____18. Brief psychodynamic therapy (BPT) generally has a time limit of
     a. 10 to 25 sessions.
     b. 1 to 6 sessions.
     c. never more than 6 sessions.
     d. 52 sessions.

_____19. Brief psychodynamic therapy (BPT) is
     a. mainly designed for borderline personality disorders.
     b. suitable for all clients regardless of diagnosis.
     c. appropriate for a variety of clients' needs.
     d. primarily aimed at working with narcissistic personality disorders.

_____20. Brief psychodynamic therapy (BPT) calls upon the therapist to
     a. assume a nondirective and even passive role.
     b. assume an active role in quickly formulating a therapeutic focus that goes beyond the surface of presenting problems.
     c. deal exclusively with a single presenting problem.
     d. avoid treating any underlying issue.

---

*Note:* Another suggestion for feedback and for review is to retake the prechapter self-inventory. All 10 of the items are true statements as applied to the particular therapy, so thinking about them is a good way to review.

---

# CHAPTER SEVEN

# Adlerian Group Counseling

## Prechapter Self-Inventory for the Adlerian Approach

Directions: Refer to page 57 for general directions. Indicate your position on these statements using the following code:

**5** = I *strongly agree* with this statement.
**4** = I *agree,* in most respects, with this statement.
**3** = I am *undecided* in my opinion about this statement.
**2** = I *disagree,* in most respects, with this statement.
**1** = I *strongly disagree* with this statement.

_____ 1. People are best understood by looking at their movement toward goals and at where they are going rather than at where they have been.

_____ 2. Group counseling is especially appropriate as an intervention because people are strongly motivated by social connectedness and because they cannot be fully understood apart from their social context.

_____ 3. Although people are influenced by their early childhood experiences, they are not passively shaped and determined by these experiences.

_____ 4. A useful focus in group counseling is the interpersonal and social nature of a member's problems.

_____ 5. Because people are primarily motivated by a need to belong, it is mostly within the group that they can actualize their potentialities.

_____ 6. Recalling one's earliest memories is an important group technique.

_____ 7. People have a basic need to strive for completion, that is, to overcome feelings of inferiority.

_____ 8. Each person develops a unique lifestyle that can be examined in group sessions.

_____ 9. The group leader's goals and the members' goals need to be aligned for effective work to occur.

_____10. An analysis of each member's family constellation is highly useful to successful group work.

## Summary of Basic Assumptions and Key Concepts of the Adlerian Approach to Groups

1. The underlying assumptions of the Adlerian approach are as follows: humans are primarily social beings, motivated by social forces and influenced largely by social interactions; conscious, not unconscious, processes account for much of behavior; people are creative,

active, self-determined, and autonomous beings, not the victims of fate; people are significantly influenced by their perceptions and interpretations of past events; as people gain awareness of the continuity of their lives, they are able to modify their faulty assumptions.

2. All people have basic feelings of inferiority that motivate them to strive for superiority, success, mastery, power, and perfection or completion. Their lifestyles comprise unique behaviors and habits that they develop in striving for power, meaning, and personal goals. Lifestyle is influenced first by the family constellation and family atmosphere, especially by relationships among siblings. This lifestyle, which is formed early in life to compensate for perceived feelings of inferiority, also influences a person's view of the world.

3. The goals of Adlerian group counseling correspond to the four phases of group work, which include establishing and maintaining the proper therapeutic relationship, exploring the dynamics operating in the individual, communicating to the individual an understanding of self, and seeing new alternatives and making new choices.

4. Adlerian group counselors make use of several assessment techniques. Assessments of the members' family constellation, relationship difficulties, early recollections, dreams, and art work provide clues to life goals and lifestyle. The leader's task is to integrate and summarize themes from the lifestyle investigation and to interpret how mistaken notions are influencing group members. Adlerian group leaders tend to encourage members to become actively involved with other people and to develop a new lifestyle through these relationships.

5. Leaders challenge members to have faith and hope, to develop the courage to face life actively, and to choose the kind of life they want. Group members are encouraged to live as if they were the way they want to be.

## Glossary of Key Terms for Adlerian Therapy

**Basic mistakes**  Faulty, self-defeating perceptions, attitudes, and beliefs that may have been appropriate at one time but are appropriate no longer. These myths are influential in the development of personality. Examples include overgeneralizations, misperceptions of life and its demands, denying one's worth, an exaggerated need for security, and impossible goals.

**Brief therapy**  An intervention that is concise, deliberate, direct, efficient, focused, short-term, and purposeful.

**Community feeling**  An individual's awareness of being part of the human community and the individual's attitudes in dealing with the social world; a sense of striving for a better future for humanity.

**Convictions**  Conclusions based on life experiences and the interpretation of such experiences.

**Courage**  The willingness to take risks without being certain of the consequences; facing difficult or challenging problems or tasks instead of avoiding them.

**Democratic living**  Personal freedom must exist within a social order, which is developed through mutual respect.

**Early recollections**  Specific, detailed childhood memories that can be thought of as capsule summaries of one's present philosophy of life.

**Emotional intelligence**  A concept related to social interest that relates to the ability to control impulses, empathize with others, form responsible interpersonal relationships, and develop intimate relationships.

**Encouragement**  The process of increasing members' courage to face life tasks; used throughout therapy as a way to counter discouragement and to help people set realistic goals; implies faith in people as they are and focuses on assets and strengths to build self-esteem.

**Family atmosphere**  The climate of relationships among family members.

**Family constellation**  The social and psychological structure of the family system; includes parental relationships, birth order, the individual's perception of self, sibling characteristics, and ratings.

**Fictional finalism**  An imagined central goal that gives direction to behavior and unity to the personality; an image of what people would be like if they were perfect, perfectly secure, or complete.

**Holism**  Characterizes the whole, indivisible person; all parts work together in harmony in movement toward goals. People are integrated beings who proceed with others through life; a reaction against separating personality into parts and a focus on the unity of personality.

**Individual Psychology**  Adler's term for his approach, reflecting his belief in the uniqueness and unity of the individual.

**Inferiority feelings**  The ever-present determining force in behavior; the source of human striving. Humans attempt to compensate for both imagined and real inferiorities, which helps them overcome handicaps.

**Insight**  Understanding that can be translated into constructive action.

**Interpretation**  The process by which individuals are helped to gain insight into their lifestyle.

**Lifestyle**  The individual's basic orientation to life and the themes that characterize the person's existence; a blueprint for living that each individual develops based on a subjective view of self and the world. The convictions individuals develop during the first six years of life to help them organize, understand, predict, and control their life experiences.

**Life tasks**  Adler's notion that all humans must face and solve certain problems universal in human life, including the tasks of friendship (community), work (making a contribution), and intimacy (love and marriage).

**Mistaken goals**  Related to patterns of misbehavior such as attention getting, power struggle, revenge, and inadequacy or withdrawal.

**Mutual respect**  Respect for the dignity of others and for oneself.

**Other-esteem**  Directed toward promoting personal and social responsibility; involves respect, acceptance, caring, valuing, and promoting the welfare of others.

**Phenomenology**  The belief that humans actively and creatively interpret their life experiences in a personal and unique way; a focus on the subjective fashion in which people perceive their world.

**Priorities**  Characteristics that involve a dominant behavior pattern with supporting convictions that an individual uses to cope; examples include significance, control, comfort, and pleasing.

**Private logic**  Basic convictions and assumptions of the individual that underlie the lifestyle pattern and explain how behaviors fit together to provide consistency.

*(Glossary continues on page 74)*

| Dimension | Initial Stage | Working Stage | Final Stage |
|---|---|---|---|
| Key developmental tasks and goals | Central developmental tasks are establishing empathy and creating acceptance, setting goals and making commitments, understanding one's current lifestyle, and exploring one's premises and assumptions. The psychological investigation that occurs in the group involves exploration of the family atmosphere and subjective interpretation of childhood events. | Members are helped to understand their beliefs, feelings, motives, and goals; they develop insight into their mistaken goals and self-defeating behaviors; they work through interpersonal conflicts; and they explore the beliefs behind their feelings. A goal is to create meaning and significance in life. | This is a time when members explore multiple alternatives to problems and make a commitment to change. They translate insights into action and make new decisions. A goal is to facilitate members' awareness of their mistaken notions through observation of fellow group members and reality testing. A main goal is to promote social interest of members. |
| Role and tasks of group leader | Main goal of the group leader is to establish a collaborative relationship and to decide with clients on the goals of the group. Leader's tasks include providing encouragement, offering support and tentative hypotheses of behavior, and helping members assess and clarify their problems. Role of leader is to observe social context of behavior in group and to model attentive listening, caring, sincerity, and confrontation. Leader helps members recognize and use their strengths. | Functions of leader at the working stage include interpreting early recollections and family patterns, helping members identify basic mistakes, helping members become aware of their own unique lifestyles, challenging them to deal with life tasks, and helping them summarize and integrate what they've learned so that they can make new plans. Leader assumes that members can best be understood by looking at their goals. | At the final stage, the focus is on reeducation. Leader helps members challenge attitudes and encourages them to take risks and experiment with new behavior by translating their new ideas into actual behavior outside the group. Leader's tasks include helping members recognize their mistaken beliefs and become aware of their own self-defeating beliefs and behaviors. Leader offers encouragement as members put their insights into action. Leader assists in fostering social interest. |
| Role of group members | Members state their goals and may establish contracts. They are expected to be active in the group and begin to assume responsibility for the ways in which they want to change. Members begin to work on trust issues, which are important in the encouragement process and in developing good morale within the group. Because of the way the group is structured, members meet their needs for belonging. Through group interaction, members' values and lifestyles become evident. | Members become increasingly aware of their lifestyles. They analyze the impact of the family constellation; they also begin to recognize that they are responsible for their own behavior. Members support and challenge others so that they can explore their basic inferiority feelings. Participants learn to believe in themselves by taking action to change their lives. They explore their mistaken attitudes and faulty motivations. | Members are expected to establish realistic goals. They see new options and more functional alternatives. They learn problem-solving and decision-making skills. This is a time of reorientation. Members encourage one another to redirect their goals along realistic lines. Members help one another in considering alternatives and in making new choices. Members are encouraged to act *as if* they were the persons they want to be. |

| Techniques | Basic listening skills are crucial at this time. Analysis and assessment of one's lifestyle and how it affects current functioning are conducted. Other techniques include questioning, reflection, and clarification. | Some of the techniques used at this stage are confrontation, interpretation, modeling, paraphrasing, encouragement, "catching oneself" in old patterns, acting "as if," and teaching. | Basic procedures at the final stage consist of encouraging members to act and to change. Contracts are reestablished and role-playing techniques are used to help members reorient their goals. |
|---|---|---|---|
| Questions to consider | How can you as a leader establish a collaborative relationship with the members?<br><br>Adlerians are concerned with the ways in which people strive for significance. How can the group itself be used to help members understand how they find meaning and how they meet the challenge of life?<br><br>How well are the members dealing with current life tasks? Why are the members seeking this group now?<br><br>In obtaining the lifestyle assessment of members, how would you address:<br><br>• Parental influences?<br>• Family information?<br>• Memories of each sibling?<br>• Role in the family?<br>• Earliest recollections?<br>• Critical turning points in life?<br>• Basic mistakes? | What are the values of focusing on members' beliefs and motives with the intention of helping them develop insight into their mistaken goals?<br><br>How can early recollections and family patterns be interpreted in light of the members' current behavior in the group situation?<br><br>Leaders might think of this question in helping members become aware of their lifestyle: Under what circumstances does the person acquire a particular lifestyle, and how is it being maintained currently?<br><br>What are some techniques for helping members catch themselves in old patterns and begin to behave in new and more effective ways?<br><br>How can the cultural context best be taken into consideration so that techniques can be applied in flexible ways? | How can members be challenged to make a commitment to change? How can insights be translated into action?<br><br>What are some ways members can apply problem-solving and decision-making skills acquired in the group to actual behavior outside of the group?<br><br>To what degree are the members behaving as active and autonomous beings as opposed to acting as victims of fate?<br><br>To what extent have the members become actively involved with other people and developed a new lifestyle through relationships?<br><br>Can members summarize changes in attitudes, beliefs, goals, and behaviors? Are they feeling encouraged to take risks by acting on these changes? |

Reactions: Summarize your reactions to the Adlerian perspective on group developmental stages. What do you like *most? Least?* What aspects of this approach would you incorporate in your style of group leadership?

**Reorientation**  The phase of the counseling process wherein members are helped to redirect their mistaken goals and basic mistakes.

**Social interest**  The sense of connectedness with others and the desire to contribute usefully to society by dealing with the tasks of work, friendship, and intimacy—a sense of identification and empathy with others, a feeling of belonging, a striving for a better future for humanity.

**Socioteleological approach**  Implies that people are primarily motivated by social forces and are striving to achieve certain goals.

**Striving for superiority**  A strong inclination toward becoming competent, toward mastering the environment, and toward self-improvement; this striving for perfection or completion is a movement toward enhancement of self and is known as the "growth force."

**Style of life**  An individual's way of thinking, feeling, and acting. A conceptual framework by which the world is perceived and by which people are able to cope with life tasks; the person's personality.

**Teleology**  The study of goals and the goal-directedness of human behavior. Humans live by goals and purposes: they are moved by anticipation of the future; they create meaning.

## Exercises and Activities for the Adlerian Group

### Rationale

Many of the Adlerian concepts relevant for group practice involve issues such as the influence of one's family on one's current personality, reviewing one's past to determine its present impact, striving for goals that define a unique lifestyle, and identifying ways of developing social interest and community feeling. The basic concepts of the Adlerian approach will assume a more concrete meaning for you if you personalize them. It is up to you to decide how personal you want to be in sharing aspects of your life with others in your class or group. Remember that you can be personal without sharing your deepest and most private experiences. The following exercises and questions give you opportunities to experience some of the themes stressed in Adlerian groups.

### Lifestyle Assessment

Adlerians often begin a group with a structured interview to obtain information about the members' family constellation, early recollections, life goals, and childhood experiences. If you have a basic grasp of the concepts of Adlerian psychology, you can develop your own inventory for getting some of this information. Although there are set formats for the lifestyle questionnaire, the purpose of this exercise is to provide you with the experience of gathering data about yourself that you could use if you were a member of a group. By practicing on yourself I hope you will gain some ideas for what to look for in interviews with members of the groups you will lead. Assume that you are interested in joining an Adlerian group *as a member,* and answer these questions as directly, simply, and honestly as you can.

1. What would you tell others about who you are? What are three adjectives that describe you?

2. How well are you dealing with current life tasks? In addressing this question, examine these areas of your life: leisure, friendship, being part of a family, relationships with others, meaning in life, being a parent, adjustment to work, finding hobbies, your feelings about self, the spiritual dimension of your life, and any other areas important to you.

3. How have your parents influenced your life? Answer these questions for each parent:
   a. Describe the parent. What kind of person is he or she? What three adjectives describe this person?
   b. What ambitions did the parent have for you?
   c. What relationship did this parent have with each child in the family?
   d. What were your main feelings toward the parent when you were growing up? What are your feelings toward him or her now?
   e. In what ways are you similar to and different from the parent?
   f. How would you describe the relationship your parents have with each other?

4. What other family information do you recall? What aspects of your family life are relevant to the person you are now?

5. Describe your brothers and sisters (from the oldest to the youngest). What do you remember about each sibling? How would you compare yourself with each sibling? Who is most like you, and in what respect? Who is most different from you, and in what way? How would you describe your position in the family? What expectations did you have for each sibling? What were their expectations for you?

6. What are your earliest recollections? What specific incidents stand out for you? Do you recall how you felt in selected situations? Can you recall any reactions that you had in these situations?

7. What do you recall about your growth and development? In addressing this question, think about specific areas such as physical development, major changes in childhood and adolescence, social development, sexual development, childhood fears, ambitions and goals, special talents, assets, liabilities, school experiences, and work experiences.

8. Can you identify any basic mistakes (self-defeating perceptions) that you acquired in childhood or adolescence? Some examples include the following:
   a. Faulty generalizations, such as "Nobody really cares about me" and "I am always singled out as the one nobody likes."
   b. Denial of your value as a person, such as "I am basically unlovable" and "I will never accomplish what I want to in life."
   c. Misperceptions of reality, such as "Since people expect so much of me, I'll never measure up, and I'll always be frustrated."

9. Write a brief summary of the key characteristics of your family constellation and your early recollections. From what you know of yourself, what might you select to explore in a group?

10. What do you see as your major assets? What about your liabilities? What would you most want to change in your past if you could relive your childhood?

## Personal Exploration and Suggested Activities

1. Adlerians use a technique known as "the question." It consists of asking a client "How would you be different if _____?" The end of the sentence refers to being free of a problem or a symptom. If you were troubled with migraine headaches, for

example, you would be asked how you'd be different if you no longer had them. Apply this question to a specific problem you have. Explore how your life might be different without this problem. How do you think your problem may be useful to you? Are you "rewarded" for some of your symptoms?

2. What are some of your earliest memories? Are they mainly joyful or painful? Consider sharing one specific early memory in your group or class and talking about the significance it has for you. What value do you see in the Adlerian technique of having clients recall their earliest memories? Can you think of ways to use this technique in groups you may lead?

3. Adlerians stress birth order and the family constellation. Share with others in your class or group what it was like to be the firstborn child, the last-born, the middle child, or the only child. What does your group think are the advantages and disadvantages of each of these positions?

4. According to Adler, each of us has a unique lifestyle, or personality, that starts to develop in early childhood to compensate for and overcome some perceived inferiority. How does this notion apply to you? In what ways might you feel inferior? Could you interpret what you do as your way to strive for mastery and significance and to overcome basic inferiority? In describing your lifestyle, consider these questions: What makes you unique? How do you strive for power? When do you feel the most powerful? What goals do you most strive for? What do you most often tell others about yourself on a first meeting? How do you typically present yourself?

5. Adlerian therapists often ask group members to live as if they were the person they wanted to be. For example, you may want to be far more creative than you are now. Assume that you are more creative, and then describe yourself to your group. Think of other ways to present yourself as if you were the person who you would ideally like to be. What stops you from being this kind of person? What can you do to begin moving in this direction? What ways can you think of to use this "as if" technique in a group? What value do you see in it?

6. Adlerians center on "basic mistakes," or faulty assumptions, that people make about themselves. These mistaken ideas lead to self-defeating behavior. For example, you may believe that to feel successful you must be perfect. Since you'll never feel perfect, you will constantly put yourself under needless stress and experience little joy in your accomplishments. Select one faulty assumption you have made about yourself or the world. In your group discuss how this mistake affects you. If you were to change this assumption, how might your life be different? Can you identify any ways in which your basic mistakes affect the kind of group leader you are?

7. Adlerians stress self-determination by maintaining that we are not the victims of fate; rather, we are creative, active, choice-making beings whose every action has purpose and meaning. How does this notion fit you as you look at the patterns in your life?

8. In Adlerian groups the members are best understood by looking at where they are going. Apply this statement to yourself and talk about what direction you are striving toward. How do you see your goals as influencing what you are doing now? How do you think your past has influenced your future goals? In what ways can you apply this purposive, goal-oriented approach in your work with groups?

9. An Adlerian group emphasizes developing social interest, which includes satisfying a need for social connectedness. What are some of the most important relationships in your life that meet your need for this sense of belongingness? Apply the concept of social interest to

yourself by considering the five life tasks that Adlerians contend we must face and resolve: How do you relate to others (friendships)? At work, what contributions do you make, and what meaning do you derive? What sense of belonging and acceptance do you experience with members of your family and those you love? How well do you get along with yourself? How satisfying is the spiritual dimension of your life (including your values and your relationship to the universe or cosmos)?

10. Adlerians place a great emphasis on family processes, especially the family atmosphere and the family constellation. Consider describing what it was like for you to grow up in your family. How would you characterize your relationship with each of your siblings? Focus on what you learned about yourself and others through these early family experiences. How do these experiences affect the kind of helper you are or the kind of group leader you are?

## Questions for Discussion and Reflection

1. What are your thoughts about Adler's idea that inferiority can actually be the basis for success? Can you relate the striving for superiority to your own life? What are some possibilities of introducing the concept of inferiority and striving for superiority in group work with children or with adolescents? What therapeutic value might there be in encouraging young people to share ways they experience inferiority?

2. Adler talks about the family constellation and birth order as important factors that influence one's personality. What implications do these concepts have for group counseling? How can a group replicate a family? To what extent would you explore family constellation issues in the groups you lead? With what kind of age population or client population might you not be inclined to explore family constellation matters?

3. Social interest is a key Adlerian concept. How can a group increase social interest, and how is the group an appropriate form of intervention in light of Adlerian principles? In what ways can you think of addressing the implications of social interest if you were leading a group with school-age students?

4. How might you work with the concept of style of life in a group setting? In what ways could you get information about the development of a member's style of life by observing this person's interactions in the group?

5. What is your evaluation of Adler's view that we can be understood only by looking at our goals and our future strivings? How might you integrate this idea in actual practice in a group? With what client populations would you particularly focus on goals and future strivings?

6. Adlerians do not tend to conduct pregroup screening interviews. Why? What do you think about prescreening? What advantages might you see in screening members for your groups? Any disadvantages? Can you think of any potential misuses of screening?

7. Adlerians see group counseling as a form of teaching and learning, and because of this they make use of advice and information. What possible advantages and disadvantages do you see in this focus? How would this educational focus fit if you were leading a group with school-age children?

8. What is one Adlerian principle you could use to understand your own life better? How might you incorporate this one principle in the group work you do?

9. What are your thoughts about the value of the four phases of the Adlerian group? How could they apply to groups you might want to lead?
10. For what kind of clients do you think Adlerian groups would be best suited? Do you think they would be appropriate for all populations? Explain. What are the implications for working with multicultural populations?

## Quiz on Adlerian Theory: A Comprehension Check     Score ____%

*Note:* Please refer to Appendix I for the scoring key. Count 5 points for each error, and subtract the total from 100 to get your percentage score.

*True/false items:* Decide if the following statements are "more true" or "more false" as they apply to the Adlerian approach to groups.

T   F   1. According to Adler, feelings of inferiority are the wellspring of creativity.
T   F   2. In the Adlerian group, interpretation is done in relationship to the lifestyle.
T   F   3. Insight and interpretation are basic aspects of Adlerian group counseling.
T   F   4. In the Adlerian group, little attention is paid to one's past experiences.
T   F   5. Encouragement is one of the most distinctive procedures used in Adlerian group work.
T   F   6. Phenomenology implies an objective approach to therapy.
T   F   7. The Adlerian group leader functions in a very nondirective manner.
T   F   8. Another label for Adlerian psychology is ego psychology.
T   F   9. Adler asserts that the earliest impressions lay the foundation for one's lifestyle.
T   F  10. Adlerians contend that people remember only those past events that are consistent with their current view of themselves.

*Multiple-choice items:* Select the *one best answer* among the alternatives given. Consider each question within the framework of Adlerian therapy.

_____11. Which of the following did Adler *not* stress?
   a. the unity of personality
   b. a focus on reliving early childhood experiences
   c. the direction in which people are headed
   d. a unique style of life that is an expression of life goals
   e. feelings of inferiority

_____12. The phenomenological orientation pays attention to
   a. the events that occur at various stages of life.
   b. the manner in which biological and environmental forces limit us.
   c. the manner in which people interact with one another.
   d. the internal dynamics that drive a person.
   e. the way in which individuals perceive their world.

_____13. The concept of fictional finalism refers to
   a. an imagined central goal that guides a person's behavior.
   b. the hopeless stance that leads to personal defeat.
   c. the manner in which people express their need to belong.

      d. the process of assessing one's style of life.

      e. the interpretation that individuals give to life events.

_____14. The "question" technique can be used to

      a. uncover repressed memories.

      b. work through transference relationships.

      c. increase social interest.

      d. determine how birth order affects current behavior.

      e. determine if a symptom is due to organic causes.

_____15. Adlerians value early recollections as an important clue to understanding

      a. one's sexual and aggressive instincts.

      b. the bonding process between mother and child.

      c. the individual's lifestyle.

      d. the unconscious dynamics that motivate behavior.

      e. the origin of psychological trauma in early childhood.

_____16. Who developed Adlerian group methods?

      a. Viktor Frankl and Rollo May

      b. Rudolf Dreikurs and Manford Sonstegard

      c. Abraham Maslow and Carl Rogers

      d. J. L. Moreno and Fritz Perls

      e. Alexander Wolf and Alexander Lowen

_____17. Adler stressed

      a. the value of transference for group therapy.

      b. the importance of the group leader's being a "blank screen."

      c. mother/child bonding as a foundation for later interpersonal relationships.

      d. the purposeful nature of behavior.

      e. the power of the group leader.

_____18. Which of the following is *not* a key concept of the Adlerian approach?

      a. holism

      b. creativity and choice

      c. psychic determinism

      d. teleology

      e. social interest

_____19. Which concept helps us explain how all human behavior fits together so that there is some consistency to actions?

      a. holism

      b. fictional finalism

      c. ego integrity

      d. lifestyle

      e. social interest

_____20. Goal alignment refers to the state whereby

      a. all the members develop common goals.

      b. both the leader's and the members' goals are the same.

      c. members are willing to carry out new behavior beyond the group session.

      d. members accept the goals of society by adjusting to the dominant norms.

      e. members are willing to abide by the group leader's rules governing the group.

# CHAPTER EIGHT

# Psychodrama in Groups

## Prechapter Self-Inventory for Psychodrama

Directions: Refer to page 57 for general directions. Indicate your position on these statements using the following code:

**5** = I *strongly agree* with this statement.
**4** = I *agree,* in most respects, with this statement.
**3** = I am *undecided* in my opinion about this statement.
**2** = I *disagree,* in most respects, with this statement.
**1** = I *strongly disagree* with this statement.

_____ 1. There is therapeutic value in releasing pent-up feelings, even if this process does not lead to changing external situations.

_____ 2. Much can be learned from acting out one's conflicts rather than merely talking about them.

_____ 3. The use of fantasy techniques in a group can increase members' awareness of themselves.

_____ 4. Group members can learn a great deal about themselves by observing and experiencing the psychodramas of other members.

_____ 5. It is important to "warm up" a group before moving into action.

_____ 6. Playing both one's own role and the role of a significant other person can increase awareness of oneself.

_____ 7. After intensive group work it is very important for members to share their feelings and discuss how they perceive the work.

_____ 8. A group leader's task is both to encourage catharsis and to help members understand emotional experiences.

_____ 9. Group members (protagonists) should always have the right to choose what conflict they will portray, and it is their right to decide how far they will explore a situation in the group context.

_____ 10. Unless a group is cohesive, it is unlikely that members will risk role playing of important problems.

## Summary of Basic Assumptions and Key Concepts of Psychodrama

1. Psychodrama frees people from old feelings so that they can develop new ways of responding to problems. Spontaneity, creativity, fantasy, and role playing are essential elements of psychodrama.

2. Psychodrama emphasizes enacting or reenacting events (anticipated or past) as though they were occurring in the present. It places importance on the past, present, *and* future; the past can come to life when it is brought into the here-and-now, as can the future. Members are encouraged to speak in the present tense and to use action words.

3. Feelings are released through verbally and physically dramatizing emotion-laden situations. After a catharsis, members often gain a new perspective on an old problem, and they begin to think and feel differently about a situation. Participants gain insight and are provided with the opportunity to test reality. Group members suggest alternatives for action.

4. The psychodrama director's tasks include being a producer, catalyst/facilitator, and observer/analyzer. One of the tasks of the leader is to provide members with opportunities to challenge stereotyped ways of responding to people and to break out of behaving within a rigid pattern.

5. A basic assumption underlying psychodrama is that members of the group can benefit vicariously by identifying with a protagonist. Many people can become involved in dramatizing the individual's struggle.

6. Psychodrama has three phases: the warm-up process, which is designed to get the participants ready for the therapeutic experience; the action phase, which includes enacting and working through a past or present situation or an anticipated event; and the discussion phase, in which members are asked to share their reactions.

7. Psychodrama has many techniques designed both to intensify feelings and to bring about increased self-understanding by working through and integrating material that has surfaced in a psychodrama.

## Glossary of Key Terms for Psychodrama

**Action phase**  The stage of psychodrama characterized by an enactment of a member's concern; this includes acting out and working through a past or present situation or an anticipated event.

**Audience**  Includes others in the group, before whom the problem is explored.

**Auxiliary ego**  Anyone in a psychodramatic enactment who helps the protagonist explore and understand a problem. Auxiliaries are supporting players who portray the roles of significant others in the life of the protagonist.

**Behavioral practice**  The process of replaying a scene until a member discovers a new response that is appropriate for dealing with a situation.

**Classical psychodrama**  An approach that requires specialized training on the director's part, adequate time for orientation and follow-up, a supportive group atmosphere, and members who are appropriate for these methods.

**Closure**  The phase in a psychodrama where members have an opportunity to talk about how they were affected and what they learned from a protagonist's work.

**Catharsis**  The expression of stored-up feelings that are released by verbal and physical acting out of an emotion-laden situation.

**Director**  The facilitator of an enactment in psychodrama.

**Double technique**  The use of an auxiliary ego who stands to the side and behind the protagonist and acts with or speaks for the protagonist. The double gives expression to the protagonist's thoughts and feelings about a situation.

*(Glossary continues on page 84)*

| Dimension | Initial Stage | Working Stage | Final Stage |
|---|---|---|---|
| Key developmental tasks and goals | The key task of the initial stage is the warm-up, which fosters spontaneity. This warm-up period develops a readiness to participate in the experience. Emphasis is on forming common bonds by identifying common experiences. Director suggests relationships that might be explored and scenes that might be enacted. | A major task of psychodrama is to facilitate expression of feelings in a spontaneous and expressive way through role playing. Full expression of conflicts leads to new awareness of problems. During this phase, a corrective emotional experience occurs through enactment and catharsis leading to insight. Reality testing can follow using a variety of techniques. | Major tasks of this phase are working through conflict situations by behavioral practice and by getting feedback, developing a sense of mastery over certain problems, receiving support from the group, and integrating what is learned into life outside the group. Through a process of sharing reactions, increased cohesion is generated. |
| Role and tasks of group leader | Director introduces the nature and purpose of psychodrama and warms up the audience (group) by using techniques. Members are briefly interviewed and asked what kind of situation they would be willing to work on. A protagonist is selected. Director's main task is to create a climate of support and prepare the group drama. Director may select a theme (such as loneliness, dealing with intimacy, and so on) on which the group can focus. Main task is to create a safe and supportive climate. | During this phase, the director's task is to encourage members to enact scenes involving conflicts. Emphasis is on action, keeping the members focused on the present, and helping them fully express feelings. Director facilitates and interprets the action and encourages spontaneity and expression. Director brings members forward to take the parts of other significant figures in the protagonist's drama. Director helps these auxiliary egos learn their roles. | After the main action, director helps the protagonist integrate what has occurred. Director asks for feedback and support from other members; in this way all members get involved in the psychodrama. Care is taken so that those who participated in the psychodrama are not left without adequate closure. Director may summarize the session and help everyone integrate the psychodramatic events. Director encourages a personal sharing and consolidation of learnings. |
| Role of group members | Members discuss goals, get acquainted with one another, and participate in exercises to get them focused. They may decide on a theme of common interest, which in turn leads to the selection of a protagonist. Members decide what personal issues they will explore. | Members define in concrete terms a situation to be enacted; they reconstruct an anxiety-causing event from the past or one anticipated in the future. They fantasize and express themselves as fully as possible both verbally and nonverbally. Members serve as auxiliary egos for the protagonist. | Members share with the protagonist feelings they had as the enactment took place. The sharing is done in a personal way, not an analytical way. Members give feedback to the protagonist and they offer support. They share the personal experiences that the psychodrama reminded them of. |

| Techniques | The warm-up period may be directed or undirected. Warm-up techniques include the use of guided fantasy, dance, and music; the use of artistic materials; the sharing of drawings; and brief interviews of each member. Members share their here-and-now reactions as a way to create trust. | A wide range of action-oriented techniques is used. These include self-presentation, presentation of the other, role reversal, soliloquy, doubling, the mirror technique, dream work, and future projection. Techniques assist members in exploring their conflicts and concerns. | After the action phase of a psychodrama, certain closure techniques may be used, such as sharing techniques, the magic shop, feedback, repeating the drama with new approaches, and discussing alternative behaviors and possible solutions. |
|---|---|---|---|
| Questions to consider | As a leader of a psychodrama, how can you tap into the creativity that exists within the group? Are you alert to connecting one person's work with others in the group as a way of promoting group cohesion?<br><br>What are some ways in which trust can be established, and how can members be encouraged to participate in role playing?<br><br>How can the members best be prepared for taking an active part in the group? How can you help them overcome their resistance to role playing?<br><br>What are some ways of finding themes and concerns that most members share? Once these common problems are identified, how can you facilitate the group so that members can work on these issues together?<br><br>How can cultural differences best be recognized and accepted? | As the group progresses, you might ask yourself these questions:<br><br>• Do I have the courage to experiment with methods even though I do not know the possible outcome?<br><br>• Do I trust my clinical hunches to try out a technique and to flow with what the member produces?<br><br>• Do I have control of the group without dominating it? Are the members able to express their spontaneity and get involved?<br><br>• Am I able to orchestrate all the members so that everyone plays a vital part in the group process? Are some members working silently but not expressing their thoughts and feelings? How can they be encouraged to bring out their reactions?<br><br>• What am I modeling by my behavior in the group? | After a psychodrama, does the member have an opportunity to put into words what he or she has experienced and learned? Is care taken so that the person is not left feeling unfinished? Are some steps taken to help the member translate what was learned in the group to situations in his or her everyday life?<br><br>After catharsis, how can the members be helped to give words to their emotional experience? How can a cognitive component be integrated with emotional work? How can members see a link between past emotional issues and options for change of current behavior?<br><br>As a leader, are you alert to ways in which others in the group might have been affected by a person's work?<br><br>How can you help members attain a vision of changes desired in the future? And how can this be practiced?<br><br>How could you assist members in developing plans for change that they can continue working on after they leave the group? |

Reactions: Summarize your reactions to the psychodramatic perspective on group developmental stages. What do you like *most? Least?* What aspects of this approach would you incorporate in your style of leadership?

**Empty chair**  Instead of another person (an auxiliary) playing the complementary figure in a protagonist's enactment, a chair represents this figure.

**Encountering**  A process at the very core of psychodrama through which people not only meet but understand one another on a deep and significant level.

**Future projection**  A technique designed to help members clarify and express concerns about a future situation. Members act out a version of the way they hope a given situation will unfold.

**Insight**  An increased awareness of a problem situation, which often allows for an emotional release.

**Magic shop**  A technique whereby group members bargain with each other by exchanging an imaginary quality.

**Mirror technique**  A method in which an auxiliary ego assumes the role of the protagonist by mirroring his or her postures, gestures, and words as they appeared in the enactment.

**Multiple double**  Two or more doubles help a protagonist express different parts of him- or herself.

**Protagonist**  The subject of a psychodramatic enactment; the member who is the focus of therapeutic exploration.

**Psychodrama**  Primarily a group therapy approach in which clients explore their problems through role playing, enacting situations using various dramatic devices to gain insight, discover their own creativity, and develop behavioral skills.

**Reality testing**  Providing a relatively safe setting for trying out behaviors that may not be socially accepted in "real life" situations.

**Replay**  A technique for repeating an action to refine it, play it with more expressiveness, or vary it in some other fashion.

**Role reversal**  A technique whereby the protagonist changes parts with other personalities portrayed in his or her drama.

**Role playing**  An offshoot of psychodrama that can be used in either a therapeutic or an educational context; the method does not aim at exploring a person's deepest feelings but generally deals with the less personal dimensions of a problem.

**Role theory**  J. L. Moreno's idea that people play multiple roles in everyday life; members are given the freedom to try out a diversity of roles, thereby getting a sharper focus on parts of themselves they would like to present to others.

**Role training**  As part of working through a problem, members acquire and rehearse specific interpersonal skills, which are often learned by modeling other members.

**Self-presentation**  A technique in which protagonists portray themselves and talk about their problem.

**Sharing phase**  The stage after an enactment by a protagonist; other members are asked to share their personal reactions to the protagonist's work.

**Soliloquy**  A technique in which protagonists imagine that they are alone and speak their thoughts and feelings out loud.

**Spontaneity**  An adequate response to a new situation or a novel response to an old situation.

**Stage**  The area where a psychodrama enactment takes place.

**Surplus reality**  The opportunity to replay an unfortunate or traumatic event with a more empowered and positive ending, or a chance to more fully express feelings in ways that might not be socially acceptable.

**Tele**  The two-way flow of feelings between people.

**Theater of spontaneity**  Playing out in a spontaneous manner events from the daily newspaper or topics suggested by an audience.

**Unconscious**  The source of wisdom and creativity as well as a repository of disowned emotions.

**Warm-up phase**  Initial activities designed to attain trust and involvement within a group.


## Exercises and Activities for Psychodrama

### Rationale

Psychodrama is based on the rationale that therapeutic work is enhanced by dealing with problems as though they are occurring in the present. The following exercises, activities, and problems are designed to give you some experience with psychodrama; experiment with them as much as possible in your group. These exercises will help you directly experience your concerns. They can also help you increase your awareness of others' experiences and thus help you develop more sensitivity to others. As you work through these activities in small groups, think of imaginative ways to modify them.

### Exercises

1. You are setting up a psychodrama for your group. What warm-up techniques will you use? Practice these techniques in your group, and get feedback on your effectiveness from fellow group members.

2. You encourage a member of the group you are leading to role-play a situation involving a conflict with her father. She says: "I won't role-play, because that seems phony. Role-playing always makes me self-conscious. Is it OK if I just talk about my problem with my father instead?" How would you respond? (You might act this out in your own class group; have one person role-play the reluctant member, and another person, the leader. Group members should take turns playing the roles, so that several ways of working with reluctance can be demonstrated.)

3. As a group leader, how would you encourage members to select significant personal issues to explore in a psychodrama without coercing them to participate?

4. Assume that a member tells you that he'd like to get involved in a particular psychodrama because he has a lot of anger stored up against women. He tells you, however, that he is afraid that if he does get involved, he will lose control and perhaps even make the women in the group the target of his rage. How would you respond?

5. A man in your group wants to explore his relationship with his daughter, which he describes as being strained. How would you proceed with him? What specific techniques might you suggest? What would you expect to accomplish with these procedures?

6. One of the women in the group describes her conflicts with her daughter as follows: "My daughter tells me that I simply don't understand what it's like to be 16. We fight continually, and the more I try to get her to do what I think is right, the more defiant she becomes. I simply don't know where to begin. How can I reach her?" Act out the above situation in your class or small group. Assume you are the leader, and get another person in class to role-play the mother. Consider trying these techniques:

    a. Role reversal (mother becomes the daughter)

    b. Self-presentation (mother presents her side of this conflict)

    c. Presentation of the other (mother presents the daughter's side)

    d. Soliloquy (mother verbalizes uncensored feelings and thoughts)

    e. What other techniques can you think of to practice in this situation?

7. Assume that the woman in the above case is role-playing with another member, who is playing the daughter. All of a sudden the mother stops and says: "I'm stuck; I just don't know what to say now. Whenever she gets that hurt look in her eyes and begins to cry, I feel rotten and guilty, and I freeze up. What can I do now?" In this instance try the *double technique*. (Another member becomes an auxiliary ego and stands behind the mother and speaks for her.) You could also use the *multiple double technique* (where two or more people represent different facets of the mother). One double might represent the guilty mother who attempts to placate her daughter, and the other double could be the firm mother who deals directly with the daughter's manipulation.

8. One of the women in your group seems aloof and judgmental. Members in the group pick up nonverbal cues such as frowning, glances, and positioning of her head, and other indications of superiority. She says that people outside of the group have the same impression of her, yet she does not feel judgmental, nor does she perceive herself as others do. Assume that this woman wants to explore this issue, and use the *mirror technique*. Someone in your class or group can play the role of the woman who is perceived as aloof and judgmental, and you or another member can imitate her posture, gestures, and speech. Can you think of other techniques to help this woman explore the discrepancy between her self-image and the view others have of her?

9. Think of a situation in which the use of the *magic shop technique* would be appropriate. Think of another case in which you'd be likely to employ the *future projection technique*. If possible, set up these situations in your class or group and practice using these techniques.

10. Select a personal problem that you are concerned about or a relationship that you'd like to understand better. (It is important that you be willing to share this problem with your class or group. If dealing with a current problem seems too threatening, consider working on a past problem that you have resolved.) Then set up a psychodrama in your group in which you are the protagonist. This exercise, if done properly, will give you a sense of what it's like to be a member of a psychodrama group. As an alternative, you can assume a role and portray a conflict. This role playing can help you identify with the problems others might present.

## Questions for Reflection and Discussion

1. For what populations do you think psychodramatic techniques would be most appropriate? Can you think of any clients you would not recommend for psychodrama?

2. What are your reactions to dealing with both the past and the future as though these events are happening in the present? What are some advantages you can see in this present-centered focus? Do you see any problems with bringing all experiences into the "now" and asking clients to reenact a past event or act out some expected future event? How might you encourage clients to stay in the present if they were reluctant to do so?

3. How might you respond to a group member who refused to get involved in any type of role playing and said: "Why do you want me to go back and relive a painful period in my life?

I've tried to forget about those difficult times. What good will it do me to open up that can of worms?"

4. What are some specific psychodramatic techniques that you find most interesting and potentially useful? To what degree are you likely to include various psychodrama techniques in the groups you are leading or might someday lead? How can you incorporate some basic concepts and practices of psychodrama into the model of group counseling you favor?

5. Role playing has many uses in many different kinds of groups with various age populations. How inclined are you to introduce role-playing interventions when members struggle with interpersonal concerns? What kind of explanation would you give to members regarding the purposes and values of engaging in role playing?

6. There are many forms of dramatic role playing that can be done through the medium of play, art, movement, the use of puppets, and other nonverbal methods. How might you incorporate art, dance, music, and play into group work with children or adolescents? What value do you see in using these expressive approaches in conjunction with verbal communication?

7. Psychodrama consists of verbally and nonverbally releasing pent-up feelings such as anger, hatred, and despair. Do you feel able to deal with the release of your own intense feelings? Have you already experienced a similar catharsis? Do you think you have the knowledge and the skills to deal effectively with a client who expresses such intense emotions? Could you deal with the emotional effects that catharsis might trigger in other group members?

8. What are some possible psychological risks associated with psychodrama? What might you want to say to members before they participated in a psychodrama? What kind of orientation would you provide? How do you think the potential risks can be reduced?

9. If you were using psychodrama, what steps would you take to see that members were not left with unfinished business? What would you do if a group member said that she felt unresolved after an enactment?

10. Do you think psychodrama has equal therapeutic value for people from all cultures? What framework would you use in deciding how to modify certain psychodramatic techniques in working with individuals from diverse cultural backgrounds?

## Quiz on Psychodrama: A Comprehension Check
Score _____%

*Note:* Please refer to Appendix I for the scoring key. Count 5 points for each error, and subtract the total from 100 to get your percentage score.

*True/false items:* Decide if the following statements are "more true" or "more false" as they apply to psychodrama.

T  F  1. In a psychodrama, participants are asked to enact their conflicts or crisis situations as if they are occurring in the present moment.

T  F  2. Catharsis and insight are not considered important in psychodrama.

T  F  3. Psychodrama has many major limitations in working with people who are emotionally inhibited.

T  F  4. Psychodrama is considered to be an experiential and action-oriented method.

T   F   5. In the soliloquy technique, the protagonist speaks directly to the audience by expressing some uncensored feelings or thoughts.

T   F   6. Past events or traumatic childhood experiences are not generally explored in psychodrama because nothing can be done to change these events in the present.

T   F   7. The concepts of *encounter* and *tele* are polar opposites.

T   F   8. Psychodrama places importance on the past, present, and future.

T   F   9. During the sharing phase, members are encouraged to offer interpretations and clinical hunches about the meaning of the protagonist's behavior.

T   F  10. Dreams are generally not explored in a psychodrama format.

*Multiple-choice items:* Select the one best answer among the alternatives given. Consider each question within the framework of psychodrama.

_____11. Psychodrama emphasizes
   a. spontaneity and creativity.
   b. an intellectual understanding of the causes of conflicts.
   c. a way of challenging irrational beliefs.
   d. understanding of life scripts.
   e. working therapeutically with early recollections.

_____12. Psychodrama was developed by
   a. Alfred Adler.
   b. Rudolf Dreikurs.
   c. Rollo May.
   d. J. L. Moreno.
   e. Fritz Perls.

_____13. The technique whereby a protagonist speaks directly to the audience by expressing some uncensored feeling or thought is
   a. the mirror technique.
   b. soliloquy.
   c. projection.
   d. role reversal.
   e. self-presentation.

_____14. Through which technique can participants rehearse in a fresh way an approach to someone with whom they would like to interact?
   a. the mirror technique
   b. the magic shop
   c. future projection
   d. the double technique
   e. the soliloquy

_____15. Which of the following techniques is the most useful for helping members clarify and prioritize their values?
   a. the mirror technique
   b. the magic shop
   c. future projection
   d. the double technique
   e. the soliloquy

_____16. According to psychodrama,
    a. unless a problem is solved, the enactment is a failure.
    b. members of the group can profit only if they are directly involved in reenacting an event.
    c. members of the group can benefit in vicarious ways by observing the work of others.
    d. members will change their behavior only if they develop a contract that specifies homework assignments.
    e. unless members resolve their transference relationship with the group leader, they will be fixated at an immature level of development.

_____17. Which of the following is *not* a key concept of psychodrama?
    a. encounter and tele
    b. catharsis
    c. dealing with the present
    d. exploring unexpressed emotions
    e. free association with the dreams of other members

_____18. In psychodrama, the past is dealt with
    a. by bringing it into the present.
    b. by reenacting the event and reexperiencing earlier feelings.
    c. by dwelling on causal factors of current problems.
    d. by talking about possible reasons for hurts in the past.
    e. both (a) and (b).

_____19. The third phase of a psychodrama consists of
    a. some type of nonverbal exercise.
    b. encouraging a protagonist to act out a conflict.
    c. sharing by members of their personal reactions to what they observed during the action phase.
    d. an assessment by the members of the possible interpretations for the protagonist's behavior and difficulties.
    e. the leader's giving an interpretation of the protagonist's behavioral dynamics and assigning homework to be carried out before the next meeting.

_____20. The ventilation of stored-up feelings is known as
    a. breaking out.
    b. breaking down.
    c. working through.
    d. acting out.
    e. catharsis.

# CHAPTER NINE

# The Existential Approach to Groups

## Prechapter Self-Inventory for the Existential Approach

*Directions:* Refer to page 57 for general directions. Indicate your position on these statements using the following code:

**5** = I *strongly agree* with this statement.
**4** = I *agree,* in most respects, with this statement.
**3** = I am *undecided* in my opinion about this statement.
**2** = I *disagree,* in most respects, with this statement.
**1** = I *strongly disagree* with this statement.

_____ 1. Group work best focuses on the subjective aspects of a member's experience.

_____ 2. The central issues in counseling and therapy are freedom, responsibility, and the anxiety that accompanies being both free and responsible.

_____ 3. Anxiety and guilt are not necessarily disorders to be cured, for they are part of the human condition.

_____ 4. Being aware of death gives meaning to life and makes each person realize that he or she is ultimately alone.

_____ 5. The basic task of group therapy is to expand consciousness and thus extend freedom.

_____ 6. The meaning of death is a productive focus for group sessions.

_____ 7. The group leader's function is not to tell members what life should mean to them but to encourage them to discover this meaning for themselves.

_____ 8. An inauthentic existence consists of living a life as outlined and determined by others rather than a life based on one's own inner experience.

_____ 9. The effective counselor is less concerned with "doing therapy" than with "living therapy" by being with another.

_____10. Therapists' major tasks are fostering self-disclosure, creating a working relationship, and providing a model for clients.

## Summary of Basic Assumptions and Key Concepts of the Existential Approach to Groups

1. People become what they choose to become; although there are factors that restrict choices, self-determination is ultimately the basis of their uniqueness as individuals. The group leader focuses on choice and freedom, the potential within humans to find their own way, and the search for identity.

2. In the existential group, basic human themes constitute the content of interactions. Existential crises are seen as a part of living and not something to be remedied. These crises frequently concern the meaning of life, anxiety and guilt, recognition of one's aloneness, the awareness of death and finality, and the fear of choosing and accepting responsibility for one's choices. Because these "crises" aren't necessarily pathological, they can't be externally alleviated; they should be *lived through* and understood in the context of a group.

3. The leader's major tasks are to grasp the subjective world of members and to establish authentic relationships in which they can work on understanding themselves and their choices more fully. The leader's ultimate goal is to enable clients to be free and become responsible for the direction of their own lives. Therefore, group members are largely responsible for what occurs in therapy.

4. Group leaders do not behave in rigid or prescribed ways, for they can't predict the exact direction or content of any group. Leaders are not technical experts who carry out treatment plans with specialized techniques; rather, they establish real relationships with the members of the group.

5. The *presence* of the leader, or the leader's willingness to be there for others and to confront them when appropriate, is a major characteristic of the effective group. Group leaders must be willing to take responsibility for their own thinking, feeling, and judging. They are present as *persons* with the members and become active agents in the group.

6. Existential therapy is best considered as an invitation to members to recognize the ways in which they are not living fully authentic lives and to make choices that will lead them to become what they are capable of being. This approach does not focus on curing sickness or merely providing problem-solving techniques for the complexities of authentic existence.

## Glossary of Key Terms for the Existential Approach

**Anxiety**  A condition that results from being aware that we are ultimately responsible for the consequences of our actions.

**Authenticity**  The process of creating, discovering, or maintaining the core deep within one's being; the process of becoming the person we are capable of becoming.

**Existential anxiety**  The feeling, viewed as a core characteristic of humans, resulting from having to make choices without clear guidelines and with no guarantees about the outcomes.

**Existential group**  People making a commitment to a lifelong journey of self-exploration.

**Existential guilt**  The result of, or the consciousness of, evading the commitment to choosing for ourselves; a condition that is rooted in the realization that we inevitably fall short of becoming what we could become.

**Existential neurosis**  Feelings of despair and anxiety that result from inauthentic modes of living, the failure to make choices, and an avoidance of responsibility.

**Existential tradition**  Seeks a balance between recognition of the limits and tragic dimensions of human existence and the possibilities and opportunities of human life.

**Existential vacuum**  A condition of emptiness and hollowness that results from meaninglessness in life.

*(Glossary continues on page 94)*

STAGES OF DEVELOPMENT OF THE EXISTENTIAL GROUP

| Dimension | Initial Stage | Working Stage | Final Stage |
|---|---|---|---|
| Key developmental tasks and goals | Focus is on how members perceive and experience their world; thus, the approach is experiential and subjective. Main goal is to increase awareness of options to widen everyone's freedom. Initial task of a group is making a commitment to explore personally meaningful and significant issues concerning human struggles. Members decide how they want to use time in the group and what issues to explore. | Members explore a wide range of universal human concerns such as loneliness, the anxiety of recognizing that one is free to make choices and that freedom is always accompanied by responsibility, the meaning of life and death, and so on. Participants consider alternative ways of dealing with issues they are facing. Emphasis is on taking responsibility *now* for the way one chooses to be. Focus is on self-discovery, which often leads to giving up defenses and living authentically. | Group counseling or therapy is seen as an "invitation to change." Members are challenged to re-create themselves. In the group, they have opportunities to evaluate their lives and to choose how they will change. Toward the end of a group, termination is another issue to face, for the ending of a group brings on anxiety. The termination of a group must be dealt with fully. Members are challenged with finding new ways of being. |
| Role and tasks of group leader | The leader's tasks are to confront members with the issue of dealing with freedom and responsibility and to challenge them to recognize that regardless of the limits there is always some element of choice in life. Leader helps members see the ways in which they are not living fully. Leader makes use of self as a way to create a safe climate for exploration. A key task is to create a safe climate that allows for taking risks. | Emphasis is on creating a quality relationship, which entails the leader's full presence. Leader's task is to be there as a person for the members; he or she embarks on an unknown journey with the members and is open to where they will go together. Leaders must understand and adopt the members' subjective world. They also engage in self-disclosure and model authentic behavior. | At the final stage of a group, the leader challenges members to go into the world and be active. Leader helps members integrate and consolidate what they've learned in the group so that the maximum transfer can occur. Rather than "doing therapy," leader lives it through the openness of ongoing existential encounters with the members. Leader helps members see their contribution to the changes they've made. |
| Role of group members | Members always have a part in the group process. They look at *who* and *what* they are; they clarify their identities and make decisions concerning how they can achieve authenticity. Members decide what they will explore in the group, as well as how they want to change. They define their personal goals. | Members decide what struggles or existential concerns they will share. Typical concerns include changing roles, creating new identities when old identities are no longer meaningful, value conflicts, emptiness, dealing with loneliness, and working on the fear of freedom and responsibility. | To change, members must go out into the world and *act*. Since members are responsible for their own lives, they decide if and how they want to live differently. If a group is successful, members achieve an authentic identity and become aware of choices that can lead to action. |

| | | |
|---|---|---|
| Techniques | There are no prescribed techniques, and therapeutic procedures can be borrowed from many approaches. More than a group leader's technique or skill, the leader's *attitude* and *behavior* are crucial for the group's results. Group leaders are not viewed as technical experts who apply therapeutic treatment plans. There is no assessment, nor is there a predetermined treatment plan for the group to follow. Emphasis is on understanding the members' world. | Emphasis is not so much on doing therapy by using techniques but rather is on being fully present. Thus, leaders may work with dreams; they may work with the current interaction in the group; they may explore the past with members; and they may be both supportive and challenging. Emphasis is on constructive confrontation so that members can learn how to confront themselves. | Group counseling or therapy is seen as a spontaneous encounter between members. The leader uses the here-and-now of the group to illustrate how members are in daily life. Although the focus is on the *encounter* that occurs in the group, specific techniques can be developed to challenge members to recognize the choices they have and their decisions to make a new life. |
| Questions to consider | An existential group can be described as people making a commitment to begin and to continue a lifelong journey of self-exploration. Ask yourself the degree to which you are willing to embark on this journey. Are you willing to do in your own life what you ask your members to do?<br><br>Are you able to experience the suffering and despair that is sometimes necessary?<br><br>Are you able to tolerate the unknown yet still take action? Can you exercise your freedom without guarantees?<br><br>How do you deal with anxiety in your own life? Do you face it, or do you try to avoid it? How might this affect the way you lead a group?<br><br>What value do you see in encouraging members to focus on their here-and-now reactions within the group? | To what degree are you able to be present for those in your group? Are you willing to travel down whatever path a member might lead you?<br><br>Can you adopt members' subjective views of the world?<br><br>Do you model in the group those attitudes and behaviors you hope the members will develop? What do you model?<br><br>Are you able to borrow techniques from other approaches and apply them to the struggles of members? Do you use techniques within the context of the relationship that you have established with members and in the climate of trust?<br><br>Are you aware of ways that your techniques may or may not fit for a member's cultural background? | Are the members willing to take action? Are they able to act on what they have learned? Are they committed to making changes in their lives? How will they make certain changes?<br><br>Are the members able to see that they do have choices? That there is a price to pay for acting on their choices? That they must choose for themselves in the face of uncertainty? Are they moving in the direction of trusting their decisions and relying less on others to decide for them?<br><br>Are members more aware of the options for action available to them?<br><br>Are members now better able to cope with the anxiety that comes with freedom than when they entered the group?<br><br>How will you assist members in evaluating their experiences in a group? |

Reactions: Summarize your reactions to the existential perspective on group developmental stages. What do you like *most*? *Least*? What aspects of this approach would you incorporate in your style of leadership?

**Freedom**  An inescapable aspect of the human condition, making each of us the author of our life and, therefore, leaving us responsible for our destiny and accountable for our actions.

**"Givens of existence"**  Core themes in the therapeutic process: death, freedom, existential isolation, and meaninglessness.

**Life-changing psychotherapy**  An effort to help clients examine how they have answered life's existential questions and challenge them to revise their answers and begin to live authentically.

**Logotherapy**  Developed by Viktor Frankl, a brand of existential therapy that literally means "healing through reason"; focuses on challenging members to search for the meaning in life.

**Phenomenology**  A method of exploration that uses subjective human experiencing as its focus.

**Restricted existence**  The state of functioning with a limited degree of awareness of oneself and being vague about the nature of one's problems.

**Self-awareness**  The capacity for consciousness that enables us to make choices.

**Solitude**  A time we choose to make to be with ourselves, to discover who we are, and to renew ourselves.

## Exercises and Activities for the Existential Approach

### Rationale

The existential approach does not provide a ready-made set of techniques for group practitioners. It is more an orientation to group counseling than a system of therapeutic procedures. Practitioners can adhere to the existential perspective and at the same time use many other therapeutic techniques.

Here are examples of activities that are in some way related to existential themes. Use these exercises both on your own and in your group or class, and then you'll have a better idea of how to integrate existential concepts in your leadership style. Think about what you can learn about both yourself and group processes through these exercises.

### Exercises

1. *Self-awareness.* Group members often say that they are afraid of learning too much about themselves. They may accept the notion that "ignorance is bliss" or that "what you don't know won't hurt you." What is your position? Are you clearly open to learning all that you can about yourself? Or do you have reservations about expanding your self-awareness? What concerns might you have about opening doors to your life that are now closed? What are some examples that illustrate your own struggles with becoming more self-aware? How do you see your willingness or unwillingness to increase your awareness as related to your potential effectiveness as a group leader? Discuss these questions in your class or group.

2. *Freedom and responsibility.* Freedom of choice entails accepting the responsibility for influencing the direction of your life. Being free means that as long as you are alive you are making choices about who it is you are becoming. Do you believe you are what you are now largely as a result of your choices, or do you think that you are the product of circum-

stances? What are some *major choices* you've made that have been crucial to your present development? Discuss some of these crucial decisions in your group. How do you imagine your life would be different now if you had decided differently? What struggles have you had between desiring freedom and fearing it? To what degree do you see yourself as being ready to accept the responsibility that accompanies your freedom? Think of specific ways in which the answers to these questions have an effect on the way you lead groups. Discuss how your concerns about your choices might affect your group leading.

3. *Anxiety.* Anxiety is not only an impetus to change but also a result of recognizing that you are responsible for your choices. What kind of anxiety have you experienced in making key life decisions? Do you agree with the existential notion that anxiety produces growth? In what situations do you experience the most anxiety? Do you tend to manage your anxiety by directly facing the consequences of your choices? by attempting to make others responsible for you? by avoiding making choices? by attempting to deny reality? In your group or class, discuss how your ways of dealing with anxiety in your own life will either help or hinder you in working with clients who are also wrestling with anxiety.

4. *Death.* How well are you able to accept the fact of your own death? Do you see any relationship between how you view death and the degree to which you are living fully now? To clarify your thoughts and feelings about death and to examine how it affects the way you live, try some of these exercises in your class or group:
   a. What do you think the significant people in your life would write on your tombstone? What would you like them to say?
   b. Write the eulogy you'd like delivered at your funeral. Bring it to the group and share it with other members.
   c. Assume that you know you are going to die within 24 hours. What would you most like to do during these final hours? What does this say about your values?
   d. Tell others in your group what you'd most like to accomplish before you die.
   e. What are your fears, if any, about your own death and dying or about the loss of those you love? How do you deal with these fears?
   f. If you have lost someone close to you, consider sharing what this has been like for you. What did you learn about yourself through this experience?
   g. As you reflect on your answers to the above questions, think about the implications for your ability as a group counselor to assist members in facing and dealing with the reality of their own death.

5. *Meaning in life.* Confronting our mortality makes us think about how meaningful our lives are. In your group, let yourself imagine a typical day in your life five years ago. What was it like, and what were you like then? Are there any major differences between your life then and now? Share with others in your group some of the most significant changes you've made over the past five years. Then project yourself five years into the future. What do you *hope* you'll be like then? What do you *fear* you might be like then? Explore in your group what you are experiencing in your life that contributes to or detracts from a meaningful existence. Again, how might your answers to these questions have implications for your ability to challenge clients to discover the meaning in their lives?

6. *Authenticity.* The existential perspective stresses that affirming ourselves is an ongoing process. We are authentic if we face the anxiety of choosing for ourselves and accept the consequences of our choices. Inauthentic people allow others to determine who and what

they are. Discuss some crucial incidents in your own personal struggles to define yourself. Consider some of these questions as you construct your personal identity road map:

a. Who am I? What has contributed to the way I am?

b. What roles have I typically played? How have I seen myself?

c. What choices did I make? What choices did others make for me?

d. Have I lost contact with myself by looking to others for answers and direction? Do I trust others more than myself?

e. How has my life been shaped by past actions, people, influences, and so on?

f. What more do I want from life? What kind of identity am I searching for?

g. If some of the elements I depend on for a sense of my identity were taken away, what would I be like?

7. *Loneliness.* Share in your group some ways in which each member has experienced loneliness. Can you recall the time in your life when you felt most alone? What was this like for you? Select a poem, a picture, or an excerpt from a book that captures the loneliness you have felt at some point in your life. Bring this to the group and share it. Think of some ways to help the members of a group you are leading deal with their own loneliness.

8. *Creative solitude.* Existentialists believe that unless we can enjoy solitude creatively we cannot develop genuine intimacy with others. Do you make time for yourself to be alone? When you are alone, what is this generally like for you? Do you welcome it or flee from it? Select a song, poem, poster, or picture that represents peaceful solitude to you. In what ways might you want to learn how to enjoy time alone? Do you have the quality of time alone that you would like?

9. *Role and functions of the group leader.* The existential approach emphasizes the role of the leader not so much as a doer of therapy but as a person to be fully present with the group members. Discuss in your group the degree to which you feel personally equipped to challenge others to look at the important issues in life. For instance, do you feel ready to challenge others to look at the choices they've made as well as the ones now open to them? Have you done this in your own life? Could you be psychologically present with another person who was exploring a life/death issue? Have you been willing to face such issues in your life?

10. *Personal evaluation and critique.* In your group or class discuss the concepts of the existential approach that you find most valuable. Consider some of these questions in your discussion:

a. What key themes would you take from this approach and apply to groups you lead?

b. What are the limitations of the approach? What disadvantages do you see in limiting yourself strictly to an existential orientation?

c. Do you think this perspective has something to offer every client? For what people do you think it is the most appropriate?

d. What do you see as both the strengths and limitations of the existential approach in working with groups composed of culturally diverse populations? What are some ways that you could link existential themes with certain cultural values of members?

e. How are you able to relate in a personal way to the existential approach? In what ways can you understand yourself better by reflecting on the key existential themes? How is your self-understanding related to your ability to encourage group members to explore their personal lives?

f. An existential approach can form a philosophical foundation for group work. This approach allows for incorporating methods from various theoretical orientations. What therapeutic techniques from other models would you apply to existential concepts in the groups you lead or will lead?

g. In what kind of group (therapy group, psychoeducation group, counseling group, support group) do you think existential notions have a place?

h. With what age populations and client populations might existential notions best fit? Can you think of ways to apply existential themes in group work with children? Adolescents? The elderly?

## Questions for Reflection and Discussion

1. What are some key concepts of the existential approach that you find personally meaningful? Which of these basic ideas, if any, would you most want to include in your framework in approaching a group?

2. In this chapter, the statement is made that anxiety results from having to make choices without clear guidelines and without knowing what the outcome will be. What implications are there for you as a group leader if you accept this view of anxiety? What are your thoughts on the role anxiety plays in a group?

3. According to Frankl, it is not the therapist's job to tell clients what their particular meaning in life should be but rather to encourage them to discover meaning for themselves. What are some ways you might challenge members to find meaning in their life? How might you deal with a member who continued to look to you for answers and direction?

4. Some existential therapists assume that the driving force behind many interpersonal relationships is existential isolation. If you accept this notion that humans are ultimately alone in the world, what are the implications for group counseling? To what degree might groups contribute to members' avoidance of their aloneness? How might a group help a person feel less isolated and less alienated?

5. As an existentially oriented group leader, you should make your emphasis more on understanding the world of the members and less on techniques. What techniques might you use from other therapeutic approaches?

6. According to Yalom, four ultimate concerns make up the core of existential therapy—freedom, isolation, death, and meaninglessness. From your vantage point, what meaning do these existential themes have for you personally? How are these human concerns related to your life and your struggles? Based on your experiences in life, what would you hope to be able to teach members of your groups? What meaning do these existential concerns have for the focus you might want to bring to a group you were leading?

7. How might you deal with those group members who spent a great deal of time trying to convince you that they are not responsible for their lives? If they attempted to hold others in their life responsible for their current problems, what might you be inclined to say or do in the group?

8. Consider the relevance of group work within an existential orientation in school counseling. If you were leading a crisis-oriented group in the schools, how might you use the crisis situation a member is experiencing as a way to understand existential concerns? In working with school-age students, can you think of ways to assist members in accepting personal

responsibility for their choices? What are some ways you could assist children and adolescents in creating an internal locus of control and increasing their potential for choices in a group?

9. If you were leading a bereavement group with the elderly, how could you draw upon existential notions in assisting members make sense of their losses? What specific existential themes might you draw from in working with older persons in your group?

10. In applying an existential approach to group work with culturally diverse individuals, what universal human concerns could link members? What value do you see in helping members come to an understanding of what they have in common with each other while respecting and valuing their differences?

## Quiz on the Existential Approach to Groups: A Comprehension Check

Score _____%

*Note:* Please refer to Appendix I for the scoring key. Count 5 points for each error, and subtract the total from 100 to get your percentage score.

*True/false items:* Decide if the following statements are "more true" or "more false" as they apply to the existential approach to groups.

T   F   1. The existential group focuses on techniques designed to assist members in experiencing catharsis.

T   F   2. Anxiety can be an impetus to change and thus can be a positive characteristic.

T   F   3. The fact that we will die can actually motivate us to create a meaningful existence.

T   F   4. Existentialists believe we are not ultimately alone if we establish intimate ties with others.

T   F   5. An existential group might be described as people making a commitment to begin and complete a lifelong journey of self-exploration.

T   F   6. The existential view is that since we are thrust into the world, life is basically hopeless.

T   F   7. The basic goal of an existential group is to treat symptoms so that members can be free of existential anxiety.

T   F   8. The existential group leader sets the tone for the group by introducing techniques and doing something to get people talking openly.

T   F   9. The existential approach has some distinct advantages in working with members from diverse cultural backgrounds.

T   F   10. Existential group work aims at curing people in the traditional medical sense.

*Multiple-choice items:* Select the *one best answer* among the alternatives given. Consider each question within the framework of existential therapy.

_____11. Existential therapy is best described as a

    a. systematic approach to behavior modification.

    b. philosophy with which a therapist operates.

    c. set of techniques designed to change behavior.

    d. form of psychoanalytic therapy.

    e. separate school of therapy.

_____12. An existential group works toward all of the following goals except
   a. enabling people to become truthful with themselves.
   b. widening clients' perspectives on themselves and the world around them.
   c. helping people adjust to the dominant norms in society.
   d. finding clarity on what gives meaning to present and future living.

_____13. Two of the most significant spokespeople for the existential approach in the United States are
   a. Heinz Kohut and Otto Kernberg.
   b. Medard Boss and Ludwig Binswanger.
   c. Rollo May and Irvin Yalom.
   d. Martin Buber and Jean-Paul Sartre.
   e. Erik Erikson and Margaret Mahler.

_____14. The existential group focuses on
   a. unresolved conflicts that were repressed in childhood.
   b. here-and-now forces within the group.
   c. techniques designed to assist members in gaining catharsis.
   d. measuring the observable outcomes of a group.
   e. working through the transference relationship with the leader.

_____15. Which of the following is a limitation of the existential approach in working with culturally diverse client populations?
   a. the focus on understanding and accepting the client
   b. the focus on finding meaning in one's life
   c. the focus on death as a catalyst to living fully
   d. the focus on one's own responsibility rather than on social conditions

_____16. Existential therapy places emphasis on
   a. a systematic approach to changing behavior.
   b. the quality of the relationship between the leader and members.
   c. teaching clients cognitive and behavioral coping skills.
   d. uncovering early childhood traumatic events.
   e. working through the transference relationship.

_____17. All of the following are considered key concepts guiding the functioning of an existential group except
   a. the search for authenticity.
   b. discovering the patterns of one's lifestyle.
   c. death and nonbeing.
   d. the search for meaning.
   e. aloneness and relatedness.

_____18. The existential view of death is that it
   a. renders us hopeless.
   b. makes life less meaningful.
   c. gives meaning to every moment.
   d. creates an existential vacuum.
   e. motivates us to seek organized religion as a source of values.

_____19. In an existential group the leader would tend to
   a. challenge members to become aware of their freedom and responsibility.
   b. urge members to free themselves of guilt and anxiety.

  c. aim for a deep catharsis for each member.

  d. encourage a regression to one's early past.

  e. help each member see how his or her lifestyle has a bearing on present interactions with others in the group.

_____20. The view in existential groups is that techniques

  a. should be secondary to understanding members.

  b. are specified to bringing about change.

  c. interfere with the therapeutic process.

  d. imply a loss of faith in the client's ability to find his or her own way.

  e. lead to inauthenticity on the part of members.

CHAPTER TEN

# The Person-Centered Approach to Groups

## Prechapter Self-Inventory for the Person-Centered Approach

*Directions:* Refer to page 57 for general directions. Indicate your position on these statements using the following code:

**5** = I *strongly agree* with this statement.
**4** = I *agree,* in most respects, with this statement.
**3** = I am *undecided* in my opinion about this statement.
**2** = I *disagree,* in most respects, with this statement.
**1** = I *strongly disagree* with this statement.

_____ 1. The group members, not the leader, have the primary responsibility for the direction the group takes.
_____ 2. The attitudes of genuineness, positive regard, and accurate empathy are both necessary *and* sufficient for therapeutic change to occur.
_____ 3. A leader's direction is not necessary for a group to move in a constructive direction.
_____ 4. A major function of the group leader is to establish a climate of trust in the group.
_____ 5. A group leader can be effective without attending to transference.
_____ 6. Self-disclosure by the leader tends to increase trust and self-disclosure on the part of the members.
_____ 7. Effective group leading is best considered as a "way of being" rather than a "way of doing."
_____ 8. The group leader is more a facilitator than a director.
_____ 9. Directive intervention by the leader can interfere with the group process.
_____10. It is well for group leaders to avoid giving advice.

*True for the theory*

*main ideas, concepts of the approach*

## Summary of Basic Assumptions and Key Concepts of the Person-Centered Approach

1. Clients are basically trustworthy and have the potential for self-direction. The group can become aware of problems and the means to resolve them if the facilitator encourages members to explore present feelings and thoughts. Because the group has the potential for self-direction, there is a minimum of direction on the leader's part, for this would undermine respect for the group members.
2. The person-centered approach emphasizes the personal qualities of the group leader rather than techniques of leading, because the primary function of the group facilitator is

to create a climate in which healing can occur. The therapeutic relationship between the facilitator and members helps the members grow and change.

3. The therapeutic core conditions for growth are genuineness, or realness, of the facilitator; unconditional positive regard, which is an acceptance of the members; and empathic understanding of the members' subjective world. To the extent that facilitators experience and demonstrate genuineness, warm regard, and accurate empathy for the members and to the extent that the members perceive these conditions, therapeutic change and growth will occur.

4. External measures such as diagnosis, testing, interpretation, advice giving, and probing for information are not useful in group work. Instead, group counseling comprises active listening, reflection and clarification, and understanding the inner world of the members. Accurate empathy is a core dimension in a person-centered group.

5. A basic characteristic of this approach to group work is the focus on the members as the center of the group. Members of a person-centered group are often as facilitative as the group leader.

## Glossary of Key Terms for Person-Centered Therapy

**Accurate empathic understanding**  The act of perceiving the internal frame of reference of another, of grasping the person's subjective world, without losing one's own identity.

**Actualization tendency**  An intrinsic source of growth or a tendency toward self-realization, which means that the individual moves inherently toward self-regulation, self-determination, and inner freedom.

**Congruence**  The state in which self-experiences are accurately symbolized in the self-concept. As applied to the therapist, congruence is matching inner experiencing with one's external expressions; genuineness.

**Empathic understanding**  The ability to sense accurately the personal meanings others are experiencing.

**Expressive arts therapy**  An approach that makes use of various arts—such as movement, drawing, painting, sculpting, music, and improvisation—in a supportive setting for the purpose of growth and healing.

**Formative tendency**  A central source of energy that seeks fulfillment and actualization, involving both maintenance and enhancement of the organism.

**Genuineness**  The quality of realness of the group leader; being without pretenses; congruence.

**Humanistic psychology**  A movement, often referred to as the "third force," that emphasizes freedom, choice, creativity, spontaneity, values, growth, self-actualization, humor, and peak experiences.

**Internal locus of control**  The ability to give oneself credit and appreciation when it is due and to be guided by one's own beliefs and standards.

**Openness to experience**  Involves a lack of defensiveness and an ability to perceive the present moment as it is without prejudgment; includes a lack of rigidity, openness to new concepts and beliefs, and a tolerance for ambiguity.

**Personal power**  A state in which individuals are aware of and can act on their own feelings, needs, and values rather than looking outside of themselves for direction.

**Presence**  The ability to "be with" someone fully in the present moment.

**Self-actualizing tendency**  A growth force within us, leading to the full development of one's potential; the basis on which people can be trusted to identify and resolve their own problems in a therapeutic relationship.

**Therapeutic conditions**  The characteristics of the client/therapist relationship necessary and sufficient for change to occur. These core conditions are therapist genuineness, unconditional positive regard, and accurate empathic understanding.

**Unconditional positive regard**  The nonjudgmental expression of a fundamental respect for the person as a human; acceptance of a person's right to his or her feelings.

## Exercises and Activities for the Person-Centered Approach

### Rationale

As is true for the existential approach, the person-centered approach emphasizes the group leader's attitudes far more than the techniques employed to facilitate a group. The most important consideration is the quality of the relationship you are able to create among the members and between yourself and the members. As you practice the exercises, do your best to keep within a person-centered framework. Attempt to attend to, listen to, and clarify what you hear, and *facilitate* more than *direct* the group process in these exercises.

### Exercises

1. Think about what you have learned about yourself to this point that will either enhance or restrict your effectiveness as a group facilitator. What do you see as your single most important personal quality or strength? Can you identify at least one specific personal characteristic that is likely to get in the way of your effectiveness? If you are exploring these issues in a group, it would be a good idea for everyone to assume responsibility for the direction of the group. This could be an interesting exercise in itself to see what occurs in the absence of structured leadership for a session. As an alternative exercise, one or two members can assume the responsibility for being the facilitator of the group. In this facilitation do your best to keep within the framework of the person-centered approach. Allow some time before the end of the exercise to share your reactions to being a member and a facilitator during the session.

2. One of the cornerstones of the person-centered approach is accurate empathy. Use the following questions as catalysts for discussion in your class or group: What is your understanding of empathy? How can you become empathic? What are the barriers? Do you expect to have the problem of overidentification, or losing your own identity by immersing yourself in another's world? What part does leader self-disclosure play in the expression of this empathy? How can you improve your ability to develop appropriate empathy for others? What kind of person do you have a hard time empathizing with, and what does this tell you about yourself?

3. This exercise is designed to help you increase your empathy for people you might identify as "problem group members." Think about a particular kind of person (especially a group member) you are likely to have the most difficulty understanding or accepting. It can be

*(Text continues on page 106)*

STAGES OF DEVELOPMENT OF THE PERSON-CENTERED GROUP

| Dimension | Initial Stage | Working Stage | Final Stage |
|---|---|---|---|
| Key developmental tasks and goals | Early stage of a group is characterized by some floundering and a search for direction. Typically, members present a socially acceptable facade or reveal the "safe" sides of themselves; they describe themselves in a "there-and-then" manner. There is a milling around and a sense of confusion concerning the purpose and the function of the group. A key task is to build trust and a supportive climate that will allow for genuine encounters. | Negative feelings often surface over the lack of leadership. Then a more accepting and trusting climate may prevail. Members show more of themselves, cohesion develops, and members find support in the group. Some confrontation may occur, especially when members sense that others are not being genuine. False fronts give way to a real expression of self. There is a willingness to explore significant personal concerns. | The group develops a healing capacity, and members are able to move forward based on the support offered. Members develop self-acceptance; they offer feedback to one another in a climate of honesty, and a sense of community develops. Behavior changes are noticed in the group. Members show increased ease in expressing their feelings, and they gain insight into how they relate to others. |
| Role and tasks of group leader | Facilitator's main role is to grant freedom to members to develop a structure of their own. Leader places responsibility on members for the direction they will take and follows that lead. Leader is concerned with creating a climate that is psychologically safe for the members. Leader's role is to be without a role. Central function is to help members interact honestly. Leader encourages members to state and explore all reactions. | A central task of the leader is to adopt an empathic viewpoint; it is important that members feel deeply understood and cared for. Leader needs to accept and understand a wide range of feelings that members express. Leader needs to share ongoing feelings and reactions with the group. Leader listens actively, reflects, clarifies, summarizes, links members' statements, demonstrates respect, and shows acceptance and caring for members. | Central role of leader is to help members express how they have experienced this group and to encourage honest feedback. Leader helps members apply what they have learned in the group to life outside of it. Leader provides support for members in making significant changes. Leader helps members accept responsibility for these changes. Leader is mainly interested in empowering members to develop their direction. |
| Role of group members | Members are expected to develop their own goals and decide for themselves how they will spend their time together. At first members are rather confused and search for a structure. They are resistant to sharing personally significant material. They are encouraged to express whatever they are feeling. | Members decide what they will reveal about themselves; they express feelings to others in the group. They offer both support and challenge to others; they give and receive feedback. Members at this stage are usually willing to express immediate interpersonal feelings of both a positive and a negative nature. Self-exploration occurs on a deeper level. | Members move from playing roles to being real, from being relatively closed to being open and able to tolerate some ambiguity, from being out of contact with internal and subjective experience to being aware of the ongoing subjective process, from looking for external answers to looking inward for direction. |

| | | | |
|---|---|---|---|
| Techniques | Person-centered leaders tend to avoid using planned exercises and techniques to "get a group moving." They rely on the capacity of the group to decide how time will be spent. Leader's attitudes and personal characteristics are far more important than the techniques used. | Key techniques include active listening, reflection, clarification, self-disclosure, respect, and congruence. Members are encouraged to speak in an open way about whatever they are feeling at the moment. These tools do not represent techniques so much as basic attitudes/behaviors. | Leader is really not necessary at this stage if the group has been effective, for now the group is fairly self-directive and can draw on its own resources for direction. Leader may help members summarize what they have learned and encourage them to apply it to life outside the group. |
| Questions to consider | Since active listening is a basis of this approach, ask yourself how your ability to hear and to understand might be hampered. What are some barriers in yourself to hearing others? Consider the following:<br><br>• Talking too much and too soon<br>• Being too concerned with answers and not allowing members to explore feelings<br>• Being too quick to give advice or to look for an easy solution<br>• Asking too many closed questions<br>• Being overly directive and doing too much for the group<br>• Selectively listening or looking for ways to confirm your preconceived notions about members<br>• Paying too much attention to the content and to words and failing to hear subtle meanings | Are you able to tolerate the expression of a range of feelings within a group? Can you accept in a nondefensive manner negative feelings that are directed toward you?<br><br>Are you able and willing to share your own reactions in an appropriate manner with the members?<br><br>Are you able to be yourself in the group, or do you hide behind professional roles?<br><br>Do you trust the members with your feelings? Are you able to let them know how they are affecting you?<br><br>How do you demonstrate respect for the members by your behavior in the group? Does your behavior indicate understanding and acceptance?<br><br>Do you trust the group to develop in a positive direction? | Are you able to facilitate a group rather than direct it? Can you let the members lead the way, helping them look at their process when necessary?<br><br>As a person and as a group facilitator, have you allowed yourself to be changed by a group? Are you open to growth yourself? What changes do you detect in yourself?<br><br>Are you able to be both supportive and confrontive? Can you provide nurturing and challenge at the same time?<br><br>Have you facilitated the group in such a manner that the members no longer look to you for direction or answers? Is the group able to function largely independently of you?<br><br>Do you assist members in taking credit for the changes they have made? |

Reactions: Summarize your reactions to the person-centered perspective on group developmental stages. What do you like *most?* *Least?* What aspects of this approach would you incorporate in your style of leadership?

helpful to think about the kind of group member you hope would drop out of the group or, better, who would not have joined in the first place. In your class or group each member can talk about the specific behaviors of clients that present the greatest challenge. As an alternative exercise, instead of talking about these difficult group members, assume the identity of one of these clients, and role-play that person. Each person in the group stays in the role of a problem member for most of the session. Again, two members can assume the role of co-facilitating the group by staying within the person-centered spirit. Leave enough time to discuss these questions:

    a. What was it like for you to assume a particular role of a difficult member? What did you learn about this kind of member?

    b. What did you recognize about yourself in relationship to this person?

    c. What was it like to be part of a group that was facilitated in a person-centered way?

    d. What was the experience like as a group participant?

    e. What was it like for the facilitators?

4. Assume that you have joined a person-centered group. This is the first session, and each member has been asked to say what he or she wants from this group experience. Spend some time identifying the personal goals that would guide your participation in this group. If you were to talk about your hopes and expectations as a member, what might you say? After you have completed this exercise, spend some time as a group discussing these questions:

    a. Do you agree with Rogers's contention that the group has the capacity to move in constructive directions without structure, direction, and active intervention on the leader's part? Why or why not? What are the implications for practice if you accept this assumption?

    b. Do you agree that group members are the ones to formulate specific goals?

    c. What is it like for you to identify what you want from a group and talk about it in a session?

5. Form small groups in your class and participate in an unstructured group session for about one hour. The rules for this particular group are that there would be no planned agenda, no structured group exercises, no opening or closing techniques, and no probing questions. The aim of the session is to allow the group to unfold naturally. After the exercise, ask each participant to share what it was like to be in an unstructured group situation. If you were a member of this group, what was it like for you? If you were the facilitator of this group, how was it for you to function without an agenda or a preconceived structure? What possible advantages and disadvantages are there to an unstructured group?

6. This group exercise requires a collective decision to select a particular population for role playing. As a group, decide what target population or specialized type of group you want to become. Consider a group for children to increase their self-esteem, an inpatient group in a hospital, or a support group for the elderly. Once your group has decided what kind of members you will "become" for the session, each member should identify a particular role that he or she will play. If you decide to become a children's group, for example, each person would assume a particular problem of a child for the session. As in the other exercises, two members can become co-facilitators. At the end of the exercise, discuss what went on within the group session. What was it like to be part of this kind of group? What was it like to stay within a person-centered framework?

7. Sometimes we need feedback from others on how well we listen, how accepting we appear to be, how genuine we come across, and the degree to which we demonstrate respect for others. After you have had a chance to try out at least one of the exercises in this section, discuss these questions in your class or group:

    a. *Attending and listening.* How well do you listen? What gets in your way of fully attending to others? How can you improve your attending skills?

    b. *Unconditional positive regard and acceptance.* To what degree do you have these qualities? What prejudices or assumptions might you have that could make it difficult for you to accept some people? Would you put certain conditions on your acceptance of people? If so, what might some of these conditions be?

    c. *Respect.* What are some specific ways you are able to demonstrate respect for group members? Do you think it's possible to work effectively with members if you don't respect them? Why or why not? Can you think of an example of when you did not show respect for a group member?

    d. *Genuineness.* What criteria can you employ to determine your level of genuineness? Is it possible to be an effective group leader and not be genuine? What problems do you think you might have in "being yourself" as a group leader?

8. *Evaluation and research.* Rogers stresses subjective research on group processes and outcomes, consisting mainly of self-reports by the participants. What do you think of subjective measures to determine the outcomes of a group? What are some of your ideas regarding ways of finding out whether a group is successful? How would you evaluate the outcome of your groups?

9. *Critique of the person-centered approach.* Give your personal evaluation of this model using some of these questions as a guide.

    a. What would it be like for you to facilitate this type of group?

    b. What relative importance would you assign to knowledge of the theory of group process? To possession of leadership skills and techniques? To attitudes pertaining to the core therapeutic conditions?

    c. In what ways could you use many of the concepts of the person-centered approach in creating a therapeutic relationship and as a foundation for other approaches?

    d. What do you consider to be the major contribution and major limitation of the person-centered approach to groups?

    e. What are your thoughts about the contributions of Natalie Rogers with her methods and approaches based on the expressive arts?

## Questions for Reflection and Discussion

1. What specific attitudes of person-centered leaders would assist you in understanding and working with culturally diverse populations?

2. What implications do you see in using a person-centered approach in working with a mandatory group? Can you think of ways to apply the key concepts of this approach to counseling reluctant and involuntary clients?

3. What are your thoughts on the matter of selecting members to participate in a group? Can you think of both advantages and disadvantages to the absence of screening and selection procedures?

4. What are some ways you might apply person-centered concepts if you were to facilitate groups with children and adolescents?

5. What are some key concepts and basic attitudes of the person-centered approach that you think could be effectively integrated into any other theory of groups?

6. Do you think you can adopt a person-centered philosophy and still incorporate techniques from some of the directive therapies in your group leading? Can you view people from a person-centered perspective yet assume a more active and central role in leadership? Explain.

7. According to Natalie Rogers, what are some of the basic principles of expressive arts therapy? What are the basic conditions upon which the various methods are based? How can the various art forms supply some structure and direction to the work on members in groups?

8. What are your thoughts about the role of the person-centered facilitator of groups? Would you feel comfortable participating as a member in a group you were facilitating?

9. Review the basic attitudes of the person-centered group leader (genuineness, unconditional positive regard, and empathy). Which of these attitudes do you think you'd have the greatest difficulty living by and translating from a belief you hold into concrete actions? What other leader and member attitudes or qualities do you think might contribute to effective outcomes in a person-centered group?

10. With what populations, and with what types of groups, do you think the person-centered approach would be most effective? In what cases, if any, do you think this approach would be inappropriate and ineffective?

## Quiz on the Person-Centered Approach to Groups: A Comprehension Check     Score ____%

*Note:* Please refer to Appendix I for the scoring key. Count 5 points for each error, and subtract the total from 100 to get your percentage score.

*True/false items:* Decide if the following statements are "more true" or "more false" as they apply to the person-centered approach to groups.

T   F   1. Carl Rogers based some of his notions of therapeutic practice on existential principles about what it means to be human.

T   F   2. The basic encounter groups make it difficult to distinguish between "therapy" and "growth."

T   F   3. The role of a person-centered group leader is to be without a role.

T   F   4. The person-centered view of group therapy places emphasis on diagnosis and interpretation.

T   F   5. The phrase *formative tendency* refers to conditioning during the early years of development.

T   F   6. The concepts of unconditional positive regard and warmth are closely associated.

T   F   7. Unconditional positive regard implies liking and approving everything about the members.

T   F   8. During the creative connection process in the expressive arts, one art form stimulates and nurtures the other.

T  F   9. A deep faith in the individual's innate drive to become fully oneself is basic to the work in person-centered expressive arts.

T  F  10. Natalie Rogers's group work differs from Carl Rogers's approach in that she offers group guidelines at the beginning of an experiential workshop so that participants understand the concepts of creative expression and the basic guidelines for group behavior.

*Multiple-choice items:* Select the *one best answer* among the alternatives given. Consider each question within the framework of person-centered therapy.

_____11. One of the strengths of the person-centered approach is that
     a. it offers a wide range of cognitive techniques to change behavior.
     b. it teaches clients ways to explore the meaning of dreams.
     c. it places emphasis on reliving one's early childhood memories.
     d. therapists have the latitude to develop their own counseling style.
     e. clients are given a concrete plan to follow.

_____12. A limitation of the person-centered approach is
     a. the lack of research conducted on key concepts.
     b. a tendency for practitioners to give support without challenging clients enough.
     c. the lack of attention to the therapeutic relationship.
     d. the failure to allow clients to choose for themselves.
     e. the lack of any applicability in working with culturally diverse client groups.

_____13. Rogers made a contribution to
     a. developing the humanistic movement in psychotherapy.
     b. pioneering research in the process and outcomes of therapy.
     c. fostering world peace.
     d. pioneering the encounter group movement.
     e. all of the above.

_____14. As a result of experiencing person-centered therapy, it is hypothesized, the client will move toward
     a. self-trust.
     b. an internal source of evaluation.
     c. being more open to experience.
     d. a willingness to continue growing.
     e. all of the above.

_____15. Unconditional positive regard refers to
     a. liking clients.
     b. accepting clients as worthy persons.
     c. approving of clients' behavior.
     d. agreeing with clients' values.
     e. accepting clients if they meet the therapist's expectations.

_____16. The crucial factor that determines the outcome of the person-centered group is
     a. the leader's technical skills.
     b. the leader's relationship with the members in the group.
     c. the leader's knowledge of group dynamics.
     d. the members' willingness to think rationally.
     e. the accurate assessment of the members' lifestyles.

_____17. All of the following are considered to be key concepts of the person-centered approach except for the notion of
   a. social interest.
   b. congruence.
   c. unconditional positive regard.
   d. empathic understanding.
   e. nonpossessive warmth.

_____18. Empathy refers to the group leader's ability to
   a. feel exactly what the members are experiencing.
   b. sense accurately the inner world of a member's subjective experience.
   c. objectively understand the dynamics of a member.
   d. accurately diagnose the core problem of a member.
   e. approve of a member's behavior.

_____19. The basic goal of a person-centered group is
   a. to provide a climate of safety and freedom.
   b. to provide opportunities for multiple transferences.
   c. to get members to accept reality and form a commitment to change specific behaviors.
   d. to assist members in seeing the connection between their current struggles and their position in their family of origin.
   e. to remove maladaptive behavior and replace it with concrete coping behaviors.

_____20. All of the following are true of Natalie Roger's person-centered expressive arts except which statement?
   a. Any art form generated from deep emotions aids in the process of self-discovery.
   b. The expressive arts lead us into the unconscious, which allows us to express previously unknown facets of ourselves.
   c. Our society tends to promote creativity and original thinking in young people.
   d. Expressive arts methods require a safe, supportive environment created by group facilitators.
   e. This approach offers structured experiences to group members by encouraging them to use movement, visual arts, music, and journal writing to go on their inner journey.

# CHAPTER ELEVEN

# Gestalt Therapy in Groups

## Prechapter Self-Inventory for Gestalt Therapy

*Directions:* Refer to page 57 for general directions. Indicate your position on these statements using the following code:

**5** = I *strongly agree* with this statement.
**4** = I *agree,* in most respects, with this statement.
**3** = I am *undecided* in my opinion about this statement.
**2** = I *disagree,* in most respects, with this statement.
**1** = I *strongly disagree* with this statement.

_____ 1. The goal of group counseling is to help members integrate the fragmented parts of their personality enough that they can carry on the process of development alone.

_____ 2. Group work should focus on here-and-now experiencing in order to increase members' awareness.

_____ 3. Past conflicts or events are best understood by reexperiencing them in the here-and-now.

_____ 4. It is generally more productive to ask "what" and "how" questions than to ask "why" questions.

_____ 5. Unfinished business from the past tends to manifest itself in one's current behavior.

_____ 6. In a group setting it is important to explore the members' nonverbal messages and blocks to awareness.

_____ 7. Fantasy can be a potentially powerful therapeutic tool.

_____ 8. The most creative and effective experiments grow out of what is happening in the group.

_____ 9. The best way to deal with future concerns is to bring them into the here-and-now.

_____10. Exploration of group members' dreams is one of the leader's major methods of increasing members' awareness.

## Summary of Basic Assumptions and Key Concepts of the Gestalt Approach to Groups

1. The here-and-now of the group members' experience is most important. The group leader focuses on "what" and "how," instead of "why," and on anything that prevents effective functioning in the present. The past, which has a significant role in shaping current behavior, is brought into the present by reenacting earlier situations that are still unfinished.

2. The Gestalt view is that people are essentially responsible for their own conflicts and that they have the capacity to deal with their life problems. Therefore, group members tend to make their own interpretations and to discover for themselves the meaning of their experiences.

3. Gestalt therapists use experiments when assisting group members to increase their awareness. Through group interaction, members will become more aware of conflicts and places where they "get stuck" (arrive at an impasse). In the group, members can experiment with a variety of ways to work through the impasse and move to a new level of integration.

4. One of the group leader's tasks is to help members locate the ways in which they are blocking energy and expressing their resistance in their body. Through body-awareness work, members are mobilized and can take an active responsibility for their therapy. They can then be encouraged to try more adaptive behaviors.

5. Although the Gestalt leader encourages members to assume responsibility for expanding their awareness, the leader also takes an active role in creating experiments designed to help members tap their resources. The essence of creative therapy is designing experiments that grow out of the existential situation of the therapy encounter. Through these experiments, members are able to confront the crises of their lives by playing out their troubled relationships in the safety of the therapeutic setting.

## Glossary of Key Terms for Gestalt Therapy

**Awareness** The process of attending to and observing one's own senses, thoughts, feelings, and actions; paying attention to the flow of one's experiences in the moment.

**Blocks to energy** Paying attention to where energy is located, how it is used, and how it can be blocked.

**Confluence** A disturbance in which the sense of the boundary between self and environment is lost.

**Confrontation** An invitation for the client to become aware of discrepancies between verbal and nonverbal expressions, between feelings and actions, or between thoughts and feelings.

**Contact** A process of interacting with nature and other people without losing one's sense of individuality.

**Continuum of awareness** Staying with the moment-to-moment flow of experiencing, which leads individuals to discover how they are functioning in the world.

**Deflection** A way of avoiding contact and awareness by being vague and indirect.

**Dichotomy** A split by which a person experiences or sees opposing forces; a polarity (tough/ tender, open/closed).

**Experiments** Interventions designed to enhance here-and-now awareness; activities members try out in a group as a way of testing new ways of thinking, feeling, and behaving.

**Field theory** The notion of the individual being viewed in his or her environment, or in the context of a constantly changing field.

**Figure-formation process** Describes how the individual organizes the environment from moment to moment and how the emerging focus of attention is on what is figural.

**Group exercises** Leaders prepare some kind of structured technique before the group meets as a way to promote interaction.

**Group experiments** A creative happening that grows out of the group experience; experiments are not predetermined, and the outcome cannot be predicted.

**Holism** A core concept in Gestalt theory that implies that all nature is a unified and coherent whole.

**Introjection** The uncritical acceptance of others' beliefs and standards without assimilating them into one's own personality.

**Organismic self-regulation** Pertains to the relationship between the individual and the environment and the tendency to restore equilibrium and contribute to change.

**Paradoxical theory of change** A concept that implies that individuals change when they become aware of what they are, as opposed to attempting to become what they are not.

**Projection** The process by which we disown certain aspects of ourselves by ascribing them to the environment; the opposite of introjection.

**Rehearsal** Internal processing about the roles we think we are expected to play. As a technique, members are asked to "rehearse out loud" so that others can experience the internal process of thinking and censoring.

**Relational Gestalt therapy** A supportive and compassionate style that emphasizes dialogue in the therapeutic relationship.

**Retroflection** The act of turning back onto ourselves something we would like to do (or have done) to someone else.

**Techniques** Exercises or procedures that are often used to bring about action or interaction, sometimes with a prescribed outcome in mind.

**Unfinished business** Unexpressed feelings (such as resentment, guilt, anger, grief) dating back to childhood that now interfere with effective psychological functioning; needless emotional debris that clutters present-centered awareness.


## Exercises and Activities for Gestalt Groups

### Rationale

Gestalt therapy makes use of a variety of action-oriented methods that are designed to intensify what members are experiencing. Instead of discussing conflicts, for example, members are encouraged to "become the conflict." The idea is to fully experience every dimension of oneself (to be authentic). The Gestalt therapist will suggest experiments to help members try some new behavior and thus experience everything fully.

It is important that the following exercises *not* be done mechanically. Each exercise is best if it is tailored to the unique needs of the members in your class/group. Further, it is a good idea to give members some preparation before springing an experiment on them. Enlist the cooperation of group members by giving a brief explanation of the basic purpose of each exercise. By trying many of the exercises in your own small group, you will be in a better position to know which of these techniques you might want to use when you are a group leader.

**Stages of Development of the Gestalt Group**

| Dimension | Initial Stage | Working Stage | Final Stage |
|---|---|---|---|
| Key developmental tasks and goals | A central goal is to gain here-and-now awareness of what is being felt, sensed, and thought; group members must experiment and experience. Personal goals include achieving contact with self and others and defining one's boundaries with clarity. | Members deal with unfinished business from the past that is impeding full functioning now. The task is to integrate polarities. Group therapy is aimed at helping members give expression to the side of themselves they tend to deny. | Members assume personal responsibility, which means that they integrate the fragmented aspects of their personalities. By achieving a moment-to-moment awareness of whatever is being experienced, members have the means within themselves to make changes. |
| Role and tasks of group leader | It is the leader's task to follow whatever leads are provided by group members; in this way, members are able to become aware of the "what" and the "how" of their experiencing. The leader functions much like an artist inventing techniques that arise from the material in the group. The emphasis is on creating effective relationships. | The leader's task is to pay close attention to both the verbal and nonverbal messages of members and to pay attention to the here-and-now. Leader suggests experiments designed to enhance and intensify the experiences of the members. Leader pays attention to energy and helps members recognize their patterns of avoidance. | After a piece of work is completed, the leader may ask members to say how they are feeling. There is not much emphasis on cognitive structuring or behavior modification. It is assumed that once members gain an awareness of what they are doing to prevent themselves from fully experiencing the moment, they are capable of changing. |
| Role of group members | Members are expected to focus on the here-and-now and to reexperience past conflicts as though they were going on now. Members decide what they will explore in the group. Members are challenged to accept responsibility for whatever they are experiencing and doing. They learn to live up to their own expectations, and they make decisions. | Members are expected to directly communicate to one another and to make "I" statements. They are discouraged from asking "why" questions. The focus is on exploration of feelings. To experience these feelings fully, members take part in a variety of action-oriented activities. They don't talk about problems; rather, they act out their various roles and conflicts. | Members give and receive feedback. They have the opportunity to identify unfinished business from their past that impedes present functioning and to work through impasses. By gaining awareness of areas that were out of consciousness, they become more integrated. They are increasingly able to live with their own polarities and to be more self-directed. |

114

| Techniques | Leader uses "what" and "how" questions, but not "why" questions, to help members focus on themselves and what they are experiencing. Leaders may use many experiments including fantasy approaches, asking people to pay attention to what they are experiencing physically, thinking out loud, and so on. The skilled leader avoids using techniques in a mechanical way. Rather, the leader creates experiments that express what is going on in the group now. | A wide range of experiments all have the general goal of helping members intensify their experiencing in the present moment. Members may explore dreams by becoming all parts of their dreams; they may engage in role playing in which they act out all the parts; or they may exaggerate a particular gesture or mannerism. Symbolic encounters are used to help members deal with unfinished situations. Members make their own interpretations. | Members can be asked to enact a situation the way they'd like it to be; they play all the parts. Members are often asked to give a new ending to an old and unfinished situation. Experiments help members see how past unfinished situations get in the way of effective living in the present. Members are asked to practice and experiment with new ways outside of the group. Action follows experiencing. |
|---|---|---|---|
| Questions to consider | Are you able to create a climate within the group that encourages members to try out creative experiments? Have you prepared them for Gestalt techniques? Have you earned their respect and trust? Do they see benefits in participating in a variety of experiments aimed at enhancing their awareness?<br><br>Do you avoid using planned techniques to make something happen in a group? Can you follow the process and invent a technique that will highlight members' concerns?<br><br>Do you take care to avoid being mechanical in using techniques? Are the methods you employ an extension of the person you are? | Do you invite members to take part in an experiment as opposed to commanding them?<br><br>Can you respect resistance in a group member? Are you able to work therapeutically with resistance?<br><br>Do you focus on what is going on within the group now? Are you able to pay attention to the subtle nonverbal messages and work with them?<br><br>Do you help members stay with their present experience and not talk about what they are thinking or feeling?<br><br>Do you bring yourself in as a person, and do you respond to others in personal ways? | How can you create experiments that will help members gain awareness of what they are doing to prevent themselves from being fully in the present?<br><br>How can members be helped to work through unfinished business that interferes with living now in a vital way? How can any unfinished business within the group be addressed?<br><br>Have the members recognized ways in which they block their strengths and keep themselves from living the way they want?<br><br>Are you able to help members deal with their feelings about termination? Do you encourage them to express feelings about separation? |

Reactions: Summarize your reactions to the Gestalt perspective on group developmental stages. What do you like *most*? *Least*? What aspects of this approach would you incorporate in your style of leadership?

## Exercises

1. *Here-and-now versus there-and-then.* Talk about a personal experience in the past tense for about three minutes. Then, relive the same experience as though it were happening in the present. What difference do you notice between these three-minute exercises? What value do you see in encouraging people in groups to make past experiences into present-centered ones?

2. *Bringing the future into the now.* Are you anticipating any future confrontations? This exercise can be a form of rehearsal. Using the two-chair technique, take turns being yourself and then becoming the person you expect to confront, then be yourself, and so on for a brief period of time. Make this future event happen in the here-and-now. When you are finished, discuss what this experience was like. What did you learn through the experiment? What are your fears and hopes regarding this future event?

3. *Identifying unfinished business.* Gestalt therapy emphasizes the role of old business that hangs around and gets in the way of our being effective and alive now. Do you have unfinished business that might limit your effectiveness in working with members' issues? What are some ways to explore your own unfinished business that could allow you to be more fully present for others?

4. *Avoidance.* The concept of avoidance is central in Gestalt therapy. How many ways can you think of in which you avoid things? Do you reach an impasse because you are afraid of feeling uncomfortable? Do you avoid changing by convincing yourself that you cannot change? Do you avoid trying by convincing yourself that you are perfectly satisfied? Do you avoid trying by blaming others? Try living out some of these avoidance techniques in your group. For example, really blame others for your inability to change.

5. *Nonverbal language in the group.* Exaggerate some of your typical body language. If you often frown, let yourself really get into that frown. If you have a certain mannerism, develop it fully. What can you learn from this exercise about your nonverbal language? Pay attention to others as they speak, and note their tone of voice, manner of speech, quality of voice, posture, facial expressions, gestures, speed and rate of speech, and so on. What do people tell you about themselves nonverbally?

6. *Experimenting with dialogues.* Have each person in the group experiment with the dialogue technique. You can also do this at home alone. Place two chairs facing each other. Next, choose one of your conflicts and become one side of this conflict. Talk to the other side, which is in the other chair. Now get up and sit in the other chair, becoming that other side. Carry on this dialogue for a time. If you're doing this in a group, discuss what you learned. What is it like for you to do the experiment? Which side felt dominant? Here are some examples of typical conflicts that often keep us fragmented:
   a. Part of me wants to open up; the other part of me wants to keep closed.
   b. I have a serious side; then there is the fun side.
   c. I want to love, yet I don't dare let myself.
   d. Part of me wants to take a risk; the other part wants to play it safe.
   List all the conflicts or fragmentations that exist inside of you. Do you have trouble integrating dichotomies such as tough/tender, masculine/feminine, worthwhile/worthless?

7. *Fantasy approaches.* Try some fantasy experiments in the group. For instance, allow yourself to live out some of your expectations and fears. If you are afraid of being rejected,

live out your rejection fantasies in your group. You can also use the rehearsal technique; as you think of your fantasy, repeat all your thoughts out loud.

8. *Gestalt dream work*. Try some Gestalt dream experiments in your group. Have a volunteer recount a dream as though it were happening now. After telling the dream in the present tense, others in the group can ask:

a. What part of the dream most interests you? Why?

b. What aspects of the dream most stand out for you?

c. What is the general mood surrounding the dream?

After recounting the dream, make up a dialogue between one or more parts of the dream. Act them out in the present tense, and let yourself really experience the dream. Carry on a dialogue between various parts of the dream, making sure to have several interchanges between the aspects of the dream. What does your dream teach you about yourself? Ask for feedback from others in your group. Others in the group can explore the question, "What idea does the dream give each of you about the dreamer?"

   If you are keeping a journal, I recommend that you begin to record your dreams if you are not already doing so. Simply writing your dreams down and reviewing them can give you clues about your struggles. Look for patterns in your dreams, and speculate on the meaning of these patterns. What can you learn from your dreams?

9. *Rehearsal*. Internal rehearsal saps much of our vitality. We often think so carefully about the appropriate way to be that any spontaneity is squelched. The rehearsal technique consists of saying out loud what you are thinking silently. In this exercise select a situation in which you would typically rehash all the pros and cons to yourself before deciding what to do or say, but this time allow yourself to think out loud. For example, let yourself play out in a group what you go through before you ask a person for a date, or go on a job interview, or give a speech. What are all the things you say to yourself? (The exercise can make you more acutely aware of how you are striving for approval or how you fear rejection.)

## Questions for Reflection and Discussion

1. Both Gestalt therapy and person-centered therapy share some features with the existential approach, yet they employ very different methods in a group. Although they have some common philosophical views of human nature, Gestalt therapy relies on therapist direction and interventions, whereas person-centered therapy deemphasizes techniques and therapist direction. Do you see any basis for the typically active Gestalt leader to incorporate some person-centered concepts? What are some person-centered assumptions and notions that could fruitfully be incorporated in Gestalt practice?

2. Do you see a possibility of thinking in psychoanalytic terms and using Gestalt experiments? How might you integrate psychoanalytic concepts with Gestalt concepts and methods as part of your leadership style?

3. Gestalt therapy focuses on what people are *experiencing* and *feeling* moment to moment. The focus is on highlighting awareness. It is important for the leader to follow whatever is in the client's awareness and to introduce experiments that grow out of this awareness and the existential situation. Using the principle of following whatever is in the client's awareness, how might you decide what kind of experiments to suggest?

4. What are the major ethical considerations that need to be addressed in Gestalt group work? What safeguards can you think of against the most common dangers associated with Gestalt groups?

5. What are some key Gestalt concepts and experiments you can apply to the process of understanding yourself? How might you use some Gestalt methods to increase your awareness and promote personality change in yourself? What do you think it would be like for you to be in a Gestalt group?

6. If you were to make use of Gestalt experiments in your group, in what ways might you prepare your members to increase their readiness to get involved in these experiments? What might you say to a member who asked what good it does to relive an event in the here-and-now rather than telling about a problem in the past? If you suggested to a member that she enact her dream and have dialogue with the different parts, how would you react if she thought doing so would be silly or pointless?

7. What are some ways you might work with the body in therapy? What kind of training would you want to have before you introduced body-oriented techniques? What advantages, if any, do you see in incorporating body work, as opposed to limiting the group strictly to verbal methods? What risks, if any, do you see in working with the body?

8. What are your reactions to the Gestalt approach of working with dreams in a group setting? How could you encourage members to share a dream and explore its meaning with them?

9. You are asked to design a counseling group for either children or adolescents in the school setting. What are some specific key concepts from Gestalt therapy that could be applied in this setting? What are some Gestalt techniques you might incorporate in your group with either children or adolescents? How would you prepare the members for participating in Gestalt experiments?

10. What are some advantages of using a Gestalt approach with culturally diverse client populations? How would you take into account the group members' cultural background using this approach?

## Quiz on the Gestalt Approach to Groups: A Comprehension Check

Score ____%

*Note:* Please refer to Appendix I for the scoring key. Count 5 points for each error, and subtract the total from 100 to get your percentage score.

*True/false items:* Decide if the following statements are "more true" or "more false" as they apply to Gestalt therapy.

T   F   1. Therapist interpretation is a necessary condition for change to occur.

T   F   2. The basic methodological tool in Gestalt therapy is the experiment.

T   F   3. Gestalt leaders use a wide range of cognitive behavioral techniques designed to get members to think about the origin of their problems.

T   F   4. Gestalt therapy, being concerned with the here-and-now, is not interested in and does not deal with one's past.

T   F   5. In a Gestalt framework, blocked energy can be thought of as resistance.

T   F   6. Typically, the Gestalt leader is highly active and directive.

T　F　7. In Gestalt dream work the leader interprets the hidden and symbolic meanings of the dream for the member.

T　F　8. The main goal of the Gestalt group is to assist members in resolving their dichotomies or polarities through problem-solving methods.

T　F　9. Methods of working with the body can be fruitfully combined with other techniques in Gestalt therapy.

T　F　10. Overuse of techniques in a Gestalt group can serve the function of keeping the leader hidden.

*Multiple-choice items:* Select the *one best answer* among the alternatives given. Consider each question within the framework of Gestalt therapy.

_____11. The process of distraction, or interruption of awareness, which makes it difficult to maintain sustained contact, is
   a. introjection.
   b. projection.
   c. retroflection.
   d. confluence.
   e. deflection.

_____12. The process of turning back to ourselves what we would like to do to someone else is
   a. introjection.
   b. projection.
   c. retroflection.
   d. confluence.
   e. deflection.

_____13. The tendency to uncritically accept others' beliefs without assimilating or internalizing them is
   a. introjection.
   b. projection.
   c. retroflection.
   d. confluence.
   e. deflection.

_____14. The process of blurring the awareness of differentiation between the self and the environment is
   a. introjection.
   b. projection.
   c. retroflection.
   d. confluence.
   e. deflection.

_____15. Which of the following is a limitation of Gestalt therapy as it is applied to working with culturally diverse populations?
   a. Clients who have been culturally conditioned to be emotionally reserved may not see any value in experiential techniques.
   b. Clients may be "put off" by a focus on catharsis.
   c. Clients may be looking for specific advice on solving practical problems.
   d. Clients may believe that to show one's vulnerability is to be weak.
   e. All of the above are limitations.

_____16. A primary function of the Gestalt group leader is to
    a. make interpretations for the members.
    b. serve as a blank screen to foster transference.
    c. suggest experiments that will lead to heightening awareness.
    d. confront clients' irrational thoughts and mistaken beliefs.
    e. help clients understand their unique style of life.

_____17. In Gestalt therapy awareness is best described as
    a. introspection.
    b. insight.
    c. recognition of why one struggles with a certain problem.
    d. understanding the root cause of dysfunctional behavior.
    e. recognition of current feelings, actions, and sensations.

_____18. The technique that most encourages participants to give expression to the side of themselves they rarely express is
    a. the reversal technique.
    b. paradoxical intention.
    c. systematic desensitization.
    d. future projection.
    e. the mirror technique.

_____19. Gestalt techniques are aimed at
    a. teaching members how to think rationally.
    b. integrating conflicting sides within members.
    c. teaching clients how to discover the causes of their problems.
    d. helping members understand unconscious dynamics.
    e. rewriting members' life scripts.

_____20. Gestalt therapy focuses most on
    a. exploration of the past.
    b. the here-and-now.
    c. the future.
    d. both the past and the future.
    e. getting members to talk about their basic problems.

# CHAPTER TWELVE

# Transactional Analysis in Groups

## Prechapter Self-Inventory for Transactional Analysis (TA)

*Directions:* Refer to page 57 for general directions. Indicate your position on these statements using the following code:

**5** = I *strongly agree* with this statement.
**4** = I *agree,* in most respects, with this statement.
**3** = I am *undecided* in my opinion about this statement.
**2** = I *disagree,* in most respects, with this statement.
**1** = I *strongly disagree* with this statement.

_____ 1. Decisions about oneself, one's world, and one's relationships to others are crystallized during the first five years of life.

_____ 2. Once we decide on a life position, as a rule, there is a tendency for it to remain fixed unless there is some therapeutic intervention to change the underlying decisions.

_____ 3. Contracts are both basic and necessary if the group counseling process is to be therapeutic.

_____ 4. Group members should develop independence and not rely on the group leader for guidance.

_____ 5. Relationships between the group leader and members need to be equal if the group's work is to be successful.

_____ 6. It is useful to teach group members how to explore their early decisions and the parental injunctions that are influencing them now.

_____ 7. It is the leader's function to challenge members to examine the decisions they made early in life and to determine whether these decisions are still appropriate.

_____ 8. Game playing, by its very definition, prevents the development of genuine intimacy.

_____ 9. People tend to accept uncritically the messages they received from their parents and from parental substitutes.

_____10. Contracts give direction to group sessions, increase the responsibility of members to participate actively in group work, and provide a basis for equal partnership between the members and the leader.

## Summary of Basic Assumptions and Key Concepts of the TA Approach to Groups

1. Based on messages that we receive in childhood, we make necessary decisions early in life that may later become inappropriate. The redecisional model of TA emphasizes that we react to stresses, receive messages about how we should be in the world, and make early

decisions about ourselves and others that become manifest in our current patterns of thinking, feeling, and behaving. In TA groups, the members relive the context in which they made these early decisions, and thus they can choose new decisions that are functional.

2. To make new, appropriate decisions, group members are taught to recognize ego states, to understand how injunctions and messages they incorporated as children are affecting them now, and to identify life scripts that are determining their actions. A basic assumption of TA is that we are in charge of what we do, how we think, and how we feel. People are viewed as capable of going beyond their early programming and choices by making new choices in the present that will affect their future.

3. TA is largely a didactic and cognitive form of therapy, with the goal of liberating group members from the past and assisting them to redecide how they will live based on new awareness. In a group context members can experience their life scripts unfolding before them through the interactions within the group. Group members represent family members from the past as well as people in the present. TA members have many opportunities to review and challenge their past decisions and to experiment with new decisions.

4. Members can best achieve these goals by being active in the group therapy process. To ensure that members actively and responsibly participate, they contract to work on specific issues, and these contracts direct the course of the group.

5. TA concepts and techniques are particularly appropriate for group work. It is the leader's role and function to create a climate in which people can discover for themselves how the games they are playing support chronic bad feelings and how they are clinging to these dysfunctional feelings to support their life scripts and their early decisions.

## Glossary of Key Terms for Transactional Analysis

**Adult ego state**  An ego state that is the processor of information. It is the analytic, rational, and objective part of personality.

**Autonomy**  Awareness, spontaneity, and capacity for intimacy.

**Basic psychological life position**  A stance that people assume in early childhood regarding their own intrinsic worth and that of others.

**Child ego state**  An ego state that consists of feelings, impulses, and spontaneous acts. This part of the personality can manifest itself in several ways, for example, the "Natural Child" or the "Adapted Child."

**Contract**  Specific and measurable statements of the objectives group participants intend to attain; contracts place the responsibility on members for clearly defining what, how, and when *they* want to change.

**Controlling (Critical) Parent**  An ego state that is critical, harsh, and fault-finding.

**Counterinjunctions**  The counterpart of injunctions that come from the parents' Parent ego state; messages that convey "shoulds" and "oughts."

**Decisions**  A view that people incorporate about themselves based on the injunctions they accept or reject.

**Ego state**  One of the three distinct patterns of behavior and psychological functioning: Parent, Adult, and Child.

**Games**  A series of stereotyped and predictable patterns of behavior designed to prevent intimacy and to provide a negative payoff for at least one player.

**Injunctions**  Parental messages telling children what they have to do and be to get recognition. These messages, which are usually couched in some form of "don't," may be verbal or nonverbal.

**Karpman Drama Triangle** A useful device that helps one understand the nature of games.

**Life script** An unconscious plan for life made in childhood, reinforced by parents and by subsequent events, and culminating in a chosen alternative.

**Nurturing Parent** An ego state that is supportive and caring.

**Parent ego state** An ego state that is an introject of parents and parent substitutes; combines the "shoulds" and "oughts" that individuals collect from significant people in their lives.

**Psychological strokes** Verbal and nonverbal signs of acceptance and recognition, which are necessary for people to develop a sense of self-worth.

**Racket** A habitual feeling (depression, guilt, anger, sadness) to which people chronically cling after a game.

**Redecision** The process of reexperiencing early situations in which we made basic decisions about life, evaluating these decisions, and making new and more appropriate choices about life.

**Redecision therapy** Aimed at helping people challenge themselves to discover ways in which they perceive themselves in victimlike roles and to take charge of their lives by deciding for themselves how they will change.

**Script analysis** A process that helps members become aware of how they acquired their life script; that part of the therapeutic process by which the life patterns of clients are identified, allowing them to take steps toward changing their programming.

**Strokes** A form of recognition. Strokes may be positive or negative, conditional or unconditional, physical or psychological.

**Structural analysis** A tool by which clients become aware of the content and functioning of their ego states of Parent, Child, and Adult.

**Transaction** An exchange of strokes between two or more people; the basic unit of human communication. Transactions may be complementary, crossed, or ulterior.

**Transactional analysis (TA)** Both a theory of personality and an organized system of interactional therapy; an approach that emphasizes the cognitive and behavioral aspects of change.

## Exercises and Activities for the TA Approach

### Rationale

Not all of the following exercises deal with therapeutic procedures routinely used by all TA practitioners; however, they are designed to increase your awareness of matters such as these: In what ego state do you tend to function? What kind of strokes do you typically receive? Which of the parental messages that you picked up early in life do you still live by? How do your decisions made early in life still influence you? What games prevent intimacy? What is the basis for new decisions?

Many of these exercises are cognitively oriented and are geared to get you to think about your assumptions and your behavior. I encourage you to think of imaginative ways of developing your own exercises; for example, experiment with combining some of these cognitively oriented TA concepts with some of the emotion-oriented techniques of Gestalt therapy. Use these exercises in your own small groups, and discuss specific aspects of this approach that you think you could use in the groups you lead.

| Dimension | Initial Stage | Working Stage | Final Stage |
|---|---|---|---|
| Key developmental tasks and goals | Group therapy begins with a contract, one that is acceptable to both member and leader. Group work is guided by the contract. An early basic task is to teach members the basics of TA, including how to recognize ego states, transactions, games, injunctions, rackets, and the significance of early decisions. | At the working stage, the basic developmental task is to recognize and work through impasses. Much work is done with reexperiencing early decisions and situations from childhood, with the aim of making new decisions that are more appropriate for the present. Members think about how they want to be different. | Focus at this stage is on actually making new decisions. Basic premise is that what was decided earlier can now be redecided. Members learn to thrive on positive strokes, and they recognize the power they possess. Contracts may be renegotiated, and new work may begin. Emphasis is on applying new learning in daily life. |
| Role and tasks of group leader | Leaders begin to teach members that they are responsible for how they think, feel, and act. Leaders provide structure for the group, teach the basic concepts of TA, and may use role playing and fantasy to have members relive certain scenes. Leaders help members identify and clarify goals and develop a contract that will specify the work to be done. | At this stage, the group leader helps members recognize early decisions they made from a Child ego state. Then, from this same ego state, the members are encouraged to make new and more appropriate decisions. Leaders draw on a variety of techniques to help members work through impasses. Group becomes a rehearsal for living. | At the final stage of a group, the leader mainly assists members in making new decisions and life-oriented contracts; members are encouraged to accept responsibility for changing their own lives. Leader challenges members to transfer their changes from the therapy group to daily life. Members are assisted to become their own therapists. |
| Role of group members | Members are expected to formulate a clear contract. They learn the ego state in which they are functioning, recognize the injunctions they've accepted, and see the importance of understanding and challenging early decisions. They learn the basics of TA and the key concepts they will need to know in participating in the group. Members begin to understand the games they play, along with understanding their life scripts, basic life positions, and early decisions. | Members learn about the injunction/ decision/racket complex. They identify life scripts. Members work through early experiences both cognitively and affectively. They discover the context in which they accepted injunctions and made early decisions. They explore ways in which they have given their power away, and they experiment with actions geared toward empowerment. Members are expected to refine the contracts and update them. | Members decide how they will change. They may use the group to practice new behaviors. Feedback and support are given. Group members are encouraged to tell a new story in the group to replace their old story. Members devise other support systems outside the group. Members are expected to plan specific ways in which they will change their thinking, feeling, behavior, and body. Members are empowered by choosing new decisions that are more functional. |

| | | |
|---|---|---|
| Techniques | Contracts are a basic tool. Imagery and fantasy techniques may be used. Role playing may be used to promote a here-and-now focus. The other techniques TA leaders tend to use are life script analysis and working with injunctions and decisions. | A wide range of cognitive and affective techniques is used, including structural analysis, transactional analysis, analysis of games, cognitive restructuring, empty chair, life script questionnaire, and desensitization. Techniques in TA groups are designed to help members feel more intensely and to think and conceptualize. | Homework assignments may be used as a way of helping the members to fulfill their contracts. Gestalt techniques may be incorporated into the TA group, as may techniques drawn from behavioral methods, psychodrama, and other action-oriented approaches. |
| Questions to consider | Are you able to obtain a clear and specific contract from each of the members? How can you help members formulate a therapeutic contract?<br><br>Are these contracts open to renegotiation? Are the members committed to working on them?<br><br>How does the structure of the group reflect the nature of the members' contracts?<br><br>What would you most want to teach the members about how a TA group functions? What is your role as leader in this group? What do you expect from the members? What kind of structuring do you most want to provide?<br><br>To what degree have you explored your own injunctions and early decisions? How might this influence the way you lead your group? | What kind of information would you want to include in a life script questionnaire? How might you use this life script checklist in your TA group?<br><br>What are some techniques for focusing on injunctions and early decisions?<br><br>How can you become aware of members' games, life positions, and life scripts by paying attention to their transactions with others in the sessions?<br><br>How might you draw on techniques from Gestalt therapy, psychodrama, and behavior therapy in working with concepts in the TA framework?<br><br>What are some ways in which you might help members work through early experiences that have an impact on their present behavior?<br><br>To what degree would you want to challenge members' cultural messages? | To what degree have the members recognized early decisions and the life script by which they have been living, and to what extent are they making new decisions? Are they acting on these redecisions in the group? Are they taking action outside of the sessions?<br><br>What new contracts might you make with members as a group approaches the final stage? How can you teach members to find support outside of the group for maintaining the changes?<br><br>What are some ways to reinforce redecisions by the client and by others in the group? What are some ways to prepare members for some new situations that they will face when they leave the group? How about preparing them for dealing with setbacks? |

Reactions: Summarize your reactions to the TA perspective on group developmental stages. What do you like *most*? *Least*? What aspects of this approach would you incorporate in your style of leadership?

## Exercises

1. *The ego states: Parent, Adult, Child.* TA teaches people in groups to recognize when they are operating in their Parent, Adult, and Child ego states. Each person in your group should choose an ego state and remain in it during a group exercise, thinking and speaking from the chosen state. The purpose of this exercise is to help you become aware of how you might function as a Parent without knowing it. As a variation, you might try having two group members conduct a debate between two ego states.

2. *Stroking.* TA stresses the need for strokes, both physical and psychological ones. In your group, talk about the specific types of strokes you need to sustain you. What strokes do you seek? How do you get the strokes you want? Are you able to accept positive stroking, or do you have a need to discount it and set yourself up for negative stroking? You could also experiment with asking your group members for the strokes you want. Discuss in your group the idea of conditional strokes. Were you brought up to believe you would get strokes when you behaved in the expected manner? How does this relate to the strokes you get in your group?

3. *Injunctions.* Injunctions are messages we have been programmed to accept—that is, messages we have knowingly and unknowingly incorporated into our lifestyle. In this experiment each group member "becomes" his or her parent and gives injunctions. Each person should adopt the tone of voice he or she imagines the parent would have used. Get involved in the exercise, and really tell people the way you think they should be and should live. As a second part of this exercise, discuss a few of the following injunctions as they apply to you. What are some other messages you heard as a child? Add these to the list. Which of these messages still influence you?
   a. Don't be _____.
   b. You should always do what is expected.
   c. Don't be who you are.
   d. Don't succeed/fail.
   e. Don't trust others.
   f. Be perfect—never make a mistake.
   g. Be more than you are.
   h. Don't be impulsive.
   i. Don't be sexy.
   j. Don't be aggressive.
   k. Keep your feelings to yourself.
   l. Think of others before yourself.
   m. Never have negative thoughts.
   Which of these injunctions have you accepted uncritically? Which of them do you most want to modify?

4. *Decisions and redecisions.* People tend to cling to early decisions and to look for evidence to support these decisions. However, TA assumes that what has been decided can be redecided. In your group, devote some time to identifying your early decisions. Then, determine what you are doing to keep them current. Finally, discuss what you might do to change these archaic decisions so that you are not held back by them. For example, you may have decided early on to keep all of your negative feelings inside you; you may have been told both directly and indirectly that you were unacceptable when you expressed

negative feelings. In this case you could discuss what you do now in situations where you experience negative feelings. Do you want to change your old decision?

5. *Exploring your rackets.* In TA a "racket" refers to the collection of bad feelings people use to justify their life scripts and the feelings on which they base their decisions. Some possible rackets are:

a. an anger racket

b. a guilt racket

c. a hurt racket

d. a depression racket

For instance, if you develop a depression racket, you may actually seek out situations that will support your feelings of depression. You will continually do things to make yourself feel depressed, and thus you will feel this way enough of the time to be able to convince yourself that you are right to have these feelings. In your group, spend time exploring how you maintain old, chronic, bad feelings. What might be one of your major rackets? List some recent situations that you put yourself in or found yourself in that led to old, familiar feelings of depression, guilt, or the like.

6. *Games we play.* In this group exercise, devote some time to listing some of the games that you played as a child to get what you wanted. For example, perhaps you played the Help-lessness Game. If you act helpless and pretend you cannot do something, others may treat you as helpless and do for you what you really don't want to do for yourself. Thus, if you did not want to make your own decisions as a child for fear of the consequences, you played stupid, and your parents then did for you what you were unwilling to do for yourself. True, you did get something from the game, but how does the price you paid compare with what you got? In your group, discuss some games you played as a child, then list what you got from each game and the price you paid for the gains. What games do you play now? Discuss what you get from these games. Evaluate the costs. What do you think you'd be like if you gave up these games?

7. *Life positions.* Have each person in your group briefly describe himself or herself with respect to self-esteem. Do you genuinely like and appreciate yourself? Can you feel like a winner without putting another person down? Do you think you are right and the rest of the world is wrong? Or do you continually put yourself down? Early in life you might have felt that everyone around you was just fine and that you were basically rotten to the core. What are some of the situations that led to these feelings of inadequacy? How might you challenge these feelings now? Would you classify yourself as a winner or a loser?

8. *Changes in your life circumstances.* You may have felt basically inadequate as a child, yet now you may feel very adequate in many areas of your life. What factors do you think are responsible for this shift in the way you feel about yourself?

9. *A book of you.* Write your own table of contents for a book about your life, and then give your book a title. What title best captures the sense of your life now? What would you include in the chapters? Mention the key turning points and key events of your life in your table of contents so that others in your group will have a picture of who you are. Now, assume you want to revise your book. What revisions do you want to make, chapter by chapter? Do you want a new book title?

10.. *"You are your parents" exercise.* This exercise can be done with a partner or in small groups. It will provide a format for looking at the influence your parents have on you and the quality of life you see your parents experiencing, and it will help you decide how you'd like to modify your own values and behavior. Close your eyes and see your parents at their present ages in a typical setting. Visualize the way they live. How is their marriage? How do they react to their children? What kind of life do they have? Now imagine yourself at their ages in the same setting. For a few minutes imagine that you value what they do and that your life is almost identical with theirs. In what ways would you modify the outcomes of this fantasy?

11. *Early decisions.* Assume that you are a group leader and that you determine that certain members have made the following decisions. Speculate about what factors may have contributed to each of these decisions:
    a. I'll always be a failure.
    b. I'm basically weak and helpless.
    c. I won't feel, and that way I won't experience pain.
    d. Regardless of what I accomplish, I'll never be good enough.

12. *Redecision work in groups.* Take the four statements above and assume that each of them represents a life orientation. How would you proceed in working with each of these approaches toward life? What new decisions would you like to see made? What would it take to change these decisions?

13. *Contracts.* TA groups work on a contract basis, which means that members clearly specify what they want to change as well as what they are willing to do to change. What do you think of the use of contracts in groups? If you were to become involved as a client in a TA group, what are some contracts you'd be willing to make? List one such contract, including a specific statement of some behavior you want to change and the steps you'd be willing to take to make this change.

14. *Personal critique.* What is your personal evaluation of the TA approach to group work? Consider questions such as the following in your critique:
    a. To what clients do you think TA is best suited?
    b. What contributions of TA do you think are most significant?
    c. What are the major limitations of TA? Explain.
    d. What are the strengths and weaknesses of TA as applied to multicultural populations?
    e. On what specific concepts from TA might you draw in working with ethnically diverse clients?

## Questions for Reflection and Discussion

1. To what degree do you think children are "scripted" and then destined to live out their lives in accord with this script? Do you think children actually make decisions about the messages they receive, or do you think they accept the injunctions uncritically? How does your answer influence the manner in which you would work with a group?

2. Consider the possibility that you might be a leader of a TA group. How do you think your patterns of games, rackets, and early decisions would affect the way you worked with certain members in your group? Using what you know of yourself, are there any members with whom you might have particular difficulty working?

3. TA is generally a didactic model of group therapy. Would you be comfortable in the role of teaching, along with the structuring that would be expected if you were to function within

this model? What aspects of this educational model might you incorporate into your style of group leadership, even if you did not adhere to TA theory?

4. TA is direct. As a leader you would be talking with participants about the games they play and the ways they cling to chronic bad feelings. To what degree do you think you would be able to be direct in working with members of your group recognize their games and to help them design contracts for what they would change?

5. Compare and contrast TA with psychoanalytic therapy with respect to the group leader's role and functions. Which role seems more compatible with your leadership style and view of group counseling? Why?

6. As you know, a contract is a basic part of a TA group. How do you think you'd proceed with one or more group members who refused to negotiate a contract with you? What might you do with a member who argued that making a contract seemed rigid?

7. TA concepts and techniques can be applied in counseling groups with both children and adolescents in school settings. What specific concepts do you think are especially useful in working with young people in schools? What techniques might you be inclined to use with children? Adolescents?

8. What are some of the advantages of a TA group in exploring gender-role socialization issues? What kind of messages do you think members of a TA group are likely to explore pertaining to the role that gender plays in their lives?

9. What do you see as both advantages and disadvantages of using a TA approach in working with cultural diversity in a group?

10. What are some possibilities you can see in integrating TA concepts and practices with Gestalt therapy and psychodrama techniques?

## Quiz on the Transactional Approach to Groups: A Comprehension Check

Score ____%

*Note:* Please refer to Appendix I for the scoring key. Count 5 points for each error, and subtract the total from 100 to get your percentage score.

*True/false items:* Decide if the following statements are "more true" or "more false" as they apply to TA.

T  F  1. TA tends to stress the experiential aspects of therapy and underplays the cognitive dimensions.

T  F  2. A basic premise of TA is that once we make a decision in childhood we become scripted, which means that the decision is irreversible.

T  F  3. Injunctions are given from the Child ego state of the parents.

T  F  4. The TA group leader considers it essential to recognize and fully work through transference.

T  F  5. TA shares with Gestalt therapy the basic assumption that awareness is an important first step in changing our ways of thinking, feeling, and behaving.

T  F  6. Script analysis is aimed at helping members understand ways to change their early programming.

T   F   7.  The analysis of the life script of a group member is based on the drama of his or her original family.

T   F   8.  The TA therapist will expect the members to formulate a contract to guide the sessions.

T   F   9.  According to the Gouldings, people are scripted in a passive way.

T   F  10.  Berne's position is that people are to a large degree the victims of their injunctions.

*Multiple-choice items:* Select the *one best answer* among the alternatives given. Consider each question within the framework of TA.

_____11. Redecision therapy, as introduced by the Gouldings, is done primarily in the context of
   a. individual therapy.
   b. couples therapy.
   c. family therapy.
   d. group therapy.

_____12. Redecision therapy integrates TA concepts with techniques drawn from all the following approaches except
   a. psychodrama.
   b. family therapy.
   c. fantasy and imagery.
   d. Gestalt therapy.
   e. person-centered therapy.

_____13. A contribution of TA to counseling with ethnically diverse clients is
   a. its focus on dreams.
   b. the structure it provides to help clients understand how their culture has influenced them.
   c. the abundance of research on TA theory as it is applied to working with culturally diverse client populations.
   d. the fact that TA always begins by exploring the client's cultural background.

_____14. The unpleasant feelings people experience after a game are called
   a. injunctions.
   b. parental messages.
   c. script analyses.
   d. rackets.
   e. life positions.

_____15. Looking ahead, TA seems to be
   a. getting more and more complex.
   b. going back to its psychoanalytic roots.
   c. moving toward becoming more and more cognitive.
   d. focusing more on encouraging clients to emotionally reexperience crucial experiences when early decisions were made.
   e. merging with Adlerian concepts.

_____16. Which of the following is not a key concept of TA?
   a. strokes
   b. rackets
   c. lifestyle assessment

d. life scripts

e. games

_____17. According to TA theory, strokes are

a. necessary only for highly dependent people.

b. necessary for healthy development.

c. needed for children but not for adults.

d. needed only in times of crisis.

_____18. Messages that are given from the Child ego state of the parents are known as

a. rackets.

b. life scripts.

c. games.

d. injunctions.

e. counterinjunctions.

_____19. Messages that come from the Parent ego state of the parents are known as

a. rackets.

b. life scripts.

c. games.

d. injunctions.

e. counterinjunctions.

_____20. Collections of bad feelings that people use to justify their life scripts are known as

a. rackets.

b. counterinjunctions.

c. games.

d. injunctions.

e. basic decisions.

# CHAPTER THIRTEEN

# Cognitive Behavioral Approaches to Groups

## Prechapter Self-Inventory for the Cognitive Behavioral Approaches

*Directions:* Refer to page 57 for general directions. Indicate your position on these statements using the following code:

**5** = I *strongly agree* with this statement.
**4** = I *agree,* in most respects, with this statement.
**3** = I am *undecided* in my opinion about this statement.
**2** = I *disagree,* in most respects, with this statement.
**1** = I *strongly disagree* with this statement.

_____ 1. Self-reinforcement is needed if participants hope to transfer the changes made in a group to everyday life.

_____ 2. Assessment is a necessary step in the initial phase of a group.

_____ 3. Evaluation of results is best done continually during all the phases of a group.

_____ 4. For change to occur, members must actively participate in group work, and they must be willing to practice outside of group sessions.

_____ 5. Specific goals increase the chances that members will do productive group work.

_____ 6. The use of techniques cannot be separated from the personality of the group leader.

_____ 7. Groups should aim at helping participants develop specific skills and self-directed methods of changing.

_____ 8. The group leader's attention to and interest in members serve as powerful sources of reinforcement.

_____ 9. It is the group members' role to decide on their own therapeutic goals.

_____10. Any group techniques or therapeutic procedures are best evaluated by both the group members and the leader to determine their effectiveness in meeting goals.

## Summary of Basic Assumptions and Key Concepts of Cognitive Behavioral Group Therapy

1. The specific unique characteristics of cognitive behavioral therapy include: (1) conducting an assessment, (2) precisely spelling out collaborative treatment goals, (3) formulating a specific treatment procedure appropriate to a particular problem, and (4) objectively evaluating the outcomes of therapy. Data-based assessment is a part of the treatment procedure, and there is a focus on transferring new skills learned in the group to everyday situations.

2. A basic assumption is that all problematic behaviors, cognitions, and emotions have been learned and that they can be modified by new learning. The behaviors clients express are considered to be the problem rather than merely symptoms of the problem. Group therapy is seen as a psychoeducational process whereby members are encouraged to try out more effective ways of changing their behaviors, cognitions, and emotions. The group leader does not focus on the member's past, or on unconscious material, rather, the focus is on changing dysfunctional thoughts and actions.

3. The decision to use certain techniques is based on their demonstrated effectiveness as ascertained through ongoing evaluation. The techniques used by the leader are evidenced-based practices. There is a wide variety of techniques, and cognitive behavioral group counselors have a great deal of flexibility in adapting techniques for the needs of group members.

4. The group leader is active and directive, functioning in some ways as a teacher. Some of the leader's functions include organizing the group, orienting and teaching members about group process, assessing problems and developing ways of resolving them, evaluating the progress of group sessions, planning procedures for change, modifying group attributes, and establishing transfer and maintenance programs for new behaviors. Cognitive behavioral leaders assess group problems as they arise. Data on group satisfaction, completion of assignments, participation, and attendance are typically collected and used as a basis for determining problems. Once the problems are identified and acknowledged by the members, they are dealt with by means of systematic procedures.

5. A basic assumption is that a good working relationship between the leader and members is a necessary, but not a sufficient, condition for change. The members must actively participate in the group work and be willing to experiment with new behavior by taking a role in bringing about changes in their thinking and behavior.

## Glossary of Key Terms for Cognitive Behavioral Therapy

**Acceptance**  A process involving receiving our present experience without judgment or preference, but with curiosity and kindness. Acceptance is an attitude of striving for full awareness of the present moment.

**Acceptance and commitment therapy (ACT)**  A program based on encouraging clients to accept, rather than attempt to control or change, unpleasant sensations.

**Assertion training**  A set of techniques employed in a group that involves behavioral rehearsal, coaching, and learning more effective social skills. Members are taught to express both positive and negative feelings openly and directly.

**Automatic thoughts**  Personalized notions that are triggered by particular stimuli that lead to emotional responses.

**BASIC I.D.**  The conceptual framework of multimodal therapy; based on the premise that human personality can be understood by assessment of seven major areas of functioning: behavior, affective responses, sensations, images, cognitions, interpersonal relationships, and drugs/biological functions.

**Behavioral assessment**  A set of procedures used to get information that will guide the development of a tailor-made treatment plan for each client and help measure the effectiveness of treatment.

**Behavior rehearsal**  Trying out new behaviors in a group session that are to be applied in everyday situations.

**Behavioral therapy**  Refers to the application of diverse techniques and procedures that are rooted in a variety of learning theories.

**Buddy system**  A therapeutic alliance between members whereby they monitor and coach one another both inside and outside of the group.

**Coaching**  Providing members with general principles for carrying out specific forms of effective behaviors.

**Cognitive behavioral therapy**  An approach that blends both cognitive and behavioral methods to bring about change.

**Cognitive restructuring**  Actively altering maladaptive thought patterns and replacing them with more realistic and constructive thoughts.

**Cognitive structure**  The organizing aspect of thinking, which monitors and directs the choice of thoughts; implies an "executive processor," one that determines when to continue, interrupt, or change thinking patterns.

**Cognitive therapy**  An approach that perceives psychological problems as stemming from commonplace processes such as faulty thinking, making incorrect inferences on the basis of inadequate or incorrect information, and failing to distinguish between fantasy and reality.

**Contingency contract**  A document that spells out specific behaviors to be performed, changed, or discontinued and identifies the rewards for achieving these goals.

**Coping skills**  A behavioral procedure for helping clients deal effectively with stressful situations by learning to modify their thinking patterns.

**Dialectical behavior therapy (DBT)**  A blend of cognitive behavioral and psychoanalytic techniques that generally involves a minimum of one year of treatment. This approach makes use of mindfulness and was developed to help clients regulate emotions and behavior associated with depression.

**Feedback**  The process of members providing verbal reactions to behaviors of others in the group.

**Mindfulness**  A process that involves becoming increasingly observant and aware of external and internal stimuli in the present moment and adopting an open attitude toward accepting what is, rather than judging the current situation.

**Mindfulness-based cognitive therapy (MBCT)**  A comprehensive integration of the principles and skills of mindfulness applied to the treatment of depression.

**Mindfulness-based stress reduction (MBSR)**  This is a program developed mainly by Jon Kabat-Zinn, which involves an 8- to 10-week group program applying mindfulness techniques to coping with stress and promoting physical and psychological health.

**Modeling**  Learning through observation and imitation.

**Multimethod group approach**  The use of various coping strategies for dealing with specific problems, such as cognitive restructuring, problem solving, and behavioral rehearsal.

**Multimodal therapy**  Developed by Arnold Lazarus, this is a model endorsing technical eclecticism; uses procedures drawn from various sources without necessarily subscribing to the theory behind these techniques.

**Problem solving**  A cognitive behavioral technique that teaches individuals a method of dealing with their problems.

**Reinforcement** A specified event that strengthens the tendency for a response to be repeated. In groups, social reinforcement is provided by the group leader and by other members.

**Relapse prevention** A way to predict and plan for the setbacks members may encounter after terminating a group.

**Self-management** A collection of strategies based on the idea that change can be brought about by teaching people to use coping skills in problematic situations such as anxiety, depression, and pain.

**Self-monitoring** The process of observing one's own behavior patterns as well as one's interactions in various social situations.

**Social effectiveness training (or SET)** A multifaceted treatment program designed to reduce social anxiety, improve interpersonal skills, and increase the range of enjoyable social activities.

**Social learning theory** A perspective, developed primarily by Albert Bandura, holding that behavior is best understood by taking into consideration the social conditions under which learning occurs.

**Social skills training** Behavioral techniques that are aimed at teaching members how to interact effectively with others.

**Stress management training** An approach that teaches clients how to detect sources of stress and to learn methods of coping adequately with stress.

**Stress inoculation training** A form of cognitive behavior modification developed by Meichenbaum that involves educational, rehearsal, and application phases. Clients learn the role of thinking in creating stress and are given a set of skills to deal with future stressful situations.

**Technical eclecticism** The drawing of strategies from a variety of approaches without having to embrace any of the diverse theoretical positions.

**Therapeutic collaboration** A process whereby the therapist strives to engage the client's active participation in all phases of therapy.

**Therapeutic homework** Aimed at putting into action what members explore during a group session; the attempt to integrate what takes place within the group with everyday life.

## Exercises and Activities for the Cognitive Behavioral Approaches

### Rationale

Cognitive behavioral group leaders use a variety of specific techniques. These evidence-based practices are used systematically to accomplish particular goals, and both the group members and the leader determine whether these methods are producing positive results. If members are not making progress, the therapeutic procedures can be modified. It is basic to the cognitive behavioral approach that therapeutic procedures and evaluation of these techniques proceed simultaneously.

Most of the cognitive behavioral techniques are designed to effect specific changes in thinking and bring about behavioral changes—that is, either to decrease or eliminate undesirable behaviors or to acquire or increase desired behaviors. The following exercises will show you ways to use learning principles in your work to change members' thoughts and behavior. You can apply

(*Text continues on page 138*)

STAGES OF DEVELOPMENT OF THE COGNITIVE BEHAVIORAL THERAPY GROUP

| Dimension | Initial Stage | Working Stage | Final Stage |
|---|---|---|---|
| Key developmental tasks and goals | Responsibilities and expectations of both the leaders and the members are outlined in a contract. Preparation of members is stressed. At the early stages the focus is on building cohesion, getting familiar with the structure of group therapy, and identifying problems to explore. Assessment is a vital aspect as is setting clear goals. A treatment plan, including procedures to be used to attain the stated goals, is developed and is constantly evaluated to test its effectiveness. Collaborative relationships are stressed from the beginning. | Treatment plan is implemented. A wide range of treatment procedures is used to solve specific problems, and the focus is on learning skills. Central part of this phase is work done outside of the group. The group is used as a place to learn and perfect skills and to gain support and feedback so that progress continues. Much of the learning in the group takes place through modeling and observation along with coaching. The emphasis is on identifying dysfunctional thoughts and behaviors and learning new skills as opposed to the exploration of feelings. | At this phase, the transfer of learning from the group to everyday life is critical. Situations that simulate the real world are used so that this transfer is facilitated. Focus is on learning self-directed behavior and developing plans for maintaining and using new coping skills. It is assumed that the generalization of learning will not occur by chance, so sessions are structured in such a manner that transfer of learning will be maximized. Relapse prevention is emphasized at the ending stage. |
| Role and tasks of group leader | Leader's tasks are to conduct pregroup interviews and screen members, organize the group, prepare the members by telling them how the group will work, establish group trust and cohesion, assess the nature of the problems to be explored, and provide a structure for the group. Leaders are active, and they provide information. They assist members in formulating specific goals. Leaders model appropriate behavior and values. They offer reinforcement to members for acquiring newly developed skills and behaviors. They emphasize the importance of members taking action and planning for change. | Leaders develop an appropriate treatment plan based on the initial assessment, and they monitor those behaviors identified as problematic. They continually assess progress and teach the members self-evaluation skills. Leaders reinforce desired behavior, and they assist members in learning methods of self-reinforcement. Leaders model, coach, and provide corrective feedback. They encourage members to form therapeutic alliances with one another. Leaders help members gradually increase their participation and involvement in setting new goals and making decisions. | Main function of leaders at this phase is to assist members in learning ways to transfer new skills to situations in daily life. They prepare members for dealing with setbacks and teach them skills needed to meet new situations effectively. Leaders arrange for follow-up interviews to assess the impact of the group and to determine the degree to which members have fulfilled their contracts. Leaders help members in preparing for generalization and maintenance of change. They overtrain members in the desired target behaviors. They devise ways of evaluating the effectiveness of a group and help members make a self-evaluation. |

| | | | |
|---|---|---|---|
| Role of group members | Members are involved in formulating the contract. They make a list of behaviors they want to change, or they clarify the problems they want to work on in the group. They determine baseline data for certain behaviors and begin to monitor and to observe their behavior in the group as well. The members are involved in the assessment process, which continues throughout the group. Members learn to identify their self-defeating cognitions. | Members report on the nature of their progress each week. Group time is used to define problem areas to work on in the group. Role playing of a behavioral nature is done to assist members in learning new skills. Members provide models for one another; they must carry out specific behavioral assignments, keep records of their progress, assess their progress in light of the baseline data collected at the initial sessions, and report to the group each week. | Members decide what specific things they've learned in the group situation, and they practice new roles and behaviors, both in the group and in daily life. Feedback is provided so that skills and new behavior can be refined, and suggestions are made for maintaining these new behavioral changes. Members act as a support system for one another. They typically agree to carry out specific assignments at the end of a group and then report back at a follow-up meeting. |
| Techniques | Basic techniques include contracts, checklists, role playing, and assessment devices. There are a variety of cognitive techniques to assess thought patterns. | Many behavioral techniques are used, including reinforcement, modeling, desensitization, cognitive methods, cognitive restructuring, and homework. | Feedback is a main technique, as are role playing and developing self-reinforcement. Follow-up sessions are scheduled to assess outcomes. |
| Questions to consider | Central function of leader is to create trust needed for work on issues. In doing this, leader must strive to make the group attractive to members, create many functional roles that they can play in the group, and find ways to involve all members in the group interactions. How can you best carry out these tasks?<br><br>Are the goals that are established meaningful for the members? Have they been developed by the members and leader in a spirit of cooperation? | In what ways will you assist members in assessment, monitoring, and evaluation throughout the working stage?<br><br>How might you involve the members in developing a treatment plan for a group? What kind of structuring would you want to provide in a cognitive behavioral group?<br><br>What specific behaviors would you most want to reinforce in members?<br><br>In what ways might you involve other members in one person's work? How could you use members to provide assistance to one another between sessions? What ways could you think of to use a buddy system? | How can you change your role from that of a direct therapist to a consultant during the final stage? How can you encourage the members to assume an increasing share of the leadership tasks?<br><br>What self-help skills and problem-solving strategies would you want to teach members as a group is approaching termination?<br><br>What kinds of short-term and long-term follow-up sessions might you consider setting up before a group ends?<br><br>Along with members, how can you evaluate the effectiveness of a given group? |

Reactions: Summarize your reactions to the cognitive behavioral perspective on group developmental stages. What do you like *most*? *Least*? What aspects of this approach would you incorporate in your style of leadership?

many of the techniques presented in these exercises to your own life. As you experiment with these techniques in your small group or in class, determine which aspects of the cognitive behavioral approaches you would incorporate in your work as a group leader, regardless of the theoretical model you might be working with.

## Exercises

1. *Setting up a cognitive behavioral group.* Assume that you are a cognitive behavioral group leader and are giving a talk to a community gathering where you hope to begin a group. What points would you emphasize to give these people a good picture of your group, your functions and role as a leader, and the things that would be expected of them as participants? Assume that they respond enthusiastically and want to join your group. Where would you begin, and how would you proceed in setting up this group? What pregroup concerns would you have? What would you do during the initial meeting?

2. *Terminating and evaluating a group.* Assume that the above group meets for 20 weeks. It is now the 18th week. What would you be concerned with as a group leader? Mention specific issues with which you'd want the group to deal. What evaluation procedures would you employ at the end of the group? What follow-up procedures would you use?

3. *Group leaders as skilled technicians.* Cognitive behavioral group leaders must be skilled technicians who also possess the human qualities that lead to the climate of trust and care necessary for the effective use of therapeutic techniques. From a cognitive behavioral perspective, what emphasis would you place on your relationships with the members of your groups? What specific skills do you see yourself as having that would be useful in a group? What are a few examples of skills that you would either like to acquire or refine as ways of enhancing your ability to function from a cognitive behavioral perspective? Discuss this in a group, and collectively generate a list of skills cognitive behavioral leaders need to possess.

4. *Relaxation exercises.* Many cognitive behavioral group therapists use self-relaxation techniques. Members are taught how to systematically relax every part of their body. They practice in the group and also daily at home. In your own group, one member can volunteer to lead a tension/relaxation procedure, going from head to foot. After the exercise, discuss the possibilities for using relaxation procedures in any group. What are the values of such procedures? Consider practicing these exercises to reduce stress. Give them at least a three-week trial to determine some personal benefits.

5. *Social reinforcement.* Observe in your own class or group how social reinforcement works. For what are members reinforced? Pay attention to *nonverbal* responses, such as smiles, head nodding, and body posture, as well as verbal support and approval. Do you see ways you can systematically use social reinforcement in a group situation? What social reinforcers have the most impact on your behavior?

6. *Modeling.* Think about the importance you place on your role as a leader in modeling for members. Consider factors such as clear and direct speech, self-disclosure, respect, enthusiasm, sensitivity, respect for diversity, and caring confrontation. In your group, discuss how you can model positive behavior. Also, observe the effect of a certain behavior on your group (for example, speaking enthusiastically). Do you notice that members tend to assume some of the traits of the leader? What are the implications of this influence? In addition to your own modeling as a group leader, the participants can function as models. Since people

tend to imitate more rapidly and thoroughly those with whom they share common features, modeling by peers in the group enhances observational learning on the part of other members. In what ways can you shape a group norm for this type of modeling? What behaviors would you like to see modeled in your groups?

7. *Social skills training in groups: An introduction.* Assume that you are giving a talk to people who might be interested in joining the social skills training group you are forming. What would you tell them about your group? What are some examples of social skills that members might learn and practice? For whom is the group intended? How can it help them? What would they do in this group? What are some of the techniques you'd use during the group sessions? For this exercise, two of those in your group can be the co-leaders and explain the group to the potential members; the others in the group can ask questions relating to what they will be expected to do in the group, how these activities will help them in daily life, and how they can apply what they learn.

8. *Applying assertiveness training procedures to yourself.* In an exercise related to the preceding one, think of an area where you have difficulty being assertive. This difficulty may involve dealing with supervisors, returning faulty merchandise, or expressing positive feelings. In your own group, you can experiment with improving your assertiveness in this area, using specific procedures that are described in the textbook such as behavior rehearsal, role playing, coaching, cognitive restructuring, and so on. Practice with these procedures *as a member* first, so that you can get some idea of the values and applications of assertive behavior training.

9. *Stress management training in groups.* Review the section in the textbook on a group approach to stress management, especially Meichenbaum's stress inoculation program. Think about yourself as a participant in such a training group. What are a couple of factors in your life that contribute to your experience of stress? Identify some of your cognitions (beliefs or self-talk) that play a role in creating and maintaining stress. Consider keeping an open-ended diary in which you systematically record specific thoughts, feelings, and behaviors for at least two weeks. This process can be useful in teaching you to become aware of your own role in creating your stress. If you are in a group at this time, consider bringing into a session a specific concern about stress. After working on this concern in your group, develop a plan that will lead to practice in daily situations. Assume that you want to begin a stress management group in your agency. What specific steps would you take in forming this group? What cognitive behavioral techniques would you use? How would you explain the purpose of your group to prospective members?

10. *Mindfulness and acceptance-based approaches in groups.* Acceptance-based approaches that typically incorporate mindfulness skills training are becoming an increasing part of cognitive behavioral groups. Mindfulness practice involves training ourselves to bring our attention on our present experiencing. This practice is aimed at helping us to be alive to the moment and accepting, rather than judging, our experience. Some mindfulness skills include focusing on breathing, noting our present activity, identifying and labeling feelings, accepting all feelings, letting thoughts flow, assuming a nonjudgmental stance, and doing one thing at a time. What do you think about this relatively recent broadening of the cognitive behavioral approaches to include mindfulness and acceptance-based skills into therapeutic practice? What are some ways that you would like to incorporate mindfulness in your daily life? What are some specific ways that you might want to use mindfulness and acceptance-based strategies in your groups?

11. *Working on specific goals.* A real value of the behavioral approach is its specificity—its ability to translate broad goals into specific ones. State some broad goals you'd like to attain. Then, in your group, practice making these goals concrete. Make them specific to the degree that you actually *know* what it is that you want and can thus measure progress toward them. As a second part of this exercise, assume that members in one of your groups make broad and vague statements such as the following. Can you think of ways to make these goals clear and concrete?

a. "I'd like to be more spontaneous." Concrete goal is: _____

_____

b. "I need to learn how to get in touch with my feelings." Concrete goal is: _____

_____

_____

c. "My goal is to become a more autonomous and actualized person." Concrete goal is: ___

_____

_____

d. "I have many fears that get in my way of living the way I want." Concrete goal is:

_____

_____

e. "I'd like to be able to relate better." Concrete goal is: _____

_____

_____

f. "I'm all messed up, and I need a major overhaul." Concrete goal is: _____

_____

_____

g. "My goal is to get to know myself better." Concrete goal is: _____

_____

_____

h. "I want to live more in the present moment." Concrete goal is: _____

_____

_____

12. *Groups designed for self-directed behavior change.* Assume that you want to organize a group for people who are interested in self-directed change. For example, they may be interested in stopping smoking, taking weight off and keeping it off, or improving their self-discipline in study or work. How would you design a group of this nature?

13. *Applying a self-directed behavior change program to yourself.* In your group or class, discuss the specific behavior you want to work on during the semester. Next, decide what you are willing to do to change this behavior. Draw up a specific contract, and include details. (For instance, "I will lose 10 pounds by the end of the semester, regulate my eating habits, and ride a bicycle for an hour a day for the rest of the semester.") Then practice your program, and report your progress to your group. Ask a fellow student to support you if you get discouraged or find that you have difficulty sticking to your program. You can apply self-directed behavior modification methods to areas such as developing better patterns of organization, reducing stress through meditation and relaxation exercises, changing what you consider to be negative behavior patterns, and so on.

14. *Cognitive restructuring in groups.* Identify a few major cognitions that have a negative impact on the way people behave. Think of common self-defeating statements that you have heard. Can you think of some methods for helping group members challenge negative cognitions and also develop a new and more effective set of beliefs and thoughts? Can you think of possible homework assignments to supplement the work done in the group sessions? What steps might you suggest to members in learning new ways of thinking?

15. *Self-reinforcement methods.* Cognitive behavioral group work teaches members how to reinforce themselves so that they are not dependent on external rewards to maintain newly acquired skills. In your class or group, experiment with ways you can *reinforce yourself* after successes. Brainstorm this topic in your group. Self-reinforcement may involve learning ways to praise yourself *and* at the same time remind yourself of certain realities that you tend to forget. An example is writing notes to yourself and putting them on the mirror. These notes could say "I am worthwhile," "I am enough," "I have a right to my own feelings," "I'll like myself better if I treat myself with regard," "I can take time for myself."

16. *Guidelines for applying cognitive behavioral methods with children and adolescents.* A number of cognitive and behavioral concepts and strategies are useful in group work in the schools. Here are some suggestions for working within a behavioral framework with a variety of groups in the school setting:

    a. Cognitive behavioral groups fit well with the restrictions often imposed on group counseling in the schools. Create formats that capitalize on the educational components, especially imparting information and teaching a range of coping skills.

    b. As a group leader, you can model many of the specific behaviors you hope members will acquire.

    c. Strive to create a collaborative spirit between you and the members of the group. Students will become more motivated to actively participate in the group if they have an opportunity to contribute to the goals and the procedures to attain them.

    d. Make use of homework methods to maximize learning. Involve group members in creating their own homework. Make sure the homework fits their goals.

    e. Assist members in formulating concrete personal goals, and teach members how to assess the degree to which they are accomplishing their goals. At each session, ask members to reflect on what they have done in the group to make it productive for them.

f. Employ a variety of cognitive behavioral strategies to teach young people how they might more effectively cope with problems.

g. Even if the group is structured around a particular theme or topic, it is still important to pay attention to the process issues that are occurring within the group. Allow time to talk about matters such as trust, interpersonal relationships within the group, and the cohesion level in the group.

h. Use cognitive behavior rehearsal methods to summarize key learnings and helping members translate what they are learning in the group sessions to various facets of daily life.

i. Teach members how to give and receive feedback. Specific feedback can be most useful in groups with children and adolescents. Oftentimes the feedback in these groups will be of a global nature. Apply a behavioral format in giving feedback.

Form small groups within your class and choose a specific type of group that you want to design (either for children or adolescents). In your small group, decide on the specific focus and purpose of your group and outline the structure of the group. How long will your group last? How might you best apply these guidelines to the group you are designing? This activity is aimed at helping you think about ways you can concretely apply behavioral methods to working with a group in the school setting.

17. *Personal evaluation and critique of cognitive behavioral groups.* Discuss in your class or group what you consider to be the major strengths and weaknesses of the cognitive behavioral approaches to groups. Consider questions such as these:

a. How can any group leader (regardless of theoretical orientation) draw on cognitive behavioral concepts and procedures?

b. How would it be for you to use cognitive behavioral techniques as a group leader?

c. If you were leading a group composed of members with culturally diverse backgrounds, what cognitive behavioral techniques do you think might be particularly effective?

d. What do you see as the major strengths and limitations of cognitive behavioral group approaches in working with multicultural populations?

e. From a cognitive behavioral perspective, what kind of teaching would you want to do if you were beginning a group with culturally diverse clients?

## Questions for Reflection and Discussion

1. What are some of the distinguishing features of a cognitive behavioral group that separate it from many of the other models covered in this book? To what extent do you think you could incorporate some cognitive behavioral concepts and techniques into relationship-oriented and experiential therapies?

2. What role does assessment play in a cognitive behavioral group? Explain how assessment is an ongoing process. Again, how could you include the focus on assessment in other therapeutic models?

3. What cognitive behavioral techniques would you most want to include in your groups? How might you broaden the base of your style of leadership by including cognitive and behavioral methods?

4. What are some practical advantages of pregroup interviews and follow-up individual interviews and group sessions? In what ways might you build these into the design of a group?

5. Select a particular kind of group you would be interested in organizing. Thinking from a cognitive behavioral perspective, what are some of the factors you would consider from the time you announced the group to the final session? How would you design this group at each of its stages? Consider discussing your proposal with others in your class.

6. What are your thoughts about the "new wave" of the cognitive behavioral field that includes the mindfulness and acceptance-based approaches? What are the main advantages of combining the various mindfulness and acceptance-based approaches with the more traditional behavioral approaches? What are some of the mindfulness techniques you would like to learn more about?

7. What are your reactions to the focuses of cognitive behavioral therapy—its emphasis on cognition and behavior rather than feelings and insight, interest in current problems rather than exploration of the past, and reliance on empirical validation as a basis for clinical practice?

8. Identify as many elements as you can from the cognitive behavioral perspective that will be operative in any group. For example, discuss the role of modeling, social reinforcement, and feedback in a group. How can systematically paying attention to some of these factors enhance a group?

9. What are the major shortcomings and limitations of the cognitive behavioral model? What is your major criticism of this theory as it is applied to group work?

10. What do you consider to be the most important contributions of the cognitive behavioral approaches?

## Quiz on the Cognitive Behavioral Approaches to Groups: A Comprehension Check

Score _____ %

*Note:* Please refer to Appendix I for the scoring key. Count 5 points for each error, and subtract the total from 100 to get your percentage score.

*True/false items:* Decide if the following statements are "more true" or "more false" as they apply to cognitive behavioral group therapy.

T   F   1. An assumption of the cognitive behavioral orientation is that the behaviors clients express *are* the problem and not merely symptoms of the problem.

T   F   2. Cognitive behavioral therapy operates on the assumption that insight is a prerequisite to behavior change.

T   F   3. Cognitive behavioral group therapy is generally long term.

T   F   4. In cognitive behavioral therapy, assessment and treatment proceed simultaneously.

T   F   5. The cognitive behavioral leader typically assumes an inactive style of leadership to allow members to direct the group process.

T   F   6. There is no single model that, strictly speaking, can be called a "cognitive behavioral group."

T   F   7. One of the group leader's functions is to collect data to determine the effectiveness of treatment, both for the individual members and for the group as a whole.

T   F   8. Mindfulness-based cognitive therapy is a comprehensive integration of the principles and skills of mindfulness applied to the treatment of depression.

T   F   9. One of the drawbacks of the mindfulness and acceptance approaches that are a part of cognitive behavioral therapy is that none of them have been empirically validated.

T   F   10. Mindfulness-based stress reduction programs aim to teach people how to live more fully in the present, rather than ruminating about the past or being overly concerned about the future.

*Multiple-choice items:* Select the *one best answer* among the alternatives given. Consider each question within the framework of cognitive behavioral group therapy.

_____11. Which of the following mindfulness-based programs involves teaching participants sitting meditation, mindful yoga, and a body scan meditation that helps a client to observe all sensations in his or her body?
   a. Dialectical behavior therapy
   b. Acceptance and commitment therapy
   c. Mindfulness-based cognitive therapy
   d. Mindfulness-based stress reduction

_____12. A limitation of cognitive behavioral therapy is
   a. its lack of research to evaluate the effectiveness of techniques.
   b. its deemphasis of the role of feelings in the therapeutic process.
   c. its lack of clear concepts on which to base practice.
   d. its lack of attention to a good client/therapist relationship.
   e. its overemphasis on early childhood experiences.

_____13. Contemporary cognitive behavioral therapy places emphasis on
   a. the interplay between the individual and the environment.
   b. helping clients acquire insight into the causes of their problems.
   c. a phenomenological approach to understanding the person.
   d. encouraging clients to reexperience unfinished business with significant others by role-playing with them in the present.
   e. working through the transference relationship with the therapist.

_____14. Which is *not* true as it applies to multimodal therapy?
   a. Therapeutic flexibility and versatility are valued highly.
   b. Therapists adjust their procedures to achieve the client's goals in therapy.
   c. Great care is taken to fit the client to a predetermined type of treatment.
   d. The approach encourages technical eclecticism.
   e. The therapist makes a comprehensive assessment of the client's level of functioning at the outset of therapy.

_____15. Which of the following is *not* considered one of the modalities of human functioning in multimodal therapy?
   a. sensation
   b. affect
   c. interpersonal relationships
   d. unfinished business
   e. drugs/biology

_____16. Which of the following statements is *false* as it is applied to the multimodal approach to group therapy?

a. Leaders function as trainers, educators, consultants, and role models.

b. Leaders provide information, instruction, and feedback.

c. Leaders generally avoid using techniques.

d. Leaders offer constructive criticism and suggestions.

e. Leaders are appropriately self-disclosing.

_____17. From a multimodal therapy perspective, enduring change is seen as a function of

a. gaining emotional and intellectual insight into one's problems.

b. a client's ability to experience catharsis.

c. the level of self-actualization of the therapist.

d. combined techniques, strategies, and modalities.

e. getting clients to change their early decisions.

_____18. Which of the following is *not* a characteristic of cognitive behavioral approaches?

a. reliance on the principles and procedures of the scientific method

b. specifying treatment goals in concrete and objective terms

c. a focus on the client's current problems and the factors influencing them

d. an emphasis on observing overt behavior

e. application of the same procedures to every client with a particular dysfunctional behavior

_____19. Dialectical behavior therapy (DBT) is a blend of cognitive behavioral therapy and

a. psychoanalytic concepts and techniques.

b. the mindfulness training of Eastern psychological and spiritual practices.

c. traditional behavior therapy.

d. Adlerian therapy.

e. both (a) and (b).

_____20. Like analytic therapy, dialectical behavior therapy emphasizes

a. the importance of the psychotherapeutic relationship.

b. validation of the client.

c. the etiologic importance of the client having experienced an "invalidating environment" as a child.

d. all of the above.

e. none of the above.

# CHAPTER FOURTEEN

# Rational Emotive Behavior Therapy in Groups

## Prechapter Self-Inventory for Rational Emotive Behavior Therapy (REBT)

*Directions:* Refer to page 57 for general directions. Indicate your position on these statements using the following code:

**5** = I *strongly agree* with this statement.
**4** = I *agree,* in most respects, with this statement.
**3** = I am *undecided* in my opinion about this statement.
**2** = I *disagree,* in most respects, with this statement.
**1** = I *strongly disagree* with this statement.

_____ 1. Our beliefs are the primary cause of emotional disturbances; therefore, an appropriate focus of group work is examining these beliefs.

_____ 2. For group leaders to be effective, they need to challenge and convince members to practice activities both inside and outside the group.

_____ 3. It is the group leader's task to show members *how* they have contributed to and are perpetuating their emotional and behavioral problems.

_____ 4. Because we have a tendency to make and keep ourselves emotionally disturbed, we are likely to sabotage our best efforts at changing.

_____ 5. Once irrational beliefs have been discovered, they can be counteracted in a variety of ways and replaced with a rational set of beliefs.

_____ 6. A large part of the leader's task is to be a teacher, especially of ways to detect and dispute irrational beliefs.

_____ 7. Homework assignments are a valuable part of group counseling.

_____ 8. Effective group therapy includes cognitive, emotional, and behavioral elements.

_____ 9. A major function of the group leader is to enable members to recognize their "shoulds," "oughts," and "musts."

_____10. A warm and personal relationship between the group leader and the members is not essential to the group's success.

## Summary of Basic Assumptions and Key Concepts of the REBT Approach to Groups

1. People's belief systems result in emotional disturbances. Situations alone do not determine emotional disturbances; rather, it is people's evaluations of these situations that are crucial. People have a tendency to fall victim to irrational beliefs, and although these beliefs were

originally incorporated from external sources, people internalize and maintain them by self-indoctrination.

2. The leader plays the role of a teacher and not that of an intensely relating partner. REBT stresses the importance of the therapist giving and showing unconditional acceptance of members. It emphasizes the group therapist's skill in challenging, confronting, and convincing the members to practice activities that will lead to positive change. REBT employs a wide variety of cognitive, behavioral, and emotive techniques, and it is therefore a truly eclectic approach to group counseling.

3. To overcome the indoctrination process that results in irrational thinking, group therapists use active cognitive methods such as disputing, teaching, and challenging group members to substitute a rational belief system.

4. Emotive methods in REBT groups are aimed at alleviating emotional disturbances. It is assumed that the best way to change feelings is by changing self-defeating thoughts. Some emotive techniques include role playing, unconditional acceptance, rational emotive imagery, and shame-attacking exercises.

5. Behavioral methods in groups are designed to motivate members to take actions that will result in thinking and feeling differently. REBT stresses that meaningful cognitive change is unlikely unless clients are willing to behave differently. Some of the techniques include behavioral homework assignments, use of reinforcements and penalties, skill training, and feedback.

## Glossary of Key Terms for Rational Emotive Behavior Therapy

**A-B-C model**  The theory that people's problems do not stem from activating events but rather from their beliefs about such events. Thus, the best route to changing emotions is to change one's beliefs about situations.

**Cognitive therapy**  An approach and set of procedures that attempts to change feelings and behavior by modifying faulty thinking and believing.

**Distortion of reality**  Erroneous thinking that disrupts one's life; can be contradicted by the client's objective appraisal of the situation.

**Internal dialogue**  People's self-talk, or inner speech; the debate that often goes on "inside their head."

**Irrational belief**  An unreasonable conviction that leads to emotional and behavioral problems.

**Musturbation**  A term coined by Albert Ellis to refer to behavior that is absolutist and rigid; self-constructed, self-repeated, and self-learned "musts," "oughts," and "shoulds."

**Psychoeducational methods**  The use of audiotapes, videotapes, and books as adjuncts to group counseling.

**Rationality**  The quality of thinking, feeling, and acting in ways that will help us attain our goals. Irrationality consists of thinking, feeling, and acting in ways that are self-defeating and that thwart our goals.

**Rational emotive behavior therapy (REBT)**  A cognitive behavioral model of therapy that stresses the reciprocal interactions among cognition, emotion, and behavior.

**Rational emotive imagery**  A form of intense mental practice for learning new emotional and physical habits. Clients imagine some of the worst things they can think of and then train themselves to develop appropriate emotions in place of disruptive ones.

*(Glossary continues on page 150)*

STAGES OF DEVELOPMENT OF THE RATIONAL EMOTIVE BEHAVIOR THERAPY GROUP

| Dimension | Initial Stage | Working Stage | Final Stage |
|---|---|---|---|
| Key developmental tasks and goals | Key task is to teach members the A-B-C theory of how they create and can "uncreate" their own disturbances, how they can detect their irrational beliefs, and how they can attack these faulty beliefs. Members need to learn that situations themselves do not cause emotional problems; rather, their beliefs about these situations cause the problems. Thus, changing beliefs (not situations) is the road to improvement. | Group focuses on identifying and examining members' "musts," "shoulds," and "oughts." Members learn that if life is not the way they want it to be, this may be unfortunate but not catastrophic. In place of self-defeating assumptions, members incorporate beliefs that are grounded in reality. Members learn a variety of ways to continue challenging their *musturbatory* philosophy. | Ultimate aim is that participants internalize a rational philosophy of life, just as they internalized a set of irrational beliefs. This phase is one of reinforcement of new learning to replace old patterns. Emphasis is on teaching people better methods of self-management. It is important for members to commit themselves to continue to work and practice new behavior in real life. |
| Role and tasks of group leader | Group leader shows members *how they have caused their own misery* by teaching them the connection between their emotional and behavioral disturbances and their beliefs. Leader teaches members how to dispute irrational beliefs and ways to substitute rational beliefs. | Leader confronts members with the propaganda they originally accepted without question and with which they continue to indoctrinate themselves. Leader strives to modify members' thinking by challenging their underlying basic assumptions about reality. | Therapist continues to act as teacher by showing members methods of self-control, giving them homework assignments that involve active practice in real life, and correcting any lasting faulty patterns. Leader encourages use of self-help methods for continuing change. |
| Role of group members | Members need to be willing to discipline themselves and work hard, both during the sessions and between sessions. They are active, both in and out of the group, for they learn by practicing and doing. Members gain awareness of specific ways in which they perpetuate the dysfunctional thinking that creates their problems. They learn how they disturb themselves and how to become undisturbed. | Members learn how to analyze, dispute, and debate by using scientific methods to question their belief systems. Members ask, "What evidence supports my views?" Members learn a new, rational set of beliefs. They learn how to dispute dysfunctional and self-defeating self-talk. Members carry out activity-oriented homework assignments as a way of challenging their beliefs. | Group members integrate what they have learned and continue to make plans for how they can practice overcoming self-defeating thinking and emoting outside of the group. They continue giving themselves cognitive, emotive, and behavioral assignments in daily life. They acquire a more rational and effective philosophy of life that allows them to face new challenges with confidence. |

| | | |
|---|---|---|
| Techniques | Educational methods: use of tapes, books, and lectures; suggestions; information giving; interpretation; group feedback and support; other directive, confrontational, didactic, philosophic, and action-oriented methods. Therapist employs a wide range of cognitive, emotive, and behavioral techniques to fit the needs of the client. | Forceful techniques that emphasize cognitive factors are used. These include persuasion, homework assignments, desensitization, role playing, modeling and imitation, behavior rehearsal, operant control of thinking and emoting, group feedback and support, cognitive restructuring, and assertiveness training. |

There is continued use of emotive/evocative and cognitive behavioral techniques that people can use on their own after therapy terminates. Members can continue working with and practicing new ways of thinking and behaving as they encounter new problems. Members are encouraged to use self-help resources such as reading.

| | | |
|---|---|---|
| Questions to consider | What would you want to teach members about the ways they create their own disturbances? | To what degree have you recognized and challenged your own "musts," "shoulds," and "oughts"? To what extent have you looked at your self-defeating assumptions and behavior? |

What are some common irrational beliefs that you might expect members to bring to a group?

Do you agree that the role of leader is to challenge members with beliefs they have accepted without thinking and questioning?

In what ways do you think a member's belief system is connected to how the person behaves and feels?

What are some specific methods you might teach the members for analyzing, disputing, and debating unexamined assumptions?

How can you confront members and help them recognize their faulty thinking without adding to their defensiveness?

What are some examples of REBT homework that you are likely to use during the working stage?

What kind of relationship would you want to create with the members before you attempted to use forceful and directive procedures?

Can you keep from imposing your values on members? Do you challenge them to think for themselves?

What behavioral techniques would you employ in an REBT group at the early stage?

If you employ directive strategies and encourage members to take a specific course of action, are you clear about your own motives? Are you willing to state your motivations to your clients? Do you share with them your values that pertain to choices they might make?

How can you teach members ways to maintain constructive thinking once they leave a group? How can you help members maintain gains they have made in challenging self-defeating attitudes?

Might you want to integrate any other therapeutic techniques from other approaches during the final stages? If so, what?

What are some ways you could evaluate the effectiveness of your group as it moves toward termination?

Reactions: Summarize your reactions to the rational emotive behavior approach to group developmental stages. What do you like *most? Least?* What aspects of this approach would you incorporate in your style of leadership?

**Self-instructional therapy**  An approach to therapy based on the assumption that what people say to themselves directly influences the things they do. Training consists of learning new self-talk aimed at coping with problems.

**Shame-attacking exercises**  A strategy encouraging people to act in ways that make them feel uncomfortable due to their fear of looking foolish and feeling embarrassed. The aim of the exercise is to teach people that they can function effectively even if they might be perceived as doing foolish acts.

## Exercises and Activities for the REBT Approach to Groups

### Rationale

The rationale underlying most of these exercises and REBT techniques is that most of us make irrational assumptions about ourselves and the world that lead to emotional and behavioral disturbances. The essence of REBT is that rational thinking can lead to more effective living. To combat persistent irrational beliefs, it is necessary to work and practice diligently and to replace faulty thinking with logical thinking.

The following activities and exercises are designed to help you experience the process of challenging your own thinking and to become aware of the consequent feelings of your belief system. As you work through these exercises on your own, with another person, and with a small group, think about ways in which you, as a group leader, could incorporate them in group practice.

### Exercises

1. *Learning to recognize and challenge your internal dialogue as a group counselor.* Leaders often incorporate a wide range of dysfunctional beliefs that impair their capacity to function as effectively as they might in their groups. In a number of his writings (cited in Chapter 14 of the textbook), Ellis has identified several irrational ideas that we often internalize and that inevitably lead to self-defeat. Here are a few typical irrational beliefs that can be applied to group counselors:
   a. "I *must* have love and approval from *all* of the members in my group. My worth as a counselor and as a person is dependent on the affirmation of each client."
   b. "As a group facilitator, I *must* always perform competently and perfectly. There is *absolutely* no room for any mistakes, for this implies failure, and any failure is catastrophic."
   c. "Because I strongly desire that group members treat me considerately and fairly, they *absolutely must* do so! If they don't, I will certainly feel miserable and be unable to function effectively."
   d. "If I don't get what I want from each member, it's terrible, and I *can't stand it*. The group *must* act exactly the way I want when I want it."
   e. "It's easier to avoid facing life's difficulties and responsibilities than to undertake more rewarding forms of self-discipline. I should be able to run my group without too much effort and *must not* have to change my way or style to get the group to work better."

2. *Dysfunctional self-statements.* Many group counselors have a strong tendency to make and keep themselves emotionally disturbed by internalizing self-defeating beliefs such as the ones listed above. I asked the students in one of my group counseling classes to write a list

of their own irrational beliefs, the underlying assumptions they often make, and a sample of their internal dialogue when they are co-leading groups. These self-statements included the following:

a. "I should always know what to say, and it's essential that I have the right answers."

b. "I should be able to fix all the problems posed by members of my group."

c. "I must not be weak, and I shouldn't ask for help."

d. "If I'm not thoroughly prepared, I'm not likely to be totally competent, as I must be."

e. "I must have the right technique for each situation, or else everything might fall flat, and the consequences would be a disaster."

f. "I mustn't lose control. I should always be perfectly in control of every situation in a group."

g. "I must be a perfect role model, which means being an outstanding group leader at all times."

h. "I fear that I may look foolish, and this should never happen!"

i. "I expect myself to be successful with all of my group members all of the time."

j. "I feel I need the approval of virtually all the people in my group."

k. "If a group session doesn't go well, I typically feel responsible and guilty."

l. "If a group member stops coming to the sessions, I tend to blame myself."

m. "I must always be available to any member who might need me."

n. "If a participant in my group is in pain, I should take it away."

o. "I should know everything."

p. "It would be terrible if I made a mistake in the groups I lead, for that would mean I'm a failure."

Review the self-statements listed here and circle the letter preceding each self-statement that you imagine you could (or do) make. Reflect on the nature of some of the beliefs you hold about who and what you think you *should be* in order to be an effective group counselor. List three of your beliefs that are not helpful to you in your development as a group leader:

1. _____

_____

2. _____

_____

3. _____

_____

3. *Your internal dialogue.* Now consider the nature of your internal dialogue regarding your functioning as a group leader. You might think about what goes on in your head just before you begin a group session. What messages do you give yourself about what you should be and must do if your group is to be successful?

4. *Challenging your internal dialogue.* How can you deal effectively with your self-defeating internal dialogue? There are no answers that will silence your internal dialogue permanently. However, by becoming aware of what you are telling yourself and by challenging your dysfunctional beliefs, you take a step in the right direction. It could be an important step to speak out in a group that you are leading, especially when you become aware of

negative thinking. Doing so can be excellent modeling for the members, for it can teach the members ways to combat their own self-defeating beliefs.

a. After you've identified a few self-defeating self-statements that you most often make, practice methods of disputing these statements. Also, attempt to replace the irrational belief with a rational and effective belief. For example, if you say, "I must be approved of or accepted by all of the members of my group," a disputation might include: "Where is it written that my own approval depends on getting approval from others? If a client disapproves of me, can't I still feel like a worthwhile person and group leader?" An example of a rational and effective belief is: "While it's true that I don't enjoy disapproval, I'm able to tolerate it. I don't have to be accepted by everyone to feel accepted by myself." Use the "REBT Self-Help Form" at the end of this exercise section as a concrete way to record and work on your beliefs.

b. Give yourself specific homework assignments to challenge some of the beliefs that interfere with your effectiveness.

c. Identifying and disputing ineffective beliefs, as well as substituting effective beliefs, could be a lively and productive group activity. Spend some time in your class or group discussing how some of your beliefs actually interfere with your effectiveness as a group leader and what you are doing to change what you are telling yourself.

d. Write constructive sentences that you might suggest to a group member who repeated self-defeating sentences such as the following:

(1) "I've always been stupid, and I suppose I'll always be that way."

(2) _____

_____

(1) "I need to please everyone, because rejection is just terrible."

(2) _____

_____

(1) "Because my parents never really loved me, I guess nobody else could ever love me."

(2) _____

_____

(1) "Basically, I'm simply an irresponsible person."

(2) _____

_____

5. Think of some in-group assignments or homework exercises for members who demonstrate problems such as the following, and write them down. Bring these assignments to your class or group and share ideas with one another.

a. A woman says very little during the group sessions because she's afraid she'll sound stupid and that other members will laugh at her. One possible assignment is:

_____

_____

_____

    b. A woman believes men are always judging her in a critical fashion. She avoids men, both in the group and outside of it, because she doesn't want to feel negatively judged. One possible assignment is:

_____

_____

_____

    c. One of the members of a group you're leading tells you that he feels and believes that he *must* gain universal approval. When someone is displeased with him, he feels like a failure. Because of this he tries hard to figure out what every person in the group wants from him, and then he goes out of his way to meet these expectations. He says he is sick of being the "super nice guy" and desperately wants to change. One possible assignment is:

_____

_____

_____

    d. A member describes his drive to be perfect and says that he carefully avoids situations and activities that make it difficult for him to feel that he's performed perfectly. He wants to relax and not be obsessed with the thought that he must be perfect in anything he attempts. One possible assignment is:

_____

_____

_____

6. Role playing with a cognitive focus can be useful in an REBT group. Think of a situation that causes you difficulty—one that you'd be willing to share in your group or class—and role-play it. For example, you may feel victimized because you can't get your father's approval. Have a person play *your role* first, and you role-play your demanding father who refuses to give approval no matter what is accomplished. After about five minutes or so, reverse roles: you be yourself while someone else plays your father as you portrayed him. Continue this for about another five minutes. Afterward, do a *cognitive evaluation* of this interchange in your group. Here are some questions you might include in your evaluation:
    a. How did you appear to others as you played yourself talking with your father?
    b. Do you need his approval to survive?
    c. What will become of you if he never gives you his approval?
    d. What might you have to do to get his approval?
    e. How do you imagine you'd feel if you did what might be required to gain his acceptance?
    f. Can you gain self-acceptance, even if acceptance is not forthcoming from him?
    g. In what ways do you treat others like your father?

7. Imagine that you want to conduct an REBT group in the agency, school, or institution in which you work (or may someday work in the future). Convince your supervisor, principal, or the agency director of the advantages of doing REBT in a group over doing it on an

individual basis. What are some unique advantages of REBT in groups in the particular setting where you expect to work? What can you say to your supervisor to increase the chances that you will be given the support to design a group? This can be a productive exercise in your group or class. Another student can play the role of the school principal or the director of the agency.

8. In small discussion groups, explore some specific ways school counselors could apply REBT concepts and techniques to group work with both children and adolescents. In your group, devise a specific kind of psychoeducational group or a group with an educational focus. Here are a few guidelines and questions to consider when creating a group to address the special needs of students:

   a. Consider your group as an approach to reeducate students. What areas would be a useful focus for reeducation?

   b. Identify some specific self-defeating beliefs of both elementary school children and high school adolescents that you would target in your group. What are some beliefs about self and others that many children and adolescents cling to, which often lead to emotional and behavioral problems?

   c. What kind of cognitive techniques might be appropriate with both children and adolescents?

   d. What kind of action plans could you think of that would assist young people in practicing new cognitive and behavioral skills outside of the group?

   e. Apply selected cognitive, emotive, and behavioral techniques that were discussed in this chapter to your group. How might you be able to increase the cooperation of the students so they are more likely to actively participate in these interventions?

9. In your class or group, discuss what you consider to be some of the major advantages and disadvantages of employing REBT techniques in working with culturally diverse groups. Consider these questions as you critique REBT in working with diverse client populations:

   a. Specifically, what cultural variables would you want to take into account in applying cognitive and behavioral techniques and concepts?

   b. Who is the judge of what constitutes a "faulty belief"? Does culture play a role in determining whether a belief is helpful or unhelpful?

   c. Clients from many cultures will be drawn to the teaching aspects of REBT and the active and directive role of the group leader. How comfortable might you be in structuring a group around educational lines and assuming the role of teacher and coach? How would you combine providing members with cognitive information and facilitating personal exploration?

   d. How might you demonstrate respect for the cultural values and beliefs of the culturally diverse members in your group, yet at the same time challenge them to evaluate the degree to which some of their values are helping or hindering them in their lives?

10. *REBT Self-Help Form.* For at least a week, pay attention to any situations that are problematic for you. Use the REBT Self-Help Form to record at least one event that contributes to an emotional upset or some self-defeating behavior. Identify any irrational beliefs that you hold about a particular event; dispute each irrational belief; and replace it with a rational belief. Bring the completed form to your class or group the following week and use it to talk about how your beliefs influence the way you feel and what you do.

# REBT Self-Help Form

## A (Activating Event)

- Briefly summarize the situation you are disturbed about (what would a camera see?)
- An *A* can be *internal* or *external, real or imagined.*
- An *A* can be an event in the *past, present, or future.*

## IBs (Irrational Beliefs)

**To identify IBs, look for:**

- Dogmatic demands (musts, absolutes, shoulds)
- Awfulizing (It's awful, terrible, horrible)
- Low frustration tolerance (I can't stand it)
- Self/other rating (I'm/he/she is bad, worthless)

## C (Consequences)

Major unhealthy negative **emotions:**

Major self-defeating **behaviors:**

Unhealthy negative emotions include:
- Anxiety
- Depression
- Shame/Embarrassment
- Rage
- Hurt
- Low Frustration Tolerance
- Jealousy
- Guilt

## D (Disputing IBs)

**To dispute, ask yourself:**

- Where is holding this belief getting me? Is it *helpful* or *self-defeating?*
- Where is the evidence to support the existence of my irrational belief? Is it *consistent with reality?*
- Is my belief *logical?* Does it follow from my preferences?
- Is it really *awful* (as bad as it could be?)
- Can I really not *stand* it?

## RBs (Rational Beliefs)

**To think more rationally, strive for:**

- Non-dogmatic preferences (wishes, wants, desires)
- Evaluating badness (it's bad, unfortunate)
- High frustration tolerance (I don't like it, but I can stand it)
- Not globally rating self or others (I—and others—are fallible human beings)

## E (New Effect)

New healthy **negative emotions:**

New constructive **behaviors:**

Healthy negative emotions include:
- Disappointment
- Concern
- Annoyance
- Sadness
- Regret
- Frustration

*Source:* © Windy Dryden & Jane Walker 1992. Revised by Albert Ellis Institute, 1996. Reprinted by permission.

## Questions for Reflection and Discussion

1. In your own experiences as a group member or a group leader, what are some of the common self-defeating beliefs you have most frequently heard? What opportunities does a group offer to challenge such ideas? What would be helpful to you in challenging some of your self-limiting beliefs?

2. REBT urges clients to examine illogical assumptions about life. Do you believe people will make changes on an emotional and behavioral level if the focus is primarily on cognitive structures?

3. As an educational model, REBT stresses teaching, learning, practicing new skills, logical thinking, carrying out homework assignments, and reading. As a group leader, to what degree would you be comfortable with such an educational focus? What aspects of REBT would you want to include in your approach to groups, regardless of your theoretical orientation?

4. Compare and contrast REBT with Gestalt therapy. What are some of the major differences? Do you see any room to integrate the differing dimensions of these two therapies? If so, what factors might you combine in a group you were leading?

5. What are some ways that you might combine aspects of REBT with TA? with cognitive behavioral therapy? Can you think of any theories that would not make a good fit with REBT? Explain.

6. REBT calls for an active/directive group leader. Compare this role with that of the person-centered group leader who gives as little leadership as possible to the members. Which leader role are you more comfortable with, and how do you think these contrasting leadership styles will change a group? Do you see any way to combine some aspects of REBT with the person-centered approach?

7. What criteria would you employ to determine whether a group member's ideas were rational and functional? How would you determine if certain assumptions were self-defeating or constructive?

8. To what degree do you think the group leader's values become a central part of REBT group therapy? How do you think the values held by the leader and by the members influence the group process?

9. Some might criticize REBT group therapy on the ground that a participant is subjected to undue group pressure, both from the leader and the other members. This pressure could take the form of persuasion, giving advice, and expecting members to do certain outside assignments. What are your reactions to this criticism? If you were to incorporate REBT concepts and methods, what safeguards might you devise so that members would not be subjected to pressure to change their way of thinking?

10. Like any other action-oriented approach, REBT insists that newly acquired insights be put into action, largely through homework assignments. What do you think of a model that is based on action outside of the sessions? In what ways might you assist members in creating and carrying out behavioral assignments? What ideas do you have that would lead to collaborative efforts in designing meaningful homework assignments?

## Quiz on Rational Emotive Behavior Therapy: A Comprehension Check

Score _____%

*Note:* Please refer to Appendix I for the scoring key. Count 5 points for each error, and subtract the total from 100 to get your percentage score.

*True/false items:* Decide if the following statements are "more true" or "more false" as they apply to rational emotive behavior therapy.

T  F  1. For Ellis, there are some distinct advantages for practicing REBT in a group context rather than in individual counseling.

T  F  2. Generally, traumatic situations, in and of themselves, cause people to be emotionally disturbed.

T  F  3. Group members need to be taught how to think logically and give themselves new internal dialogues if they hope to change.

T  F  4. Group members are expected to confront the faulty thinking of fellow members.

T  F  5. REBT is basically an educational model.

T  F  6. Clients can improve through the process of self-rating.

T  F  7. REBT considers the nature of the therapeutic relationship between the group therapist and the members to be central to the outcomes of a group.

T  F  8. Group members are taught to use logical analysis as a way of understanding their faulty premises.

T  F  9. REBT group leaders tend to be highly active and directive.

T  F  10. Ellis believes people become emotionally disturbed because stressful situations lead to a breakdown of their coping mechanisms.

*Multiple-choice items:* Select the *one best answer* among the alternatives given. Consider each question within the framework of rational emotive behavior therapy.

_____11. Cognitive therapy is based on the assumption that
    a. our feelings determine our thoughts.
    b. our feelings determine our actions.
    c. cognitions are the major determinants of how we feel and act.
    d. the best way to change thinking is to reexperience past emotional traumas in the here-and-now.
    e. insight is essential for any type of change to occur.

_____12. In REBT, the therapy techniques are designed to
    a. assist clients in substituting rational beliefs for irrational beliefs.
    b. help clients experience their feelings more intensely.
    c. help clients rate themselves as human beings as a route to self-acceptance.
    d. enable clients to deal with their existential loneliness.
    e. teach clients how to think only positive thoughts.

_____13. According to Albert Ellis, people develop psychological disturbances because of
    a. a traumatic event.
    b. failure to receive love from significant others.
    c. their beliefs about and reactions to certain events.
    d. unfinished business from their past.
    e. inadequate bonding with their mother during infancy.

_____14. All of the following are *cognitive* methods of REBT except for
    a. shame-attacking exercises.
    b. disputing irrational beliefs.
    c. coping self-statements.
    d. teaching the A-B-Cs.
    e. psychoeducational methods.

_____15. All of the following are *emotive* methods used in REBT groups except for
    a. unconditional acceptance.
    b. rational emotive imagery.
    c. the use of humor.
    d. shame-attacking exercises.
    e. the analysis of one's life script.

_____16. In an REBT group, the members would be most concerned about
    a. understanding the childhood origins of their emotional disturbances.
    b. understanding the problems of other members.
    c. merely freeing themselves of their symptoms.
    d. minimizing ways in which they create their own disturbances.
    e. reexperiencing the traumatic situations under which they made critical decisions about themselves and their place in the world.

_____17. REBT can best be considered as
    a. an educational method.
    b. a didactic process.
    c. the process of challenging ideas and thinking.
    d. a teaching/learning process.
    e. all of the above.

_____18. In an REBT group, role playing
    a. is rarely done, as it needlessly stirs up emotion.
    b. is limited strictly to cognitive aspects.
    c. is designed to evoke intense feelings.
    d. involves a cognitive/emotive evaluation of both feelings and beliefs.
    e. involves a member acting out all the various roles of a present conflict.

_____19. Which of the following would have the least applicability to an REBT group?
    a. interpretation of early memories
    b. unconditional acceptance
    c. role playing
    d. feedback
    e. reinforcement and penalties

_____20. When REBT group practitioners ask members to imagine some of the worst things they can think of and then to train themselves to develop appropriate emotions in the place of disruptive ones, this is an example of which technique?
    a. systematic desensitization
    b. teaching the A-B-Cs
    c. rational emotive imagery
    d. future projection
    e. cognitive dissonance

# CHAPTER FIFTEEN

# Reality Therapy in Groups

## Prechapter Self-Inventory for Reality Therapy

*Directions:* Refer to page 57 for general directions. Indicate your position on these statements using the following code:

**5** = I *strongly agree* with this statement.
**4** = I *agree,* in most respects, with this statement.
**3** = I am *undecided* in my opinion about this statement.
**2** = I *disagree,* in most respects, with this statement.
**1** = I *strongly disagree* with this statement.

_____ 1. The group counselor's main task is to encourage the group members to evaluate their present behavior and to make more effective choices.

_____ 2. By changing how we are acting, we inevitably change what we think and feel.

_____ 3. Blaming others and making excuses for one's behavior lead to cementing one's identification with failure.

_____ 4. Involvement and self-evaluation are at the core of therapy; without these dimensions there is no therapy.

_____ 5. The only person whose behavior we can control is our own.

_____ 6. Group work should aim to change actions rather than feelings or attitudes.

_____ 7. Generally, it is not the group leader's role to evaluate the behavior of group members; rather, the leader should challenge members to evaluate their own behavior.

_____ 8. The goal of reality therapy is to help people fulfill their needs, to make more effective choices, and to gain better control of their lives—without infringing on others' rights.

_____ 9. Unless clients are willing to accept responsibility for their behavior, they will not be able to change it.

_____10. Group members are able to change when they accept that what they are doing, thinking, and feeling is not simply happening to them but that they are making choices.

## Summary of Basic Assumptions and Key Concepts of the Reality Therapy Approach to Groups

1. Choice theory/reality therapy is grounded on the premise that human behavior is purposeful and originates within the individual rather than from external forces. All behavior is motivated by the striving to fulfill five basic psychological needs: survival, love and

belonging, power, freedom, and fun. This approach focuses on solving problems and on taking better charge of one's life. By evaluating what we are doing and what we want, we are able to achieve opportunities for choice.

2. We perceive the world against the background of our needs and wants rather than as objective reality. We create our own inner world. We are not locked into any one mode of behavior, although we must behave in some way. Behavior is the attempt to control our perceptions of the external world to fit our internal and personal world (or what we want).

3. Choice theory teaches that the only person whose behavior we can control is our own. How we feel is not controlled by others or by events. Choice theory explains how and why we make the choices that determine the course of our lives. With its emphasis on connection and interpersonal relationships, choice theory is well suited for group counseling.

4. Everything we do can be understood within the context of total behavior, which is made up of four inseparable components: acting, thinking, feeling, and physiology. All total behavior is chosen, yet we have much more direct control over the acting and thinking components than over the feeling and physiological components.

5. The reality therapy group leader assists members through a process of skillful questioning aimed at getting them to assess what they want. Leaders generally assume a verbally active and directive role in the group. Their main task is to encourage the members to evaluate their present behavior. Leaders tend to focus on the strengths and potentials of members rather than on their failures. This is done by challenging members to look at their unused potential and to use it to fulfill their needs and gain more effective control of their lives.

6. Group leaders tend to focus on what members can do now to change their behavior. Members are guided in the process of self-evaluation, and they are also taught how to make a plan for action, to commit themselves to doing what it will take to change, and to follow through with their plan. Group leaders do not encourage members to spend much time exploring the past but consistently assist members in dealing with what they are doing presently. A reality therapy group leader might say: "Because the past is over and cannot be changed, it is best that we attend to what is going on now. Let's face your present problems and search for creative solutions." Group therapists focus especially on the client's relationships, no matter what the presenting problem is, for it is assumed that the problem relationship is generally part of our present lives.

7. The practice of reality therapy involves two major components: (1) the counseling environment and (2) specific procedures that lead to changes in behavior. This is referred to as the cycle of counseling. A great deal of emphasis is placed on creating a supportive environment that allows clients to change. Through a process of skillful questioning, leaders help members recognize, define, and refine how they wish to meet their needs. The procedures that lead to change are based on the assumption that human beings are motivated to change (1) when they are convinced that their present behavior is not getting them what they want and (2) when they believe they can choose other behaviors that will get them closer to what they want. Members explore what they want, what they have, and what they are not getting.

See the charts on pages 161–162 for details of basic concepts of choice theory and reality therapy.

# CYCLE OF MANAGING, SUPERVISING, COUNSELING AND COACHING

**PROCEDURES**

**ENVIRONMENT**

**W D E P**

## E — EVALUATION (8 Types)

## P — Make "SAMIC³" Plans P (2 Types)

## D — Explore Total Behavior: Direction
"Doing" ("Acting" Aspect, and Self-Talk
Explore Two-Fold Purpose of Behavior: to impact the outer world and to communicate a message to it.

## W — BUILD RELATIONSHIPS

A. Use "attending behaviors"
B. AB-CDE
C. Suspend Judgment
D. Do the Unexpected; Paradoxical Techniques
E. Use Humor
F. Establish Boundaries & Policies
G. Share Self & Adapt to Own Personality
H. Listen for Metaphors and Use Stories
I. Listen for Themes
J. Summarize & Focus
K. Allow or Impose Consequences
L. Allow Silence
M. Show Empathy
N. Be Ethical
O. Create Anticipation
P. **Practice Lead Management**
Q. **Discuss Quality**
R. **Increase Choices**
S. Discuss problems in the past tense and solutions in present and future tenses.
T. Withdraw from Volatile Situations if helpful
U. Talk about non-problem areas
V. Connect with the person's thinking & feeling
W. Invite solutions
X. Use broken record technique

C. Get a Commitment (5 levels)
B. Share wants and perceptions
A. Explore wants, needs, & perceptions

### 4 ACT

**ESPECIALLY FOR PARENTS**

**RELATIONSHIPS TO FEFF (F F F)**

**TRUST HOPE**

**RELATIONSHIPS TO LAXTIONSHIPS**

## Follow Up, Consultation, Continuing Education

A. Argue, Attack, Accuse
B. **Boss, Manage, Blame, Belittle**
C. Criticize, Coerce, Condemn

D. Demean, Demand
E. Encourage Excuses
F. Instill Fear, Find Fault
G. Give Up Easily, Take for Granted
H. Hold Grudges

**ENVIRONMENT**

Developed by **Robert E. Wubbolding, EdD**
from the works of William Glasser, MD

**Copyright 1986 Robert E. Wubbolding, EdD**
15th Revision 2006

# SUMMARY DESCRIPTION OF THE
# "CYCLE OF MANAGING, SUPERVISING, COUNSELING AND COACHING"

The Cycle is explained in detail in books by Robert E. Wubbolding:
*Employee Motivation*, 1996: *Reality Therapy for the 21st Century, 2000*
*A Set of Directions for Putting and Keeping Yourself Together, 2001*

## Introduction:

The Cycle consists of two general concepts: Environment conducive to change and Procedures more explicitly designed to facilitate change. This chart is intended to be a **brief** summary. The ideas are designed to be used with employees, students, clients as well as in other human relationships.

## Relationship between Environment & Procedures:

1. As indicated in the chart, the Environment is the foundation upon which the effective use of Procedures is based.

2. Though it is **usually** necessary to establish a safe, friendly Environment before change can occur, the "Cycle" can be entered at any point. Thus, the use of the cycle does **not** occur in lock step fashion.

3. Building a relationship implies establishing and maintaining a professional relationship. Methods for accomplishing this comprise some efforts on the part of the helper that are Environmental and others that are Procedural.

## ENVIRONMENT:

**Relationship Tonics:** a close relationship is built on TRUST and HOPE through friendliness, firmness and fairness.

A. Using Attending Behaviors: Eye contact, posture, effective listening skills.

B. AB = "Always **Be** . . ." **C**onsistent, **C**ourteous & **C**alm, **D**etermined that there is hope for improvement, **E**nthusiastic (Think Positively).

C. Suspend Judgment: View behaviors from a low level of perception, i.e., acceptance is crucial.

D. Do the Unexpected: Use paradoxical techniques as appropriate; Reframing and Prescribing.

E. Use Humor: Help them fulfill need for fun within reasonable boundaries.

F. Establish boundaries: the relationship is professional.

**4 A C T**

- Affirm feelings
- Accept
- Show affection
- Action consequences
- Conversation (WDEP)
- Time together

G. Share Self: Self-disclosure within limits is helpful; adapt to own personal style.

H. Listen for Metaphors: Use their figures of speech and provide other ones. Use stories.

I. Listen to Themes: Listen for behaviors that have helped, value judgements, etc.

J. Summarize & Focus: Tie together what they say and focus on them rather than on "Real World."

K. Allow or Impose Consequences: Within reason, they should be responsible for their own behavior.

L. Allow Silence: This allows them to think, as well as to take responsibility.

M. Show Empathy: Perceive as does the person being helped.

N. Be Ethical: Study Codes of Ethics and their applications, e.g., how to handle suicide threats or violent tendencies.

O. Create anticipation and communication hope. People should be taught that something good will happen if they are willing to work.

P. **Practice lead management, e.g., democracy in determining rules**.

Q. **Discuss quality.**

R. **Increases choices.**

S. Discuss problems in the past tense, solutions in present and future tenses.

T. Withdraw from volatile situations if helpful.

U. Talk about non-problem areas.

V. Connect with the person's thinking and feeling.

W. Invite solutions.

X. Use broken record technique.

## Relationship Toxins:

Argue, **Boss Manage,** or Blame, Criticize or Coerce, Demean, Encourage Excuses, Instill Fear, or Give up easily, Hold Grudges.

Rather, stress what they **can** control, accept them as they are, and keep the confidence that they can develop more effective behaviors. Also, continue to use "WDEP" system without giving up.

Follow Up, Consult, and Continue Education:

Determine a way for them to report back, talk to another professional person when necessary, and maintain ongoing program of professional growth.

## PROCEDURES:

Build Relationships:

**WDEP**

A. Explore **W**ants, Needs & Perceptions: Discuss picture album or quality world, i.e., set goals, fulfilled & unfulfilled pictures, needs, viewpoints and "locus of control."

B. Share Wants & Perceptions: Tell what you want from them and how you view their situations, behaviors, wants, etc. This procedure is secondary to A above.

C. Get a Commitment: Help them solidify their desire to find more effective behaviors.

Explore Total Behavior:

Help them examine the **D**irection of their lives, as well as specifics of how they spend their time. Discuss ineffective & effective self talk. Explore two-fold purpose of behavior: to impact the outer world and to communicate a message to it.

**E**valuation – The Cornerstone of Procedures:

Help them evaluate their behavioral direction, specific behaviors as well as wants, perceptions and commitments. Evaluate own behavior through follow-up, consultation and continued education.

Make **P**lans: Help them change direction of their lives.

Effective plans are **S**imple, **A**ttainable, **M**easurable, **I**mmediate, **C**onsistent, **C**ontrolled by the planner, and **C**ommitted to. The helper is **P**ersistent. Plans can be linear or paradoxical.

**Note:** The "Cycle" describes specific guidelines & skills. Effective implementation requires the artful integration of the guidelines & skills contained under Environment & Procedures in a spontaneous & natural manner geared to the personality of the helper. This requires training, practice & supervision. Also, the word "client" is used for anyone receiving help: student, employee, family member, etc.

## For more information contact:

Robert E. Wubbolding, EdD, Director

Center for Reality Therapy
7672 Montgomery Road, #383
Cincinnati, Ohio 45236

(513) 561-1911 • FAX (513) 561-3568
E-mail: wubsrt@fuse.net • www.realitytherapy.com

The Center for Reality Therapy provides counseling, consultation, training and supervision including applications to schools, agencies, hospitals, companies and other institutions. The Center is a provider for *many* organizations which award continuing education units.

This material is copyrighted. Reproduction is prohibited without permission of Robert E. Wubbolding. If you wish to copy, please call.

## Glossary of Key Terms for Reality Therapy

**Autonomy**  The state that exists when individuals accept responsibility for what they do and take control of their lives.

**Commitment**  The act of sticking to a realistic plan aimed at change.

**Choice theory**  The view that humans are internally motivated; based on an internal control psychology that explains how and why we make the choices that determine the course of our lives.

**Counseling environment**  The practice of reality therapy that involves a leader's personal involvement with the members and those leader attitudes and behaviors that promote change.

**Cycle of counseling**  Specific ways of creating a positive climate in which counseling can occur. The proper therapeutic environment provides the foundation for the implementation of counseling strategies.

**Essential human needs**  The innate forces that motivate all behavior that consist of survival, belonging, power, freedom, and fun.

**Involvement**  Therapist's attempt to be part of the client's quality world, namely, the world of wants.

**Paining behaviors**  Choosing misery by developing symptoms (such as "headaching," "depressing," and "anxietying") because these seem to be the best behaviors available at the time.

**Picture album**  The perceptions and images we have of how we can fulfill our basic psychological needs.

**Quality school**  Applying concepts of choice theory and techniques of lead management to the classroom and to groups in the schools.

**Quality world**  Another phrase for "picture album." Our view of what we have in our present world and what we would like to have. These are intense wants, not whims.

**Reality therapy**  An approach based on the key concepts of choice theory that was founded by William Glasser.

**Responsibility**  The act of satisfying one's needs in ways that do not interfere with others' fulfilling their needs.

**Self-evaluation**  Clients' assessment of current behavior to determine whether it is working and meeting their needs.

**Total behavior**  The integrated components of doing, thinking, feeling, and physiology. Choice theory assumes that all elements of behavior are interrelated.

**WDEP system**  Key procedures applied to the practice of reality therapy groups. The strategies help clients identify their wants, determine the direction their behavior is taking them, make a self-evaluation, and design plans for change.

## Exercises and Activities for Reality Therapy in Groups

### Rationale

Reality therapy is a practical approach with many uses and applications for a variety of types of groups. As you review the basic concepts and principles of choice theory, think about ways to translate them into your practice with different kinds of groups. Also, reflect on how you could

*(Text continues on page 166)*

**STAGES OF DEVELOPMENT OF THE REALITY THERAPY GROUP**

| Dimension | Initial Stage | Working Stage | Final Stage |
|---|---|---|---|
| Key developmental tasks and goals | First task is to create member-to-member relationships and a sense of involvement in the group. Leader-to-member relationships based on trust are essential. Major goal of initial stage is to get members to look at the degree to which current behavior is meeting their needs and to determine the direction of their behavior. | Focus is on present behavior rather than feelings. Past is important only insofar as it influences present behavior. The central goal is to create a climate wherein members will learn to understand how their irresponsibility and poor choices have led to their personal problems; in this way members can make better choices. | Specific plans for achieving desirable behavior patterns must be established. Although plans are crucial for behavioral change to occur, a noncritical therapeutic milieu must be created to give members the strength to carry out their plans. It is important that the plan be "owned" by the member. |
| Role and tasks of group leader | Group leader has the task of fostering involvement among the members by being active with every member. Leader may ask question, ask others to make comments, and encourage interaction in the group. Modeling is crucial. Leader nudges members to look at what they are getting from their behavior. | Leader encourages members to evaluate their own behavior, asks members whether their behavior is meeting their needs, and firmly rejects excuses and rationalizations. Leader teaches members how to apply the basics of choice theory to their lives. Counselor avoids labeling people with diagnostic categories. | Leader assists members in formulating realistic plans for change and creates a noncritical therapeutic climate that helps them believe change is possible. Leader does not give up even if members fail to carry out plans; he or she insists on finding a short-range plan that will lead to success. |
| Role of group members | Members concentrate on current behavior and problem areas. Focus may be on how each member attempts to gain love and feelings of self-worth and success. Members are expected to face their problems and to make plans to solve them. Making these plans for change begins early in the group. Members explore their "picture album" and whether what they are doing is getting them what they want. They define what they expect and want from the leader and other members. Members examine the direction of their lives. | Members evaluate their own behavior. They must understand what they are doing *now* as well as what they are getting from this behavior. After they decide if they have what they want, members must decide for themselves if they are willing to change their patterns of behavior. The focus is on choosing better behaviors to satisfy their needs. The work is aimed at teaching members how they can gain better control of their lives. The cornerstone of the approach is to assist members in self-evaluation. | Realistic plans to change behavior are made and carried out. If members do not carry out their plans, they are expected to state when they will complete them. They are to accept responsibility for what they do and to make commitments. Plans help members change the direction of their lives. Effective plans are simple, attainable, measurable, immediate, consistent, and controlled by the planner. Action plans assist members in achieving their long-range plans. |

| | Techniques | | |
|---|---|---|---|
| **Techniques** | In keeping with the goal of establishing involvement, leader encourages members to talk about any subjects of interest to them. An attempt is made to find out what members want from the group. Leader invites members to explore their wants, perceptions, and needs. | Confrontation; insistence on importance of evaluating behavior and making decisions; avoidance of punishment. Leader uses techniques of skillful questioning. Other techniques are use of humor, use of paradox, and designing action plans. | Contracts; behavioral strategies such as role playing, behavior rehearsal, homework assignments, and so on; encouragement and support. Plans are refined and members commit to a plan to bring about changes once the group is over. Plans must be meaningful for members. |
| **Questions to consider** | Once you have established a relationship with members, you will want to focus on current behavior. In doing so, questions you may want to ask are:<br><br>• What are you doing now?<br>• What did you do this week?<br>• What did you want to do differently this past week?<br>• What stopped you from doing what you wanted to do?<br>• What will you do tomorrow?<br><br>If members seem reluctant to accept responsibility for their own problems, what might you do?<br><br>How will you help members discuss their relationships?<br><br>How would you help members establish clear and realistic goals? Would you focus exclusively on behavioral goals? Would you work with feelings and thoughts as well? | A central task is to get members to look at what they are doing to decide whether their course of action is working. How can you challenge members in a nonjudgmental way to make an evaluation of their behavior? How can you avoid lecturing and imposing your values on members?<br><br>How can you challenge members to make an honest evaluation if they seem resistant? What if the members cling to what you consider self-defeating ways of behaving?<br><br>What do you see as your role in planning with members, checking with them about how well the plan is working, and making revisions in plans as needed?<br><br>How can you use the group process in helping members make and follow through with their commitments?<br><br>What will do you if members do not follow through with a plan?<br><br>How will you get members to be more involved with people outside the group? | How might you avoid giving up on certain members, even if they fail to meet their commitments? What might you do with members who do not seem willing to carry out short-range plans?<br><br>What are some ways to use the group sessions to help members practice new behaviors that they will try out in daily situations? What methods might you employ to encourage members to practice outside the group what they are learning in the session?<br><br>What are some ways to help members express and explore their fears of failing? How can you reinforce success and small gains? Can you think of ways to encourage members to take action even though they feel defeated?<br><br>What follow-up procedures might you use to assess the extent to which members make and maintain positive changes after a group?<br><br>What are some specific ways you can evaluate your groups after termination? |

Reactions: Summarize your reactions to the reality therapy perspective on group developmental stages. What do you like *most? Least?* What aspects of this approach would you incorporate in your style of leadership?

apply choice theory to help you get what you want and to gain more effective control of your own life. Some of the following exercises, activities, and questions can be used on your own, and others can be used in small groups. After you have worked with this material and answered the questions, you will be in a better position to know which of these ideas you might want to employ in the groups you lead or will lead.

## Exercises

1. *Are you meeting your needs?* Choice theory holds that total behavior is purposeful, that it originates from within the individual rather than from external sources, and that psychological needs are powerful motivating forces. Choice theory also contends that we develop pictures in our head (an inner picture album) of specific wants. Our inner pictures make up our ideal world, or the way we want life to be. We are motivated to mold the external world to match our ever-changing inner world. Discuss the ways in which your needs are being met, as well as how you see them influencing your daily behavior. Arrange the following five needs in the order of priority to you. As you review these needs, attempt to identify what you consider to be your key strengths.

   a. *Survival.* To what degree are you maintaining vitality and good health rather than merely surviving?

   b. *Love and Belonging.* What do you do to meet your needs for involvement with others? In what ways do you feel a sense of belonging?

   c. *Power.* When do you feel a sense of power? In what areas of your life do you feel most competent? When do you feel recognized?

   d. *Freedom.* To what degree do you feel that you are in charge of your life and are moving in the direction that you want?

   e. *Fun.* What activities do you do for fun? Do you have as much fun as you would like?

2. *Choosing your total behavior.* Choice theory is based on the assumption that we choose our total behavior, which is composed of the interrelated elements of doing, thinking, feeling, and physiology. In our attempt to gain more effective control, we behave in the world to get the picture we want at that time. Every total behavior is our best attempt to get what we want. Considering this set of basic assumptions, discuss the following questions as they apply to you in your group.

   a. What experiences have you had that either support or discredit the notion that you have an almost complete ability to change what you are doing and some ability to change what you are thinking? Do you find it is easier to change what you are doing and thinking rather than what you are feeling?

   b. To what extent do you find that when you begin to act differently you also change what you are thinking and feeling? Can you provide any personal examples?

   c. Glasser contends that it is inaccurate to speak of being depressed, having a headache, or being anxious. Instead, he says that these are action states that we are choosing. Thus, it is more accurate to say that we are "depressing," "headaching," or "anxietying." In your group, provide examples of states over which you think you have some control. Are you willing to assume responsibility for these states? Or do you think that some of your behaviors (or actions, thoughts, feelings, physiology) are beyond your control?

3. *Effective and ineffective control.* How does what you say about yourself affect the way people view and treat you? Answer these questions about how you perceive yourself.

    a. To what self-fulfilling prophecies do you subject yourself?

    b. If your parents were to describe you in terms of the degree of your success, what might they say about you? What do you imagine your best friend would say? If you are in a group now, how do you think other members might perceive you?

    c. Is there a difference between the way you see yourself now and the way you'd like to be? If so, what changes would you like to make? In what ways do you restrict your possibilities by rigidly adhering to fixed notions that do not allow for change? Do you tell yourself that you can't be other than you are—that you can't change?

    d. What would you say about your current ability to control your life?

4. *Involvement.* Reality therapy stresses the importance of involvement (or a spirit of caring) as the foundation for the group process. Ask yourself these questions:

    a. If you are in a group now, to what degree do you experience a sense of involvement with the leader and the other members?

    b. Do you think the group leader should become involved with the participants? Why or why not? How would you involve yourself in your groups? With what clients would you most easily become involved? With what people would it be difficult for you to become involved?

5. *Applying WDEP to the cycle of counseling.* (Refer to the chart on the cycle in this chapter.) The cycle of counseling involves both the counseling environment and procedures; see if you can answer these basic questions.

    a. W = Explore your wants, needs, and perceptions. What is it that you want? If you had what you wanted now, how would your life be different?

    b. D = Explore the direction in which your total behavior is moving you. What are you currently doing, and is it working for you?

    c. E = It is essential to make a self-evaluation. What changes are you willing to make in your life?

    d. P = Make plans designed to change the direction of your life. It is essential that there be a commitment to the plan. What are you willing to commit to changing?

6. *Self-evaluation.* A central procedure in reality therapy consists of asking members to assess what they are doing to determine if they are getting what they want and whether their behavior is working for them. Spend some time thinking about how making an evaluation of your behavior could benefit you.

    a. As you review your behavior on a given day, what would you most want to change about yourself? Are there any specific actions or thoughts that you would like to change because they are not working for you? To what degree do you think you are getting what you want? What are you willing to do to make the changes you want? Are you committed to taking action to change?

    b. What are some values that are important to you? What difficulties do you think you may have in allowing the members in your groups to make their own evaluations?

7. *Developing a plan for change.* Think about what you would do in each of these situations.

    a. Think about a particular behavior that you want to change and are willing to change. If you are in a group at this time, work out a specific plan that will lead to change. Discuss the details of the plan with those in your group. One of the best ways to understand the process of formulating personal plans is for you to develop such a plan yourself.

    b. What commitments would you, as a leader, expect from those who participate in your groups? What methods would you use to assist them in formulating specific action plans? How do you imagine you'd handle participants who continually made plans but then returned to group without having followed through on most of them?

    c. How would you, as a group member, deal with other members who talked about wanting to change but refused to make any concrete plans to put into action outside the group?

8. *Role-playing activity with involuntary group members.* In your class or group, discuss some reality therapy strategies you might use if you were leading or co-leading an involuntary group. After this discussion, each member can assume the identity of an involuntary client and then role-play this person in your group. Two students can function as co-leaders and demonstrate ways of working with such a client. Attempt to keep within the reality therapy perspective. Allow enough time before the end of the session for processing. What was it like to lead this group by staying within the parameters of this approach? What was the experience like for those who role-played an involuntary client?

9. *Role-playing activity with a specific value issue.* Think about a specific concern of a group member that might pose difficulties for you as a group leader. Identify a particular value conflict a member is experiencing that you think would be challenging for you. Here are some issues members are likely to present:

    a. The client is an adolescent girl who is struggling with whether to have an abortion.

    b. The client is having difficulty accepting the religion with which he was brought up, yet he hesitates to leave the religion because of his fears and guilt feelings.

    c. The client discloses that he is having an affair and is not certain whether he wants to remain married and keep the affair going or leave his wife for the other woman.

    d. The client is a member of an ethnic group that values loyalty to one's family. This woman is contemplating leaving her husband because of her dissatisfaction with what she refers to as a "dead-end relationship." What mainly stops her are the "internal voices" that remind her that she would bring shame to her entire family if she were to divorce.

10. *Ideas for small group discussion.* Consider the strengths of reality therapy as it pertains to working with culturally diverse client populations. Apply the WDEP system to group work from a diversity perspective. In your groups, also consider other factors that could be strengths of reality therapy with multicultural populations such as your active role as a leader who teaches and provides structure, the emphasis on making plans for change, the emphasis on belonging, and the value of self-evaluation. Can you think of any potential disadvantages or cautions in applying reality therapy with diverse client populations?

11. *Small group discussion exercise.* As a group, develop a brief proposal for using reality therapy as the basic format for a counseling group with either elementary school children or high school adolescents. In designing your group, consider these guidelines:

    a. The group will deal primarily with present concerns of the members.

    b. The group leader teaches the members how to evaluate the direction their behavior is taking them to determine what changes, if any, they are willing to make.

    c. The group leader strives to get involved in an active and personal way with the members.

    d. The interventions are mainly directed at what members are doing and thinking.

    e. Group members spend time exploring the degree to which their basic needs of survival, love and belonging, power, freedom, and fun are being met.

    f. The group leader raises helpful questions at the beginning of a group.

    g. The emphasis is on the quality worlds of the members.

h. The group would involve considerable teaching and developing homework to carry outside of the group.

i. Considerable emphasis is given to assisting each member in developing a concrete and realistic plan of action to bring about change.

12. *Role-playing activity for a particular age group.* You can do this activity in your group or in a small group within the larger class. Pick a member age group, and think of a particular focus. For example, you might have a group for children who are coping with divorce, a group for adolescents who want to explore social and personal problems, or a group for elderly clients who are in a day-care facility. Each person role-plays a particular individual in the chosen group. Identify a concern for which you think you have empathy and with which you could get involved through role playing. Two students can volunteer to be the co-leaders. Apply what you know of choice theory and the interventions made in reality therapy to leading this group. After the session, discuss the possible advantages and disadvantages of working with this type of group with this approach.

## Questions for Reflection and Discussion

1. Choice theory is based on the premise that we can control what we do and think: If we change what we are doing and thinking, it is highly likely that we will also change how we are feeling. Do you agree with this assumption? What are the implications of this viewpoint in working with clients who suffer from depression? How does this assumption fit for you personally?

2. Choice theory assumes that everything we do, think, and feel is generated by what happens inside of us. Thus, the proper focus for therapy is not to discuss the external world but to deal with the internal world of the client. What are the implications of this perspective for your group practice? How would this view influence your interventions in a group?

3. In many respects, reality therapy is at the opposite end of the therapeutic spectrum from psychoanalytic therapy. What contrasts do you see between these two models? Do you agree or disagree with Glasser's objections to the psychoanalytic perspective?

4. What are some of the unique advantages of practicing reality therapy in groups as opposed to individual counseling? How can others in the group help a member make a behavioral evaluation, form a realistic plan, and commit to an action program?

5. Compare and contrast reality therapy with the experiential therapies (person-centered therapy, Gestalt therapy, psychodrama, and the existential therapies). To what extent do you think reality therapy incorporates or fails to incorporate elements of these approaches? How might you blend reality therapy with the experiential therapies in your groups?

6. Some of the more cognitively oriented therapies (TA, rational emotive behavior therapy, and other cognitive behavioral therapies) emphasize the role of one's thoughts, values, beliefs, and attitudes as crucial determinants of behavior. Reality therapy focuses mainly on actions. How would you blend reality therapy's emphasis on acting with the emphasis of the cognitive therapies on thinking? What kinds of interventions could you devise that would make use of both cognitive and behavioral dimensions? How might you incorporate interventions aimed mainly at exploration of feelings with this cognitive behavioral emphasis?

7. What are your reactions to those who criticize reality therapy on the ground that it is simplistic? To what extent do you agree with the reality therapist's contention that the

procedures are simple to discuss but that putting them into practice requires considerable therapeutic skill and creativity?

8. Reality therapy requires members to make an honest assessment of their current behavior to determine whether it is working for them. In considering some of the groups that you want to organize, what problems might you anticipate with respect to actually getting members to make such a self-evaluation?

9. What are a few key concepts of choice theory that have the greatest applicability in working with cultural diversity within your groups? What reality therapy techniques might you most draw from as a way to work within the framework of the diverse cultural backgrounds of the members of your groups?

10. What are some of the specific concepts of choice theory that have relevance for group work with children and adolescents? How might you modify some of the techniques of reality therapy in working with children and adolescents in groups? What particular value do you see in using a reality therapy framework in devising groups in the school setting?

## Quiz on Reality Therapy: A Comprehension Check          Score _____%

*Note:* Please refer to Appendix I for the scoring key. Count 5 points for each error, and subtract the total from 100 to get your percentage score.

*True/false items:* Decide if the following statements are "more true" or "more false" as they apply to reality therapy.

T   F   1. Reality therapy emphasizes an inner self-evaluation.

T   F   2. Reality therapy is basically an active, directive, didactic model.

T   F   3. In many ways, Glasser's approach is grounded on phenomenological and existential premises.

T   F   4. The essence of choice theory is that we are determined by events during our early childhood.

T   F   5. Reality therapists would probably encourage their clients to get into contact with their buried feelings before they would expect them to change their behavior.

T   F   6. One of the main functions of the group leader is to make an evaluation of each member's current behavior.

T   F   7. Reality therapy emphasizes discussion of feelings and attitudes, for the assumption is that behavior will not change unless attitudes change first.

T   F   8. Reality therapy in groups is well suited to adolescents.

T   F   9. Punishment is an effective way to pressure participants to meet their contracts and to change.

T   F  10. Group members are expected to make plans for change and also to commit to these plans.

*Multiple-choice items:* Select the *one best answer* among the alternatives given. Consider each question within the framework of reality therapy.

_____11. Reality therapy rests on the central idea that

    a. we need insight into the cause of our problems if we hope to change.

    b. we choose our behavior and are responsible for what we do, think, and feel.

    c. environmental factors largely control what we are doing.

    d. the way to change dysfunctional behavior is to reexperience a situation in which we originally became psychologically stuck.

    e. our family of origin sets our patterns for interacting with others.

_____12. With which one of the following conclusions would Glasser disagree?

    a. We are most likely to change if we are threatened by punishment.

    b. We do not have to be the victim of our past.

    c. We have more control over our life than we believe.

    d. We strive to change the world outside of us to match our internal pictures of what we want.

    e. We strive to gain more effective control of our life to fulfill our needs.

_____13. The core of reality therapy consists of

    a. teaching clients how to acquire rational beliefs instead of irrational ones.

    b. helping clients understand their unconscious dynamics.

    c. giving clients opportunities to express unresolved feelings.

    d. teaching clients to take effective control of their own life.

    e. identifying clients' cognitive distortions by means of a Socratic dialogue.

_____14. Glasser identifies four psychological needs (plus survival), which are the forces that drive us. Which of the following is *not* one of those needs?

    a. transcendence

    b. belonging

    c. power

    d. freedom

    e. fun

_____15. All of the following are basic concepts of reality therapy except for

    a. total behavior.

    b. musturbatory beliefs.

    c. quality world.

    d. self-evaluation.

    e. planning and action.

_____16. All of the following procedures are commonly used by reality therapy except for

    a. exploring wants, needs, and perceptions.

    b. exploring parental messages and early decisions.

    c. focusing on current behavior.

    d. planning and commitment.

    e. engaging in self-evaluation.

_____17. Which of the following is *not* emphasized in reality therapy?

    a. focus on what one is doing

    b. a time-limited focus

    c. exploration of how basic needs are being met

    d. a focus on understanding the origin of a client's problem

_____18. Another term for one's "quality world" is

    a. a basic psychological life position.

    b. personal life script.

    c. fictional finalism.

    d. inner picture album.

_____19. What is Glasser's thinking about depression?
   a. We depress or anger ourselves, rather than being depressed.
   b. Depression is due to unresolved childhood issues.
   c. The more effective way to treat depression is with the use of drugs and medication.
   d. Depression is best understood as anger turned inward.

_____20. Choice theory tends to focus on
   a. feeling and physiology.
   b. doing and thinking.
   c. coming to a fuller understanding of the past.
   d. the underlying causes for feelings of depression or anxiousness.
   e. how the family system controls our decisions.

# CHAPTER SIXTEEN

# Solution-Focused Brief Therapy in Groups

## Prechapter Self-Inventory for Solution-Focused Brief Therapy

*Directions:* Refer to page 57 for general directions. Indicate your position on these statements using the following code:

**5** = I *strongly agree* with this statement.
**4** = I *agree,* in most respects, with this statement.
**3** = I am *undecided* in my opinion about this statement.
**2** = I *disagree,* in most respects, with this statement.
**1** = I *strongly disagree* with this statement.

_____ 1. It is the therapist's role to create opportunities for the members to view themselves as being resourceful.

_____ 2. The leader has the task of moving the group from a problem focus to a solution focus, or to keep the group members on a solution track instead of a problem track.

_____ 3. If members concentrate on telling problem-saturated stories, they tend to keep themselves from moving in a positive direction.

_____ 4. A key goal is to create a group context in which the members are able to learn more about their personal abilities and then learn to solve their concerns on their own.

_____ 5. A task for group leaders is to engage in conversations with their clients about what is going well, about future possibilities, and exploring what will likely lead to a sense of accomplishment.

_____ 6. People tend to respond better to a present and future approach to counseling than they do to a past orientation that dwells on why they have certain problems that they cannot solve.

_____ 7. Small changes are crucial in the process of change.

_____ 8. Asking group members to consider that a miracle takes place opens up a range of future possibilities.

_____ 9. The group counselor supplies the optimism, but the group members generate what is possible and contribute the movement that actualizes it.

_____10. Because success tends to build upon itself, modest goals are viewed as the beginning of change.

| Dimension | Initial Stage | Working Stage | Final Stage |
|---|---|---|---|
| Key developmental tasks and goals | First task is to set the mood for focusing on solutions from the beginning. Members are given an opportunity to describe their problems briefly. Leader helps members to keep the problem external in conversations, which tends to be a relief to members because it gives them an opportunity to see themselves as less problem-saturated. | Rather than engage in detailed accounts of their problems, members have the task of shifting from a fixed problem state to a world with new possibilities that lead to creative solutions. Members can become blocked when they focus on past or present problems rather than on future solutions. People tend to respond better to a present and future approach to counseling than they do to a past orientation. | Specific plans for achieving personal goals need to be established. Members devote time in the group to talk about what they learned that they could transfer to their everyday living. |
| Role and tasks of group leader | Leader works with members in developing well-formed goals as soon as possible. Questions that might be posed are: "What will be different in your life when your problems are solved?" "What will be going on in the future that will tell you and the rest of us in the group that things are better for you?" | Leaders give primary attention to creating collaborative relationships with members because of their belief that doing so opens up a range of possibilities for present and future change. One way of creating an effective therapeutic partnership is for the facilitator to show the members how they can use the strengths they already have. | The group leader assists group members in monitoring their progress and eventually determining when they have accomplished their personal goals. Prior to ending a group experience, leaders assist members in identifying things they can do to continue the changes they have already made into the future. |
| Role of group members | Members are asked about those times when their problems were not present or when the problems were less pressing. Members explore these exceptions and talk about what they did to make these events happen. Members engage in identifying exceptions with each other. This improves the group process and promotes a solution focus rather than problem focus. Members discuss what they need to do before they see their problem as being solved and what will be their next step. | Members look for what is working in their lives, rather than talking about what cannot be changed. By zeroing in on those aspects that are working, members are able to apply this knowledge to effectively address their concerns in the shortest time possible.

The leader tries to shift the responsibility of the group dynamic toward group members noticing exceptions about each other. This allows the group leader to be assisted by members who function as co-facilitators who support and encourage each other and who also keep the focus on exceptions rather than problems. | Members design an action plan aimed at change. As a result of the group experience, the members have identified many of their competencies that they can bring to bear in attaining their plans for change. |

| | | | |
|---|---|---|---|
| Techniques | Some questions asked by SFBT group leaders during the initial stage might include:<br><br>• If a miracle happened and the problem you have was solved overnight, how would you know it was solved, *and what would be different?*<br><br>• Let yourself imagine that you leave the group today and that you are on track to acting more confidently and securely. What will you be *doing* differently?<br><br>• Talk about the times before a problem started to interfere with your lives. What were you doing at these times to keep the problem at bay?<br><br>• In the future when the problems that brought you to this group are less pressing, what will you be doing? | Leaders ask members to observe their behavior and to note any changes in feelings, moods, actions, or communication. By use of the scaling technique, members rate on a scale of zero to ten the degree to which they show improvement on specific dimensions. Scaling questions enable clients to pay closer attention to what they are doing and how they can take steps that will lead to the changes they desire. | Clients are encouraged to experiment with patterns that have a better chance of working. Leaders typically allow time in each group session for sharing feedback with one another. This kind of summary feedback assists members in carrying their learning outside of the group sessions into daily living. Members are invited to give one another feedback and identify the changes they have observed in each other over the course of the entire group. |
| Questions to consider | If members seem reluctant to talk about the times when their problems did not exist, and instead insisted on talking about their problems, what might you do?<br><br>How will you help members identify their strengths and search for possibilities?<br><br>How would you help members establish clear goals at the first session? Would you focus primarily on what members are doing? How much might you attend to feelings that members might bring up?<br><br>If members wanted to talk about the past, would you allow this? How might you re-direct the focus to present and future behavior? | Members are encouraged to engage in change—or solution-talk rather than problem-talk. The miracle question is a goal-setting technique that is useful when a member has no clue of what a miracle might look like. Leaders might ask other group members to brainstorm with the disillusioned member about what they think his or her miracle might look like. This sparks creative conversations and can create cohesion in the group. How can you get members to focus on possibilities and solutions, especially if they come to the group with the expectation of talking about their problems and finding answers to what troubles them? | What are some ways to use the group sessions to help members practice new behaviors that they will try out in daily situations? What methods might you employ to encourage members to practice outside the group what they are learning in the session?<br><br>How can you reinforce success and small gains? Can you think of ways to encourage members to take action even though they feel defeated?<br><br>What follow-up procedures might you use to assess the extent to which members make and maintain positive changes after a group? |

Reactions: Summarize your reactions to the solution-focused brief therapy perspective on group developmental stages. What do you like *most? Least?* What aspects of this approach would you incorporate in your style of leadership?

## Summary of Basic Assumptions and Key Concepts of the Solution-Focused Approach to Groups

1. SFBT is centered primarily on solutions, rather than an exploration of problems. There is very little interest in identifying and exploring the causes of a problem, and not much time is spent on taking a family history, or looking at past influences. The proper focus of therapy is almost exclusively centered on the present and future.

2. There are advantages to a positive focus on solutions and on the future. By concentrating on successes, beneficial changes are likely to occur.

3. There are advantages to keeping therapy simple and brief.

4. Participants in a counseling group have the capability of behaving effectively, even though this effectiveness may be temporarily blocked by negative cognitions. Problem-focused thinking prevents people from recognizing effective ways they have dealt with problems. There is a movement from problem-talk to solution-talk.

5. No problem happens all of the time. There are always exceptions to a problem situation, and these exceptions are important to discuss. By talking about these exceptions, members can get control over what had seemed to be an insurmountable problem. The climate of these exceptions allows for the possibility of creating solutions.

6. Small changes pave the way for larger changes. Once a change has been made, it will lead to other small changes. Any problem is solved one step at a time.

7. Group members can be trusted in their intention to solve their problems. There are no universal solutions to specific problems that can be applied to all people. Each individual is unique and so, too, is each solution.

8. Some of the major tenets of SFBT are: (a) If it ain't broke, don't fix it. (b) If it works, do more of it. (c) If it's not working, do something different.

9. Little attention is paid to pathology or to giving clients a diagnostic label. People are not viewed as being locked into a set of behaviors based on a history or a psychological diagnosis.

10. The solution-focused model emphasizes the role of group members establishing their own goals and preferences. This is done when a climate of mutual respect, dialogue, inquiry, and affirmation are a part of the group process.

11. The future is a hopeful place, and people are the architects of their own destiny. Group leaders strive to establish collaborative relationships with members, which they do by showing members how they can use the strengths and resources they already possess to construct solutions.

12. Interventions in a group are based on the assumption that people are competent, and that given a climate where they can experience their competency, they are able to solve their own problems.

13. Solution-focused therapists adopt a "not knowing" position, or a non-expert stance, as a way to put clients into the position of being the experts about their own lives. The therapist-as-expert is replaced by the client-as-expert. Therapists do not assume that they know more about the lives of clients than clients do.

## Glossary of Key Terms for Solution-Focused Brief Therapy

**Solution-focused brief therapy (SFBT)**  An approach to therapy that emphasizes helping clients find solutions rather than talking about problems. This is a future-focused, goal-oriented therapeutic approach.

**A not-knowing position** This implies that group counselors allow themselves to enter the conversation with curiosity and with an intense interest in discovery, rather than have a preconceived idea about the client.

**Questions of difference** These are questions that open up space in relationships for thinking about and understanding self and others in a new way.

**Pre-therapy change** This addresses any changes made before the initial session and is often framed by the question, "What changes have you noticed that have happened since you decided to come to this first group session?"

**Exception questions** This is a solution-focused technique of directing clients' attention to times when the problems did not occur as a way to help clients build on successful problem-solving skills.

**Miracle question** A solution-focused technique of asking clients to imagine how life would be different if they were to wake up tomorrow and no longer have a particular problem. The way this might be presented is: "If a miracle happened and the problem you have was solved overnight, how would you know it was solved, and what would be the signs that something was different?"

**Scaling questions** A technique of asking clients to rate a behavior or feeling on a scale of zero to 10 to determine changes.

**Formula first session task (FFST)** This is a form of homework a group leader might give members to complete between their first and second sessions.

## Exercises and Activities for the Solution-Focused Approach to Groups
### Rationale

Techniques in the solution-focused approach are geared to assisting clients in discovering their internal resources and competencies. There are a number of solution-focused brief therapy techniques that are frequently used: pre-therapy change, exception questions, the miracle question, scaling questions, formula first session task, homework, and summary feedback. See how some of these methods fit for you, both personally and as a group leader.

The following activities and exercises are designed to help you experience the process of applying some concepts and techniques of a solution-focused group, both as a member and as a leader. As you work through these exercises on your own, with another person, and with a small group, think about ways in which you, as a group leader, could incorporate them in your group practice.

### Exercises

1. *Pre-therapy change.* Solution-focused brief therapists often ask clients at the first session, "What have you done since you called for an appointment that has made a difference in your problem?" Asking about pre-therapy change tends to encourage clients to rely less on the therapist and more on their own resources to reach their goals. These changes cannot be attributed to the therapy process itself, so asking members about these changes encourages them to rely less on the leader and more on their own resources to accomplish their goals.

   a. Think of yourself as a member of a group. How might you address this pre-therapy change question? What value would you find in this kind of question?

b. Now, think of yourself as a facilitator of a solution-focused group. What uses might you make of asking members what they had already done since they first decided to join the group? What are some other ways that you can think of to encourage members to begin to identify the strengths they already have?

2. *Exception questions*. These questions direct clients to those times in their lives when their problems did not exist. Exploring exceptions offers group members opportunities for evoking resources, engaging strengths, and creating possible solutions. The following are examples of questions looking for exceptions: When was the last time that things were better? Talk about times when things were going well for you? What were you doing then? What are some things that you have done that help with your problem? How will you know when you are handling your problem well?

a. Put yourself in the place of a group member. Identify one problem that you would want to explore in a group. Can you think of any time in your life when you did not have the problem? What was different then? What might you do to use your resources more fully to create solutions? Explore ways that such questions could suggest multiple answers and encourage members to think of what they could do to create a different future. Do you find any personal value in thinking about this kind of question?

b. Thinking of yourself as a group leader, what advantages can you see of asking members to come up with exceptions to their problems? Can you think of ways you might be able to focus members on exceptions to their problems in your groups during the initial sessions?

3. *The miracle question*. Members can be asked: "If you were to wake up tomorrow and you no longer had your problem, how would your life be different?" Allowing group members to describe themselves without their problem involves a future focus that encourages group members to consider a different kind of life than one dominated by a particular problem. This question focuses clients on searching for solutions. Members can also be asked questions such as: How will you know when things are better? What will be some of the things you will notice when life is better?

a. From the vantage point of you being a group member, how would you answer this question: If a miracle were to happen and the problem you have was solved overnight, how would you know that your problem had been solved and what would be different? What process did you go through in imagining that a particular problem of yours would be gone?

b. As a group leader, what are some ways that you could introduce the miracle question? When would you want to do this in a group? What would you most be hoping to accomplish? Explore ways that you could use the miracle question as a strategy to help members formulate specific goals they could pursue in a group?

4. *Scaling questions*. This technique asks clients to observe changes in feelings, moods, thoughts, and behaviors. On a scale of zero to 10, clients are asked to rate some change in their experiences. Scaling questions enable clients to see progress being made in specific steps and degrees.

a. Think of as many uses as you can of the scaling technique. How might you use this in your personal life? When might you want to introduce a scaling question to members of your group?

b. What are some specific values you can think of in asking members to rate changes in their experiences, both in and out of the group?

5. *Homework.* A basic part of a solution-focused group involves often asking clients to observe events that they would like to see occur more frequently in the future. They can also practice some form of new behavior outside of the group and then report on changes or improvements at the next session.

   a. As a group member, what kind of homework is most meaningful to you? What motivates you to complete homework? Do you operate best when homework is assigned to you or when you devise your own homework?

   b. Think of yourself as leading a group. How would you introduce homework to members in your sessions? Would you be inclined to suggest homework to individual members? Would you ask members to suggest homework to each other? Would you expect members to design their own tasks to complete both in the sessions and outside the group? What are your thoughts about accountability for homework assignments? How might doing tasks outside of the group assist members in accomplishing their goals?

6. *Summary feedback.* Both group leaders and members may provide summary feedback in the form of genuine affirmations or pointing out particular strengths that certain members have demonstrated. Solution-focused practitioners typically allow time in each group meeting for sharing feedback with one another.

   a. What kind of feedback have you found helpful in the groups in which you were a member? What increases your chances of considering feedback from other members or the leader in a nondefensive manner?

   b. As a leader, how might you structure a session so that useful feedback can be shared? Do you see possible ways to combine feedback with suggesting tasks for members to complete as homework? What value do you see in arranging for feedback for each group session?

7. *Being a group member.* What do you imagine it would be like for you to be a member of a solution-focused group? What issues do you think you'd want to pursue in such a group? What kind of member do you think you'd be in such a group?

8. *Role of group leader.* Review the section in the textbook on the role of the solution-focused group leader. Solution-focused group counselors adopt a "not knowing" position as a route to putting group members into the position of being the experts about their own lives. In this approach, the therapist-as-expert is replaced by the client-as-expert. What would it be like for you to work within the framework of this model? Could you function within this model if it were your primary orientation? Why or why not?

9. *Personal evaluation and critique.* In your group or class, discuss the concepts of the solution-focused approach to group work that you find most valuable. Consider some of these questions in your discussion:

   a. What key themes or concepts would you take from this approach and apply to groups you lead?

   b. What are the limitations of the approach? What disadvantages do you see in limiting yourself strictly to a solution-focused orientation?

   c. Do you think solution-focused brief therapy has something to offer every client in a group? For what people do you think it is the most appropriate? What clients might have difficulty with this perspective?

   d. What do you see as both the strengths and limitations of the solution-focused approach in working with groups composed of culturally diverse populations? What are some ways that you could apply the notion that people are creative, resourceful, and competent with certain cultural backgrounds of members?

   e. How are you able to relate in a personal way to the solution-focused approach? What ways can you understand yourself better by reflecting on the exceptions to your problems and the times when your problems did not get the best of you? How is your self-understanding related to your ability to encourage group members to explore their own resources for creating solutions in their personal lives?

   f. In what kind of group(s) (therapy group, psychoeducation group, counseling group, support group) do you think solution-focused notions best have a place?

   g. With what age populations and client populations might SFBT best fit? Can you think of ways to apply SFBT ideas and methods in group work with children and adolescents? What value do you see in using a solution-focused framework in designing groups in a school setting?

10. *Small group discussion exercise.* As a group, develop a brief proposal for using solution-focused brief therapy as the basic format for a counseling group with either elementary school children or high school adolescents. In designing your group, consider these guidelines:

   a. The group will deal primarily with present and future concerns of the members.

   b. The group leader teaches the members how to think in terms of exceptions to their problems.

   c. The group leader strives to get involved in an active and personal way with the members and also attempts to create collaborative relationships with members.

   d. Group members spend time exploring exceptions to problems they bring to group.

   e. The group leader raises helpful questions at the beginning of a group to assist members in thinking what they did that was different.

   f. Members are given summary feedback and some homework tasks at the end of each session.

11. *Integrating solution-focused therapy with the practice of reality therapy.* In small groups, discuss some ways that you could integrate some of the basic ideas of solution-focused therapy with reality therapy, which you studied in the previous chapter. Consider the possibilities of blending concepts and techniques such as these that are common to both approaches:

   a. Deemphasis on the past, and focus on the present and the future

   b. A time-limited framework that stresses results

   c. Emphasis on members making choices about the personal goals they wish to pursue

   d. Creating an optimistic attitude of change being possible

   e. The effective use of questioning

## Questions for Reflection and Discussion

1. Solution-focused brief therapy eschews the past in favor of both the present and the future. What implications does this time perspective have for you as a group leader? What are your thoughts about getting group members to work toward present and future solutions?

2. Solution-focused brief therapists strive to get their clients away from talking about their problems, and instead, talking about solutions. What do you think of this orientation toward solutions? How would you deal with members who insisted that they wanted to talk about

the problems that brought them to your group? How natural might it be for you to focus on constructing solutions with group members rather than resolving problems?

3. What are your thoughts about the value of keeping therapy brief? How do you think that SFBT contributes to limiting the time frame of a group? With what kinds of groups do you think a brief orientation is most called for? Can you think of groups that you might lead for which a brief approach would not be appropriate?

4. What thoughts do you have about the value of asking group members to talk about the exceptions to their problems and to adopt a positive focus on what they are doing that is working in their lives? If you build your group on the notion of helping members recognize their strengths and resources, what implications does this have for the way you would work with members of your groups?

5. Solution-focused practitioners often ask clients the miracle question. What value do you see in asking group members to imagine their problems would vanish one night when they were asleep? How does the miracle question enable members to create solutions? What are some specific ways that you might make therapeutic use of how they respond to this question? What ways can you think of to use the miracle question as a way of promoting interpersonal interaction within the group?

6. Solution-focused group leaders are concerned with establishing collaborative relationships with the members of their groups. As a group leader, what kind of collaborative partnership would you want to form with your clients?

7. The solution-focused group leader replaces the therapist-as-expert with the client-as-expert. These practitioners play down the role of expert, preferring a more collaborative stance. To what degree is this a stance that you are ready to assume? If you were to assume the stance that clients are the experts in their own lives, how would this influence your way of facilitating a group?

8. Compare and contrast solution-focused brief therapy with the experiential therapies (person-centered therapy, Gestalt therapy, psychodrama, and the existential therapies). To what extent does SFBT incorporate or fail to incorporate elements of these approaches? How would you blend solution-focused therapy with the experiential therapies in your groups?

9. Some are critical of SFBT because it is a simple framework and might be overly optimistic by quickly focusing on solutions. What are your thoughts about this criticism? What limitations do you see in this approach?

10. What are a few concepts or techniques of the solution-focused approach that you think have the greatest applicability in working with cultural diversity in your groups? What specific techniques might you be most inclined to draw from as a way to work within the framework of the diverse cultural backgrounds of the members of your groups?

## Quiz on Solution-Focused Brief Therapy: A Comprehension Check

Score ____%

*Note:* Please refer to Appendix I for the scoring key. Count 5 points for each error, and subtract the total from 100 to get your percentage score.

*True/false items:* Decide if the following statements are "more true" or "more false" as they apply to solution-focused brief therapy.

T   F   1.  Solution-focused brief therapy is both future-oriented and goal-oriented.

T   F   2.  In SFBT the therapist-as-expert is replaced by the client-as-expert.

T   F   3.  A main therapeutic task is to help clients imagine how they would like things to be different and what it will take to bring about these changes.

T   F   4.  This approach is based on the assumption that talking about problems will be the path to resolving them.

T   F   5.  Behavioral tasks and homework are a basic part of this therapy approach.

T   F   6.  Solution-focused therapists generally avoid asking questions, since doing so is viewed as being confrontational.

T   F   7.  An assumption of this approach is that the future is both created and negotiable.

T   F   8.  This approach is based on giving clients an accurate diagnosis so that a treatment plan can be designed based on solutions.

T   F   9.  Members of a solution-focused group are expected to gain insight if they hope to solve their problems.

T   F   10. Solution-focused therapy does not work very well with children and adolescents in school settings.

*Multiple-choice items:* Select the *one best answer* among the alternatives given. Consider each question within the framework of solution-focused brief therapy.

_____11.  Solution-focused brief therapy rests on the central idea that

a. we need insight into the cause of our problems if we hope to change.

b. we need to explore our past to create a better future.

c. clients are competent and a therapist's role is to help them recognize the competencies they already possess.

d. the way to change dysfunctional behavior is to reexperience a situation in which we originally became psychologically stuck.

e. our family of origin experiences determine our present way of interacting with others.

_____12.  With which one of the following conclusions would a solution-focused therapist disagree?

a. People are resilient, resourceful, and competent.

b. We do not have to be the victim of our past.

c. Clients choose the goals they wish to accomplish, which reduces resistance.

d. It is best to focus on what is not working in a client's life so that the therapist can provide suggestions on more effective ways of behaving.

e. Clients can build solutions to their problems without any assessment of the nature of their problems.

_____13.  The core of solution-focused brief therapy consists of

a. teaching clients how to acquire rational beliefs instead of irrational ones.

b. helping clients understand the unconscious dynamics that block their ability to function effectively in daily life.

c. giving clients opportunities to express unresolved past conflicts.

d. assisting clients in discovering a range of solutions and enabling them to do more of what is working for them.

e. identifying clients' cognitive distortions and teaching clients methods of cognitive disputation.

_____14. The main person who is considered the founder of SFBT is
  a. Bill O'Hanlon.
  b. Steve de Shazer.
  c. Michelle Weiner-Davis.
  d. Linda Metcalf.
  e. John Peller.

_____15. All of the following are basic concepts of solution-focused brief therapy except for
  a. looking for what is not working.
  b. a positive orientation.
  c. focusing on solutions, not problems.
  d. a not-knowing position of the group leader.
  e. creating a therapeutic partnership.

_____16. All of the following are generally steps involved in a solution-focused group except for
  a. the group leader setting the tone for the group.
  b. the facilitator works with members in developing well-defined goals as soon as possible.
  c. members completing a very detailed form that identifies some of their past problems that they think are getting in the way of living effectively.
  d. searching for exceptions to the problem.
  e. the group facilitator assisting the members with task development.

_____17. Which of the following is _not_ emphasized in solution-focused therapy?
  a. a focus on the future
  b. a time-limited focus
  c. a focus more on solutions than on problems
  d. a focus on understanding the origin of a client's problem
  e. identifying small changes

_____18. Which of the following is _not_ a solution-focused technique?
  a. exception questions
  b. miracle questions
  c. scaling questions
  d. exploring with clients how they view the origin of a problem
  e. considering solutions and possibilities

_____19. Solution-focused therapists believe
  a. life is change, and change is inevitable.
  b. their function is to prescribe ways that clients can solve problems.
  c. the past is more important than the future.
  d. understanding the past is essential in working out current problems.
  e. it takes a long time for clients to begin to make substantial changes.

_____20. All of the following are characteristics of SFBT that make it an appropriate approach in working with diverse client populations except for
  a. the emphasis on uncovering and exploring intense emotions.
  b. The not-knowing position frequently assumed by solution-focused practitioners.
  c. the discussion of solutions rather than problems.
  d. the focus on strengths rather than weaknesses.
  e. The brief and structured nature of the therapy.

# PART THREE

# INTEGRATION AND APPLICATION

# CHAPTER SEVENTEEN

# Comparisons, Contrasts, and Integration

## Questions for Discussion and Evaluation

### Perspectives on Goals for Group Counseling

1. How does the theoretical orientation of a group practitioner influence the group's goals and the direction it takes? How can a leader's values and beliefs influence the direction of the group?

2. In view of the many differences among the various theoretical approaches to group therapy, how is a common ground possible among groups with a cognitive behavioral orientation and experientially-oriented groups? How can long-range goals and concrete short-term goals be integrated into group practice?

3. What value would you, as a group leader, place on the freedom of members to select personal goals? How would you strive to develop goals collaboratively with the members of your group? What problems can you foresee if a member's personal goals are not consistent with the purpose of the group?

4. How do a group's goals relate to its type of membership?

5. Consult the overview chart of goals for group counseling (Table 17-1) in the textbook. Decide which approaches come closest to your thinking with respect to goals. Which model(s) do you find least helpful in clarifying your own vision of the purpose of a group? As you review the models, determine which goals you'd choose to incorporate in your own counseling.

## Role and Functions of the Group Leader

1. In the text, review Table 17-2, which summarizes the role and functions of the group leader in the various theoretical approaches. What do you see as your specific role and functions in leading a group? To what degree does your role depend on the stage of development of your group?

2. If your group is culturally diverse, what do you see as your role in encouraging members to explore their feelings about their similarities and differences? What is your role in helping members take their cultural values into account as they explore their concerns and make decisions about their lives?

3. If you were asked in a job interview to briefly describe what you considered to be your central role as a group leader, what would you say?

## The Issue of Structuring and the Division of Responsibility

1. It is clear that a group leader will provide structure for the group. What is not predetermined is the *degree* and *kind* of structure he or she provides. The group could range from being extremely unstructured (the person-centered group) to being highly structured and directive (a rational emotive behavior therapy group). Review Table 17-3 in the textbook on the degree of structuring and division of responsibility. Which theories come closest to your view? Why? What theories do you find the least agreement with? Why? How could you combine some of these different approaches to structuring a group? How can these models stimulate your thinking regarding what type and degree of structuring you want to provide a group? How does structuring relate to the group's stage of development?

2. The division of responsibility, like structuring, can differ widely according to the theoretical approach used in a group. Some therapies place primary responsibility on the leader for the direction and outcome of the group. Other therapies give primary responsibility to the group members and tend to downplay the role of the leader. A number of approaches emphasize collaboration and partnership. What is your position on the matter of division of responsibility?

3. The group leader needs to maintain a balance between taking on too much responsibility for the group and denying any responsibility for its direction. What problems do you foresee for a group if the leader assumes either too much or not enough responsibility?

4. After reviewing Table 17-3, decide what approaches provide you with the most insight on this issue.

## Group Leader's Use of Techniques

1. Review Table 17-4 in the textbook on techniques that flow from each of the theories. Which methods are you most inclined to employ? How would your selection of techniques depend on the kind of group you were leading? How would you adapt your methods to fit the needs of culturally diverse populations? What techniques seem to be most congruent with your personality and leadership style?

2. What kinds of interventions are you most likely to use at each of the stages of a group's development? What techniques are you inclined to use in opening a group session? In closing a group session? In assisting members to evaluate their progress?

3. What is the purpose of techniques in groups? When do techniques most enhance group process? When might the use of interventions interfere with the progress of a group? What are your ideas for evaluating the effectiveness of the techniques you introduce?

## Theories Applied to Multicultural Group Counseling

1. If your groups are culturally diverse, which theoretical approaches would you find most useful in understanding the members? Identify several approaches that provide you with a conceptual framework and methods that would be helpful in addressing the diversity that is likely to characterize your group.

2. What group practices do you think might pose problems for some members because of their cultural background? One example is the expectation that the participants will disclose here-and-now feelings as they emerge within a group. Some people have been

culturally conditioned to hide their feelings and, thus, are likely to have difficulty with self-disclosure. Shame may be associated with showing feelings, especially outside of one's family setting. What help could you provide to those members who have trouble participating in your group because of a conflict between the group norms and their cultural values?

3. What do you consider to be a few of the major limitations of the theories in working with various multicultural populations? Which particular approach do you see as being the most limited in addressing ethnic diversity considerations within a group?

## Toward a Synthesis of Theories Applied to Practice

Review the sections of the chapter in the textbook that deal with developing an *integrative model* of group counseling. Strive to begin developing your own synthesis of theories applied to groups at the various stages of development. I suggest that you use the questions below as the basis for discussion in small groups. With your fellow students, think of ways to develop a conceptual framework that can account for the factors of cognition, emotion, and behavior. Also, focus on various theoretical approaches that you'd probably draw on at each of the stages in the life history of a group. Strive for a blending and an integration of theories that will provide you with a cognitive map to explain what goes on in a group as it evolves.

1. What general *group process goals* would guide your interventions at the initial, transition, working, and final stages of a group? How might the goals for a group differ with respect to the period of development?

2. How would you describe your major *role and functions* at each of the stages of a group? What changes, if any, do you see in your leadership functions at the various phases?

3. What kind of *structuring* do you most want to provide at each of the phases of a group's development? How would you describe the division of responsibility (between you as leader and the members) at each of the stages?

4. In terms of *techniques* in the facilitation of group process at the various phases of development, what possible integration can you come up with? How can you combine theories and techniques to work on the three levels of thinking, feeling, and doing? (For example, can you think of ways to combine experiential techniques with cognitive and behavioral methods? In what ways might you blend Gestalt or psychodramatic methods with REBT or cognitive behavioral techniques?)

5. During the *pregroup stage,* how could you draw on those approaches that stress therapeutic contracts? How might you help members formulate a contract during the screening and orientation interview?

6. During the *initial stage,* what aspects of the relationship-oriented approaches (especially the existential and person-centered approaches) could you use as a basis for building trust among the members and between yourself and the members? How might you look to the cognitive behavioral approaches in assisting members to develop specific personal goals? How can you apply solution-focused brief therapy to the tasks of the initial stage?

7. During the *transition stage,* how might you understand resistance from a psychoanalytic and an Adlerian perspective? How do solution-focused therapists typically view resistance? How could you work with resistance by using the group as a way to re-create the members' original family? Can you think of theories you could draw on to help you work with members from a thinking, feeling, and behaving perspective when a group is in transition?

8. During the *working stage,* what integration of theoretical perspectives will allow you to consider the thinking, feeling, and behaving dimensions? How much emphasis would you be inclined to place on the expression of emotion? How much focus would you place on what members are thinking and how their cognitions influence their behavior? What are some examples of techniques you'd employ to work on a behavioral level? Can you think of ways in which you might use role playing, behavior rehearsal, and feedback? What ways can you think of to promote interaction among the members? How could you link the work of several members? What are some ways to develop themes in a group that many members are able to work with at the same time? What ways might you use to promote an interpersonal focus in your groups?

9. During the *final stage,* how could you borrow strategies from the cognitive behavioral therapies to help members consolidate their learning and apply it to life outside of the group? What are some ways in which you might help members practice new learning? What are some ways of teaching members how to create support systems once they leave a group?

10. At the *postgroup stage,* how could you apply cognitive behavioral strategies for accountability and evaluation purposes? What specific follow-up procedures would you want to use for the groups you lead?

---

*Note:* Now that you have addressed these questions, attempt to develop your own questions on the applications of theory to group practice and look toward your own personal synthesis. Explain how you see groups from a developmental perspective, giving emphasis to those theories that most help you understand how groups function.

---

# CHAPTER EIGHTEEN

# The Evolution of a Group: An Integrative Perspective

## Synopsis of a Group in Action: Evolution of a Group

A DVD and Workbook for *Groups in Action: Evolution and Challenges,* is available from the publishers of this textbook and student manual. The DVD program is accompanied by a workbook that illustrates the therapeutic interventions used in the group. The first program (Evolution of a Group) is based on a three-day weekend residential group that Marianne Schneider Corey and I co-facilitated. Only brief segments of the weekend group could be included in the two-hour program, yet the program does illustrate significant events in the life of that group as it progressed from the initial stage to its ending.

In the initial stage, the focus is on building trust and focusing on the here-and-now. As co-leaders, we set the stage by exploring ground rules for the group and assisting members in developing goals for the three days. In the transition stage, identifying and challenging member fears, hesitations, and resistance is the main topic. During this stage, the level of trust deepens and members begin, reluctantly, to talk about personal material.

The working stage is characterized by a high level of trust, clearer goals, and members exploring feelings, ideas, and beliefs. As co-leaders, we help members explore their issues by focusing on the here-and-now so that members are not just "talking about" their issues but actually are experiencing them. Group cohesiveness is high, and members interact with each other with less reliance on the leaders. In the ending stage, the group reviews what they have learned, discussing how they will put those learnings into action and preparing for ending the group.

## Guidelines for Critiquing Various Approaches to Group Therapy

The *Evolution of a Group* program shows the stages of one group experience. Chapter 18 gives you a general picture of how different counseling approaches could be applied to the same group, providing practical examples of the advantages and disadvantages of each approach. Use the following questions as a guide in your class and discuss what aspects you like best (and least) about each approach. Then explore ways to integrate several approaches in your own leadership style—selectively borrowing concepts and procedures from all of the therapies—and begin to develop your own theory of group counseling.

### Using the Psychoanalytic Approach

1. What is the psychoanalytic view of resistance? How might resistance be explored from a psychoanalytic perspective?

2. What are some ways that focusing on the here-and-now can illuminate conflicts from the past? How can working with past themes be integrated with an exploration of what is occurring in the context of the group?
3. What examples of transference can you find in the group depicted in Chapter 18?
4. With what specific kinds of groups do you think psychoanalytic concepts and techniques are most suitable? What would you most want to incorporate in your style from this approach?

## Using the Adlerian Approach

1. If you were using the Adlerian approach, how would you go about getting early recollections from members, and how would you use them?
2. What possibilities can you see in using the group as a way to recreate the original family of the members? What are some ways in which work with the family constellation could be included in a group context? What family-of-origin issues did you see being played out in the *Evolution of a Group* program?
3. Adlerians are interested in the personal goals of members, including a focus on what they are working toward and what kind of life they want. Applied to the group members described in the chapter, how might you work with the various goals of members?
4. At what stage of a group's development do you think Adlerian concepts and techniques are most appropriate? What concepts and techniques would you want to draw from in this approach?

## Using Psychodrama

1. How could the group leaders "warm up" the group? Would you use any of these techniques in your group work?
2. What value did you see the co-leaders placing on reenacting past events or enacting anticipated situations?
3. What examples of role-playing situations stood out for you? What value do you see in encouraging members to role-play?
4. With what kinds of groups would you most be inclined to draw upon psychodrama? At what stage of a group's development would psychodramatic procedures be most effective? What do you want to take from this approach?

## Using the Existential Approach

1. How might the theme "I have a hole in my soul" be explained and dealt with?
2. What are some existential themes that most struck you in the group described in this chapter?
3. From an existential perspective, how might you work with a member who expressed problems with feeling isolated?
4. At what stage of a group's development would an existentialist approach be most appropriate? With what types of group do you think an existential orientation is most useful?

## Using the Person-Centered Approach

1. What are some specific things the co-leaders did in this group to create and maintain trust? What lessons did you learn about how to establish trust?

2. Do you think this group or any particular members in it *need* more direction and structure than is illustrated?

3. From reading this chapter, what is your sense about the direction provided by the co-leaders? Could they be seen as person-centered, and if so, how?

4. At what stage of a group's development might this approach be of the most value? What do you want to draw on from the approach?

## Using the Gestalt Approach

1. What are some ways to creatively work with the metaphors group members use? How might you explore a member's wall that keeps people at a distance? How could you work with the statement, "I feel that I've been stabbed in my core, in my heart."

2. If a member in this group wanted to work on a dream that related to emptiness, how might a Gestalt leader carry this out?

3. What are some specific examples of Gestalt methods that were used in this group?

4. At what stage of a group's development do you see Gestalt therapy as being most useful and appropriate?

## Using Transactional Analysis

1. How would the TA group leaders (as opposed to psychoanalytic leaders) work with a member's problem of feeling not good enough or of striving for perfection?

2. TA uses contracts between the leaders and the members. How do you think contracts will work in this group?

3. What role would examining old decisions and making new ones play in this group's work? What are some examples of early decisions made by some of the members in this group?

4. At what stage of a group's development do you think TA is most useful? What concepts and techniques do you want to use from TA?

## Using a Cognitive Behavioral Approach

1. If you were a cognitive behavioral leader, how would you begin the group? What are the typical steps and sequences in a cognitive behavioral group?

2. How would cognitive behavioral leaders work with this group, as contrasted with psychoanalytic leaders? Existential leaders? Gestalt leaders?

3. What are some examples of cognitive behavioral work that was done with members of this group?

4. At what stage of a group would cognitive behavioral methods be most appropriate? Which of these methods are you most likely to use in your group leading?

## Using Rational Emotive Behavior Therapy

1. What are some examples of member statements where you might apply REBT techniques?

2. What are the possibilities for dealing with a member who fears rejection?

3. How might REBT leaders deal with a member with a problem pertaining to what he or she did not get as a child? How would this intervention differ from what person-centered therapists would do? From what leaders using psychodrama would do?

4. At what stage in a group would REBT be most appropriate? What might you take from REBT and use in your style of leading?

## Using Reality Therapy

1. From the reality therapy perspective, how would you respond to members who blame their past for their current problems?
2. How might you get members to evaluate their current behavior?
3. In what ways would you assist members in formulating a plan for action? How is what members are doing in the present related to making plans for change and committing themselves to this program?
4. At what stage in the group's development would reality therapy be most useful?

## Using Solution-Focused Brief Therapy

1. From the solution-focused therapy perspective, how would you respond to members who are intent on talking about their problems?
2. How might you encourage members to shift from a problem track to a solution track?
3. In what ways would you assist members in sharing exceptions to a problem? How might this increase group cohesion?
4. At what stage in the group's development would solution-focused methods be most useful? With what kinds of groups would this orientation be most useful?

# Practice in Developing Your Own Therapeutic Approach

Now that you have thought about applying specific group counseling approaches in working with the same group, consider how you can integrate several approaches in your own leadership style. Explore these questions as a way of clarifying your personal perspective on working with groups:

1. What specific techniques would you be inclined to use in working with this group during the first few sessions? As the group reached a working stage, what are some cognitive, emotive, and behavioral methods you would be most likely to employ with each of the themes illustrated? What techniques might you use during the final stage as a way of helping these members consolidate their learning?
2. Select one of the themes explored in the group and think of ways you could work creatively with this theme by combining two or more models of group therapy. What theoretical approaches are you most likely to blend? What techniques from the various theories are you interested in learning more about? What are some ways of working with the same theme with different techniques?
3. Which themes of this group do you think you might have the most difficulty working with as a group leader? Who are the members that you would find the most challenging to work with, and why? What are some ways you could draw on your life experiences to enhance the themes illustrated in this group?
4. If you had to select one primary theoretical orientation as a guide to your practice, which would you select? Why?
5. Using a primary theoretical orientation, what would be some of the key concepts from other approaches that you would want to incorporate into your primary orientation?
6. What do you consider to be some of the advantages of drawing concepts and techniques from various theoretical approaches as a framework for guiding your practice in group work? What are some of the disadvantages of an integrative approach to group counseling?

7. What do you consider to be some of the advantages of working within the framework of a single theoretical orientation as a basis for guiding your practice in group work? What are some of the disadvantages of working with one primary theoretical orientation to group counseling?

8. If your group were composed of culturally diverse members, would you be inclined to modify any of your techniques? If so, what kinds of modifications can you see yourself making?

9. Again, in thinking of a culturally diverse group, which of the theories that you have studied do you think would be most applicable in your group? Why? Which theories do you think would have the least applicability? Why?

10. As you reflect on your personal style of group leadership, think of what kind of co-leader you would most like to work with and especially reflect on specific characteristics you would want in a co-leader. Would you look for a person who shared your primary theoretical orientation, or would you want a co-leader with a different theoretical perspective? Before you would actually co-facilitate a group, imagine that you are meeting with this person to discuss your respective perspectives. What would you most want to tell your co-leader about your approach? What would you be most interested in knowing about your co-leader?

11. In addition to reading about group work, what are some specific ways that you can think of to develop and refine your personal style of group facilitation? What are some things you can do to challenge yourself that might result in deepening your approach to group work?

12. What kind of group would you be most interested in forming and facilitating? What can you do to learn more about the population that is likely to be a part of this group? How could you learn more about organizing and actually facilitating this kind of group?

13. In what ways can you involve the members of your group in working with you collaboratively? What can you do to enlist the cooperation of the members of your group? Can you think of ways to empower the members of your group?

14. As a part of your leadership approach, think of accountability and ways to assess the on-going process of your group. What are some of your ideas regarding how you can include assessment as a part of every group session?

15. What are some ideas you have for evaluating the outcomes of your group as the group is moving toward termination? What specific things would you most want to know from the members of your group regarding their experience in this group?

# Comprehension Check and General Test

This test is designed to help you assess your understanding of the basic concepts of the textbook. Take it toward the end of the term to determine which areas you need to study further. A scoring sheet is given in Appendix II. Consider outlining the essay questions given after the objective test. Another set of questions, similar in format and content, is available to instructors.

This test will help you prepare for an objective test if such a test is given as part of your course. Select the *one best* answer.

## Multiple-Choice Items

_____ 1. A major difference between group therapy and group counseling lies
   a. in their techniques.
   b. in the group process.
   c. in the goals for the group.

_____ 2. Which of the following is *not* true of psychoeducational groups?
   a. They impart information.
   b. They teach people how to solve problems.
   c. They help clients learn to create their own support systems outside of the group.
   d. They tend to be long term.

_____ 3. Which of the following is *not* a similarity between self-help groups and therapy groups?
   a. Both are led by qualified professionals.
   b. Both encourage support and stress the value of affiliation.
   c. Both aim for behavioral change.
   d. Both make use of group process.

_____ 4. In self-help groups, the focus tends to be on
   a. discussing the external causes of members' problems.
   b. developing strategies to deal with environmental pressures and barriers.
   c. stressing a common identity based on a common life situation.
   d. all of the above.

_____ 5. If you are involved in group work with culturally diverse populations, it will be important for you to
   a. be an expert on each of the populations.
   b. accept the challenge of modifying your strategies to meet the unique needs of the members.

        c. be of the same ethnic background as the members in your group.

        d. do all of the above.

_____ 6. Which of the following is an advantage of group work with multicultural populations?

        a. Members gain from the power and strength of collective group feedback.

        b. Modeling operates in groups.

        c. In groups people learn that they are not alone in their struggles.

        d. Cross-cultural universality often exists in such groups.

        e. All of the above are advantages.

_____ 7. A limitation of group work in a multicultural context is that

        a. groups have been proved ineffective in working with ethnic clients.

        b. many ethnic clients consider it shameful to talk about their personal problems in front of others.

        c. ethnic clients will not be able to develop trust in a group setting.

        d. there is no basis for sharing common struggles or common pain.

_____ 8. Which of the following is *not* an example of Western values?

        a. interdependence

        b. freedom

        c. responsibility

        d. achievement

_____ 9. Assume that you are leading a group and a particular ethnic client tends to be very quiet. Which of the following might best explain this silence?

        a. This is surely a sign of a resistant client.

        b. This is evidence that this client does not want to be in the group.

        c. The silence may indicate politeness and a sense of respect.

        d. This hesitation is best interpreted as a stubborn refusal to be open.

_____ 10. If you are intending to form a group composed of culturally diverse members, it would be important to

        a. prepare the clients for the group experience.

        b. have a general understanding of the cultural values of your clients.

        c. develop patience in accepting differences in behavior.

        d. help members clearly identify why they are in a group.

        e. do all of the above.

_____ 11. Which of the following captures the essence of informed consent?

        a. having members sign a contract before joining a group

        b. telling members in some detail about the nature and purpose of the group

        c. having members decide on all of the activities of the group

        d. making sure that groups will always be composed of voluntary members

_____ 12. The principle of informed consent applies to

        a. voluntary groups only.

        b. involuntary groups only.

        c. both voluntary and involuntary groups.

_____ 13. On the matter of coercion and pressure in a group, members should know that

        a. some pressure is to be expected as part of group process.

        b. they have a right to be protected against undue pressure.

_____ c. coercion to make acceptable decisions may be a part of group procedure.

d. they may well be pressured to participate in threatening nonverbal exercises.

e. both (a) and (b) are true.

_____ 14. On the issue of psychological risks in groups, what can be safely said?

a. In a well-designed group, there are really no psychological risks.

b. Because groups can be catalysts for change, they also contain risks.

c. Members can be given guarantees that a group will not involve risks.

d. There are risks only when members are not properly screened.

_____ 15. Advanced competencies have been specified by the ASGW for which groups?

a. task work groups

b. psychoeducational groups

c. counseling and psychotherapy groups

d. all of the above

e. none of the above

_____ 16. A training group for beginning leaders focuses primarily on

a. problems the group leaders are having in their personal lives.

b. the skills necessary for effective intervention.

c. a discussion of theories of group counseling.

d. learning structured techniques and exercises for most problems that might arise within a group.

_____ 17. Which of the following would *not* be considered one of a group member's rights?

a. the right to expect protection from verbal or physical assaults

b. the right to expect complete confidentiality

c. the right to know the leader's qualifications

d. the right to help from the group leader in developing personal goals

e. the right to expect freedom from undue group pressure

_____ 18. What is the recommended course of action regarding freedom to leave a group?

a. Members should be able to leave at any time they wish without any explanation.

b. Members should never be allowed to leave a group once they join.

c. Members who are thinking of leaving should bring the issue up for discussion in the session.

d. Members should bring up the issue of leaving privately with the leader but not with the group.

e. All of the above are true.

_____ 19. Regarding the right to confidentiality, which statement is *false*?

a. Confidentiality is one of the key norms of behavior in a group.

b. Confidentiality is often on the minds of people when they initially join a group.

c. Members who are in an involuntary group have no rights to confidentiality.

d. It is a good practice to remind participants from time to time of the danger of inadvertently revealing confidences.

_____ 20. The key to a group leader's avoiding a malpractice suit consists of maintaining

a. reasonable practices.

b. ordinary practices.

c. prudent practices.

d. all of the above.

e. none of the above.

_____ 21. Which is the correct sequence of the stages of a group?
   a. transition, initial, working, final
   b. initial, transition, final, working
   c. initial, transition, working, final
   d. transition, initial, final, working

_____ 22. Which stage is characterized by dealing with conflict, defensiveness, and resistance?
   a. working stage
   b. transition stage
   c. final stage
   d. initial stage

_____ 23. Inclusion and identity are the primary tasks of which stage of a group?
   a. initial stage
   b. transition stage
   c. working stage
   d. final stage

_____ 24. Teaching participants some general guidelines of group functioning, developing group norms, and assisting members to express their fears and expectations are all group leadership functions during the
   a. working stage.
   b. transition stage.
   c. initial and exploration stage.
   d. final stage.

_____ 25. Which stage is generally characterized by increased anxiety and defensiveness?
   a. initial stage
   b. transition stage
   c. working stage
   d. final stage

_____ 26. Cohesion and productivity are most closely associated with the
   a. working stage.
   b. transition stage.
   c. initial and exploration stage.
   d. final stage.

_____ 27. Conflict and struggle for control are most likely to appear in the
   a. working stage.
   b. transition stage.
   c. initial and exploration stage.
   d. final stage.

_____ 28. Resistance in a group can be seen as
   a. a common form of defense.
   b. material for productive exploration.
   c. a bad attitude on the part of the member.
   d. something that should be avoided at all costs.
   e. both (a) and (b).

_____ 29. When attempting to organize and begin a group in an agency, it is important to
   a. be aware of the politics involved in the setting in which you work.

b. give up the idea if no one else on the staff seems excited about it.

c. expect the complete support and encouragement of your co-workers.

d. think of ways to outsmart the agency director.

_____ 30. When working with involuntary group members, it is important to

a. expect that they will figure out on their own the best way to participate without guidance.

b. discuss with them ways to use the time beneficially.

c. insist that they participate with enthusiasm.

d. assume that they will understand the basic group procedures after being at the first group meeting.

## True/False Items

_____ 31. Psychoeducational groups, or groups characterized by some central theme, have recently declined in popularity.

_____ 32. Structured groups are often based on a learning theory model and use cognitive behavioral procedures.

_____ 33. The terms *psychoeducational group* and *structured group* are often used interchangeably.

_____ 34. Essentially, task groups and therapy groups have the same goals.

_____ 35. Counseling groups deal with relatively normal problems.

_____ 36. The literature dealing with multicultural counseling indicates that ethnic minority clients are making full use of mental health services.

_____ 37. Group leaders may encounter resistance from clients with certain cultured backgrounds because the leaders are using traditional white, middle-class values to interpret these clients' experiences.

_____ 38. An advantage of group work with ethnic clients is that members can gain from the power and strength of collective group feedback.

_____ 39. A disadvantage of group work with ethnic clients is their reluctance to disclose personal material or to share family secrets.

_____ 40. If an ethnic client displays silence in a group, this behavior is most probably a sign of resistance.

_____ 41. It is best not to inform clients of their rights as members before they join a group, for this generally reduces their commitment to work.

_____ 42. It is clearly unethical to form groups composed of involuntary members.

_____ 43. It is a good practice to remind participants from time to time of the danger of inadvertently breaking confidentiality.

_____ 44. One way to establish trust is to reassure members that whatever they disclose in a session will never go outside of the group, under any circumstances.

_____ 45. It is realistic to assume that adequately led groups, by their very nature, eliminate all psychological risks to the participants.

_____ 46. It is unwise to forewarn participants of the psychological risks of being in a group, for this is likely to create a tense climate and lead to extreme caution.

_____ 47. It is important that group leaders be clear about their own values and express them openly when it is relevant and appropriate to the work of the group.

_____ 48. As a group counselor, you may face the need in a malpractice action to justify the techniques you have used.

_____ 49. Group leaders who possess personal power generally meet their needs at the expense of the members and are therefore unethical.

_____ 50. Research findings on leader self-disclosure clearly indicate that the more leaders disclose of their personal lives, the more their groups become self-directed and cohesive.

## Definition Items

Select the group leadership skill that is described by each phrase.

_____ 51. Identifying with clients by assuming their internal frames of reference.
a. sympathizing
b. empathizing
c. facilitating
d. reflecting
e. none of the above

_____ 52. Expressing concrete and honest reactions based on observation of members' behavior.
a. evaluating
b. initiating
c. clarifying
d. interpreting
e. giving feedback

_____ 53. Attending to verbal and nonverbal aspects of communication without judging or evaluating.
a. interpreting
b. reflecting feelings
c. active listening
d. facilitating
e. empathizing

_____ 54. Demonstrating desired behavior through actions.
a. modeling
b. clarifying
c. facilitating
d. evaluating
e. none of the above

_____ 55. Challenging participants to look at discrepancies between their words and actions, or verbal and nonverbal communication.
a. confronting
b. suggesting
c. clarifying
d. interpreting
e. initiating

_____ 56. Revealing one's reactions to here-and-now events in the group.
     a. restating
     b. empathizing
     c. confronting
     d. disclosing oneself
     e. linking

_____ 57. Promoting member-to-member interactions rather than focusing on member-to-leader interactions.
     a. summarizing
     b. linking
     c. suggesting
     d. reflecting feelings
     e. questioning

_____ 58. Safeguarding members from unnecessary psychological risks in the group.
     a. modeling
     b. linking
     c. goal setting
     d. interpreting
     e. protecting

_____ 59. Preparing a group to close a session or end its existence.
     a. restating
     b. terminating
     c. summarizing
     d. evaluating
     e. questioning

_____ 60. Planning specific goals for the group process and helping participants define concrete personal issues as the focus of work.
     a. supporting
     b. clarifying
     c. facilitating
     d. goal setting
     e. suggesting

## Conceptual Items

Items 61–85 present a series of related concepts or techniques pertaining to one therapeutic approach. *One item in the series of five does not fit with the other four items.* Identify the word or phrase that does not fit.

_____ 61. (a) life stages, (b) developmental crises, (c) psychosocial stages, (d) stress inoculation, (e) critical tasks

_____ 62. (a) fictional finalism, (b) basic mistakes, (c) A-B-C theory, (d) social interest, (e) style of life

_____ 63. (a) playing the projection, (b) the rehearsal experiment, (c) family modeling, (d) working with dreams, (e) making the rounds

_____ 64. (a) style of life, (b) openness to experience, (c) self-trust, (d) internal source of evaluation, (e) willingness to continue growing

_____ 65. (a) total behavior, (b) mistaken goals, (c) private logic, (d) early recollections, (e) family constellation

_____ 66. (a) congruence, (b) redecision, (c) internal source of evaluation, (d) unconditional positive regard, (e) accurate empathic understanding

_____ 67. (a) self-evaluations, (b) plan for action, (c) commitment, (d) unconditional positive regard, (e) quality world

_____ 68. (a) A-B-C theory, (b) irrational beliefs, (c) choice theory, (d) cognitive restructuring, (e) self-defeating thought patterns

_____ 69. (a) present-centered awareness, (b) the concept of the now, (c) unfinished business, (d) life script analysis, (e) bringing the past into the here-and-now

_____ 70. (a) relaxation training, (b) the dialogue experiment, (c) exaggeration technique, (d) reversal technique, (e) present-centered dream work

_____ 71. (a) injunctions, (b) existential anxiety, (c) early decisions, (d) games, (e) redecisions

_____ 72. (a) early recollections, (b) strokes, (c) lifescripts, (d) games, (e) early decisions

_____ 73. (a) social skills training, (b) social effectiveness training, (c) mindfulness and acceptance methods, (d) assertiveness training, (e) analysis of transference

_____ 74. (a) the dialogue experiment, (b) cognitive restructuring, (c) exaggeration experiment, (d) rehearsal experiment, (e) making the rounds

_____ 75. (a) games, (b) rackets, (c) scripting, (d) catharsis, (e) Parent, Adult, Child

_____ 76. (a) figure-ground, (b) unfinished business, (c) ego states, (d) contact and resistance to contact, (e) energy and blocks to energy

_____ 77. (a) modeling, (b) coaching, (c) imitation, (d) social learning, (e) observational learning

_____ 78. (a) multimodal therapy, (b) BASIC I.D., (c) technical eclecticism, (d) therapeutic flexibility and versatility, (e) choice theory

_____ 79. (a) Gestalt experiments, (b) assertiveness training, (c) stress management training, (d) social skills training, (e) social effectiveness training

_____ 80. (a) total behavior, (b) choice theory, (c) existential/phenomenological orientation, (d) redecisional therapy, (e) WDEP

_____ 81. (a) establishing the relationship, (b) exploring the individual's dynamics, (c) working through transference neurosis, (d) encouraging insight, (e) helping with re-orientation

_____ 82. (a) solution-focused therapy, (b) the miracle question, (c) exception questions, (d) focus on the future, (e) focus on the past

_____ 83. (a) disputation of irrational beliefs, (b) cognitive homework, (c) rational emotive imagery, (d) shame-attacking exercises, (e) dialogue experiment

_____ 84. (a) lifestyle assessment, (b) scaling, (c) exception questions, (d) miracle question, (e) questions of difference

_____ 85. (a) reexperiencing one's past, (b) developing an action plan, (c) getting a commitment, (d) refusing to accept excuses, (e) focusing on what one is doing

## Multiple-Choice Items

_____ 86. Many analytically oriented group therapists have a leadership style that is characterized by
a. objectivity, warm detachment, and relative anonymity.
b. objectivity, aloofness, and strict anonymity.

     c. subjectivity, mutuality, and self-disclosure.

     d. rationality, impersonality, and coolness.

_____ 87. Adler stresses

     a. the value of transference for group therapy.

     b. the purposeful nature of behavior.

     c. the role of biological determinants of behavior.

     d. total behavior as a concept of control theory.

     e. understanding the client's quality world.

_____ 88. Psychodrama was developed by

     a. Fritz Perls.

     b. Carl Rogers.

     c. J. L. Moreno.

     d. William Glasser.

     e. Albert Ellis.

_____ 89. The function of the existential group leader is

     a. to understand the member's subjective world.

     b. to explore the member's past history.

     c. to challenge each member to change irrational beliefs.

     d. to create experiments for group members.

_____ 90. The congruence of a group leader implies

     a. empathy.

     b. immediacy.

     c. genuineness.

     d. unconditional positive regard.

     e. objectivity.

_____ 91. Which of the following is *not* a key concept of the Gestalt group?

     a. awareness

     b. unfinished business

     c. understanding one's irrational beliefs

     d. here-and-now focus

     e. paying attention to blocked energy

_____ 92. The founder of transactional analysis is

     a. Robert Goulding.

     b. Eric Berne.

     c. J. L. Moreno.

     d. William Glasser.

     e. Albert Bandura.

_____ 93. Which of the following techniques is *not* considered a cognitive behavioral technique?

     a. mindfulness

     b. miracle questions

     c. cognitive restructuring

     d. self-reinforcement

     e. coaching

_____ 94. REBT methodology includes all of the following procedures except

     a. confrontation.

        b. emotive methods.

        c. analysis of one's lifescript.

        d. cognitive methods.

        e. behavioral methods.

_____ 95. Which of the following is *not* a key concept of reality therapy?

        a. Members must make commitments.

        b. Members focus on early childhood issues.

        c. Members make an evaluation of their behavior.

        d. Members focus on the present, not the past.

        e. Members look at ways in which they are choosing their total behavior.

_____ 96. In an analytic group, free association might be used for all of the following except

        a. working on dreams.

        b. encouraging spontaneity among members.

        c. promoting interaction between members.

        d. getting at unconscious material.

        e. getting clients to evaluate their quality world.

_____ 97. All of the following are key concepts underlying the Adlerian group except

        a. teleology

        b. social interest.

        c. creativity and choice.

        d. developing a lifestyle.

        e. the A-B-C theory of personality.

_____ 98. Which of the following techniques is least likely to be used in psychodrama?

        a. scaling technique

        b. doubling

        c. future projection

        d. role reversal

        e. soliloquy

_____ 99. In an existential group, which technique would be considered essential?

        a. role playing

        b. rational emotive imagery

        c. homework

        d. dream analysis

        e. none of the above

_____ 100. Which best captures the role and functions of a person-centered group counselor?

        a. teacher

        b. facilitator

        c. expert

        d. companion

_____ 101. Which of the following is generally *not* a technique used in Gestalt groups?

        a. experiments with dialogues

        b. making the rounds

        c. teaching rational thinking

        d. working with dreams

        e. focusing on nonverbal communication

_____ 102. Which of the following is *not* a key concept of TA groups?
    a. lifestyle assessment
    b. analysis of ego states
    c. strokes
    d. script analysis
    e. games

_____ 103. During the initial stage of a cognitive behavioral group, the concern of the group leader is to
    a. identify problematic behavior.
    b. develop baseline data.
    c. teach members about the group process.
    d. conduct an assessment of each member's current behavior.
    e. do all of the above.

_____ 104. In an REBT group, role playing involves
    a. a catharsis.
    b. a cognitive restructuring of beliefs.
    c. a return to some event during early childhood.
    d. promoting an expression of feelings between members.
    e. none of the above.

_____ 105. Which of the following is a typical procedure used in reality therapy groups?
    a. conducting an assessment of one's family constellation
    b. exploring exceptions to one's presenting problems
    c. fostering transference reactions toward the leader
    d. analyzing ego states
    e. evaluating current behavior

_____ 106. Dreams are explored in
    a. Gestalt groups.
    b. psychoanalytic groups.
    c. psychodrama groups.
    d. all of the above.
    e. none of the above.

_____ 107. The object relations theory is associated with
    a. solution-focused brief therapy.
    b. Gestalt therapy.
    c. Adlerian therapy.
    d. reality therapy.
    e. none of the above.

_____ 108. Creativity and choice are stressed in
    a. Adlerian therapy.
    b. existential therapy.
    c. person-centered therapy.
    d. all of the above.
    e. none of the above.

_____ 109. Insight is stressed in all of these approaches except
    a. psychoanalytic therapy.
    b. psychodrama.

c. solution-focused brief therapy.

d. Gestalt therapy.

e. TA.

_____ 110. The process of skillful questioning would be used mostly by a group leader with which theoretical orientation?

a. person-centered therapy

b. reality therapy

c. Gestalt therapy

d. existential therapy

e. none of the above

_____ 111. Unfinished business and avoidance are key concepts of

a. Gestalt therapy.

b. reality therapy.

c. cognitive behavioral therapy.

d. rational emotive behavior therapy.

e. none of the above.

_____ 112. Which type of group serves the function of re-creating the original family so that members can work through their unresolved problems?

a. REBT

b. behavioral

c. psychoanalytic

d. TA

e. person-centered

_____ 113. Individual Psychology is another name for

a. psychoanalytic therapy.

b. Adlerian therapy.

c. existential therapy.

d. reality therapy.

e. person-centered therapy.

_____ 114. Contracts and homework assignments are most likely to be used in

a. TA groups.

b. cognitive behavioral therapy groups.

c. reality therapy groups.

d. REBT groups.

e. all of the above.

_____ 115. Which approach would be least interested in the exploration of early childhood experiences?

a. reality therapy

b. psychoanalytic therapy

c. Gestalt therapy

d. Adlerian therapy

e. TA

_____ 116. A basic premise that we are not the victims of circumstances because we choose our behavior is emphasized in

a. existential therapy.

b. reality therapy.

c. person-centered therapy.

d. TA.

e. all of the above.

_____ 117. Concepts of introjection, projection, retroflection, confluence, and deflection are part of

a. Adlerian therapy.

b. psychodrama.

c. Gestalt therapy.

d. existential therapy.

e. TA.

_____ 118. The concept of basic psychological life positions is part of

a. psychoanalytic therapy.

b. TA.

c. psychodrama.

d. REBT.

e. none of the above.

_____ 119. Which theory would be most concerned with understanding and exploring an individual's developmental stages?

a. TA

b. psychoanalytic therapy

c. solution-focused brief therapy

d. REBT

e. none of the above

_____ 120. The socioteleological approach that holds that people are primarily motivated by social forces and striving to achieve certain goals is

a. person-centered therapy.

b. existential therapy.

c. reality therapy.

d. Adlerian therapy.

e. solution-focused brief therapy.

_____ 121. Which type of group counselor would tend to give the least degree of direction?

a. REBT therapist

b. person-centered therapist

c. Gestalt therapist

d. reality therapist

e. cognitive behavioral therapist

_____ 122. The here-and-now is emphasized in

a. psychodrama.

b. existential therapy.

c. person-centered therapy.

d. Gestalt therapy.

e. all of the above.

_____ 123. Mindfulness and acceptance methods are associated with which theoretical approach?

a. cognitive behavioral therapy

b. TA

c. reality therapy

d. Adlerian therapy

e. existential therapy

_____ 124. The A-B-C theory is associated with

a. reality therapy.

b. TA.

c. behavior therapy.

d. REBT.

e. solution-focused brief therapy.

_____ 125. A focus on ego states would occur in

a. Gestalt groups.

b. Adlerian groups.

c. TA groups.

d. psychodrama groups.

e. all of the above.

_____ 126. Which approach most relies on empirical research to validate its techniques?

a. reality therapy

b. cognitive behavioral therapy

c. person-centered therapy

d. existential therapy

e. solution-focused brief therapy

_____ 127. Cognitive homework is most likely to be assigned in

a. psychodrama groups.

b. psychoanalytic groups.

c. REBT groups.

d. reality therapy groups.

e. Gestalt groups.

_____ 128. Modeling would be important in which type of group?

a. reality therapy

b. cognitive behavioral therapy

c. REBT

d. existential therapy

e. all of the above

_____ 129. Choice theory is a basic part of the practice of

a. solution-focused brief therapy.

b. REBT.

c. reality therapy.

d. Adlerian therapy.

e. existential therapy.

_____ 130. The role of the family would be stressed mostly in which type of group?

a. psychodrama group

b. behavioral group

c. existential group

d. Gestalt group

e. Adlerian group

_____ 131. Injunctions, early decisions, and redecisions are key concepts stressed in which type of group?
   a. Adlerian group
   b. TA group
   c. Gestalt group
   d. REBT group
   e. reality therapy group

_____ 132. Which approach would be most likely to focus on an expression and exploration of feelings?
   a. cognitive behavioral therapy
   b. REBT
   c. reality therapy
   d. Gestalt therapy
   e. none of the above

_____ 133. Significant developments in dealing with borderline and narcissistic personality disorders have occurred within which theory?
   a. solution-focused brief therapy
   b. TA
   c. Gestalt therapy
   d. person-centered therapy
   e. none of the above

_____ 134. Dealing with the present is stressed in
   a. psychodrama.
   b. Gestalt therapy.
   c. existential therapy.
   d. reality therapy.
   e. all of the above.

_____ 135. Which approach does _not_ emphasize techniques?
   a. Adlerian therapy
   b. psychodrama
   c. existential therapy
   d. cognitive behavioral therapy
   e. REBT

_____ 136. Which theory focuses on cognition?
   a. Adlerian
   b. Gestalt
   c. REBT
   d. psychodrama
   e. two of the above

_____ 137. The miracle question is a technique used in
   a. TA.
   b. REBT.
   c. Gestalt therapy.
   d. solution-focused therapy.
   e. reality therapy.

_____ 138. A lifestyle investigation, which would focus on family background and would reveal a pattern of basic mistakes, would be used in
    a. psychoanalytic therapy.
    b. Adlerian therapy.
    c. cognitive behavioral therapy.
    d. REBT.
    e. existential therapy.

_____ 139. Which type of group leader is most likely to focus on energy and blocks to energy?
    a. Adlerian leader
    b. Gestalt leader
    c. psychoanalytic leader
    d. TA leader
    e. person-centered leader

_____ 140. The therapeutic conditions of congruence, unconditional positive regard, and empathy are emphasized in
    a. psychoanalytic therapy.
    b. reality therapy.
    c. TA.
    d. person-centered therapy.
    e. none of the above.

_____ 141. Role playing is likely to be used in
    a. psychodrama.
    b. Gestalt therapy.
    c. REBT.
    d. cognitive behavioral therapy.
    e. all of the above.

_____ 142. Which approach stresses the total behavior of doing, thinking, feeling, and physiology?
    a. REBT
    b. reality therapy
    c. person-centered therapy
    d. psychoanalytic therapy
    e. TA

_____ 143. Which approach emphasizes the personal qualities of the group leader rather than the techniques of leading?
    a. existential
    b. person-centered
    c. REBT
    d. solution-focused
    e. two of the above

_____ 144. The approach that teaches members how to identify irrational beliefs and substitute rational beliefs is
    a. reality therapy.
    b. REBT.
    c. TA.

_____ d. Gestalt therapy.

e. solution-focused brief therapy.

_____ 145. Social skills training groups most rely on which type of techniques?

a. cognitive behavioral

b. TA

c. psychodramatic

d. reality therapy

e. Adlerian

_____ 146. In which type of group would members focus on their lifescripts through the process of script analysis?

a. psychoanalytic group

b. reality therapy group

c. cognitive behavioral group

d. Adlerian group

e. TA group

_____ 147. Shame-attacking exercises are likely to be used in which type of group?

a. reality therapy group

b. person-centered group

c. Gestalt group

d. REBT group

e. psychodrama group

_____ 148. Which theoretical approach would most contribute to teaching members coping skills to manage stress?

a. person-centered therapy

b. reality therapy

c. Adlerian therapy

d. cognitive behavioral therapy

e. Gestalt therapy

_____ 149. The group leader assumes the role of a teacher in which approach?

a. TA

b. reality therapy

c. cognitive behavioral therapy

d. REBT

e. all of the above

_____ 150. Which approach has the goal of uncovering unconscious conflicts and working through them?

a. person-centered therapy

b. reality therapy

c. psychoanalytic therapy

d. TA

e. solution-focused brief therapy

## Essay Questions for Review and Study

*Directions:* These questions are designed as a study guide to help you pull together some central ideas in the textbook. Strive to write your answers briefly, using your own words.

1. What are the advantages of a group format for special populations (children, adolescents, or adults)?
2. Differentiate between
   a. group psychotherapy and group counseling.
   b. group psychotherapy and self-help groups.
3. If you were working in a setting with clients representing diverse cultural backgrounds, what would you see as your major challenges as a group leader? How might you meet some of these challenges?
4. What are a few of the advantages and disadvantages of multicultural group counseling?
5. What are some guidelines that could help you design and conduct groups with culturally diverse populations?
6. Assume that you are a counselor in a community agency. No groups are being offered, and you see a need for several types of groups. What course of action, if any, might you be inclined to take?
7. Review the section in Chapter 2 that deals with the group leader as a person. What are your major personal characteristics that would help you and hinder you in your work as a group leader?
8. In the same chapter, review the section dealing with special problems and issues for beginning group leaders. Discuss your single most important concern.
9. Assume that you are working in an agency and would like to form a group. The director would like you to co-lead your groups. What specific things would you look for in selecting a co-leader?
10. Discuss what you see as your major tasks at each of the stages in the development of a group.
11. Assume that you were in a job interview and were asked this question: "Tell us about the theoretical orientation that guides your practice as a group counselor." How would you answer?
12. There are different styles of group leadership. Again, in a job interview, how might you describe your own personal style of leadership?
13. Think of a particular group that you might conduct, and describe briefly what factors you would consider in forming it.
14. The stages of a group do not generally flow neatly and predictably in the order described in the textbook. Why is it important that you have a clear understanding of the characteristics associated with the development of a group?
15. If you had to select one theory that comes closest to your thinking and that helps you in your practice as a group counselor, which would it be? Explain the reasons for your selection.
16. Dreams can be fruitfully explored by using several different therapy approaches. Show how you might work with a dream in a group format from these three perspectives: psychoanalytic, psychodrama, and Gestalt therapy.
17. Compare the goals of solution-focused and Gestalt groups; contrast the differences in techniques between these two approaches.
18. Discuss some common denominators of these various approaches to group counseling: Adlerian therapy, TA, REBT, reality therapy, solution-focused therapy.
19. Select one of the following possible combinations and discuss what you see as the merits of merging the concepts and techniques of the two approaches as applied to group counseling: Gestalt with TA, Gestalt with REBT, or Gestalt with reality therapy.

20. Assume that you are leading a group with culturally diverse members. Are there any concepts and techniques from the various approaches that you would find particularly useful?

21. Discuss some of the ways of combining existential themes with cognitive behavioral techniques. What are the possibilities of a merger between the existential and cognitive behavioral approaches as applied to group counseling?

22. What are some commonalities between a person-centered group and an existential group? What are some basic differences?

23. How would you describe your role as a group counselor to a new group? What do you see as your major leadership functions?

24. How would you assess the outcomes of a group that you were leading?

25. Discuss the role that theory plays in the practice of group counseling. How does the theory that a leader holds influence the interventions he or she makes?

# Scoring Key for Chapter Quizzes

| ITEM NO. | PSYCHOANALYTIC CH. 6 | ADLERIAN CH. 7 | PSYCHODRAMA CH. 8 | EXISTENTIAL CH. 9 | PERSON-CENTERED CH. 10 | GESTALT CH. 11 | TA CH. 12 | COGNITIVE BEHAVIORAL THERAPY CH. 13 | REBT CH. 14 | REALITY THERAPY CH. 15 | SOLUTION-FOCUSED BRIEF THERAPY CH. 16 | ITEM NO. |
|---|---|---|---|---|---|---|---|---|---|---|---|---|
| 1. | F | T | T | F | T | F | F | T | T | T | T | 1. |
| 2. | T | T | F | T | T | T | F | F | F | T | T | 2. |
| 3. | F | T | F | T | T | F | T | F | T | T | T | 3. |
| 4. | F | F | T | F | F | F | F | T | T | F | F | 4. |
| 5. | F | T | T | T | F | T | T | F | T | F | T | 5. |
| 6. | T | F | F | F | T | T | T | T | F | F | F | 6. |
| 7. | F | F | F | F | F | F | T | T | F | F | T | 7. |
| 8. | T | F | T | F | T | F | T | T | T | T | F | 8. |
| 9. | T | T | F | T | T | T | F | F | T | F | F | 9. |
| 10. | T | T | F | F | T | T | T | T | T | T | F | 10. |
| 11. | a | b | a | b | d | e | d | d | c | b | c | 11. |
| 12. | b | e | d | c | b | c | e | b | a | a | d | 12. |
| 13. | e | a | b | c | e | a | b | a | c | d | d | 13. |
| 14. | c | e | c | b | e | d | d | c | a | a | b | 14. |
| 15. | e | c | b | d | b | e | d | d | e | b | a | 15. |
| 16. | c | b | c | b | b | c | c | c | d | b | c | 16. |
| 17. | e | d | e | b | a | e | b | d | e | d | d | 17. |
| 18. | a | c | e | c | b | a | d | e | d | d | d | 18. |
| 19. | c | d | c | a | a | b | e | e | a | a | a | 19. |
| 20. | b | b | e | a | c | b | a | d | c | b | a | 20. |

# Answer Key for Comprehension Check and General Test

| | | | | | | |
|---|---|---|---|---|---|---|
| 1. c | 2. d | 3. a | 4. d | 5. b | 6. e | 7. b |
| 8. a | 9. c | 10. e | 11. b | 12. c | 13. e | 14. b |
| 15. d | 16. b | 17. b | 18. c | 19. c | 20. d | 21. c |
| 22. b | 23. a | 24. c | 25. b | 26. a | 27. b | 28. e |
| 29. a | 30. b | 31. F | 32. T | 33. T | 34. F | 35. T |
| 36. F | 37. T | 38. T | 39. T | 40. F | 41. F | 42. F |
| 43. T | 44. F | 45. F | 46. F | 47. T | 48. T | 49. F |
| 50. F | 51. b | 52. e | 53. c | 54. a | 55. a | 56. d |
| 57. b | 58. e | 59. b | 60. d | 61. d | 62. c | 63. c |
| 64. a | 65. a | 66. b | 67. d | 68. c | 69. d | 70. a |
| 71. b | 72. a | 73. e | 74. b | 75. d | 76. c | 77. b |
| 78. e | 79. a | 80. d | 81. c | 82. e | 83. e | 84. a |
| 85. a | 86. a | 87. b | 88. c | 89. a | 90. c | 91. c |
| 92. b | 93. b | 94. c | 95. b | 96. e | 97. e | 98. a |
| 99. e | 100. b | 101. c | 102. a | 103. e | 104. b | 105. e |
| 106. d | 107. e | 108. d | 109. c | 110. b | 111. a | 112. c |
| 113. b | 114. e | 115. a | 116. e | 117. c | 118. b | 119. b |
| 120. d | 121. b | 122. e | 123. a | 124. d | 125. c | 126. b |
| 127. c | 128. e | 129. c | 130. e | 131. b | 132. d | 133. e |
| 134. e | 135. c | 136. e | 137. d | 138. b | 139. b | 140. d |
| 141. e | 142. b | 143. e | 144. b | 145. a | 146. e | 147. d |
| 148. d | 149. e | 150. c | | | | |

TO THE OWNER OF THIS BOOK:

I hope that you have found the *Student Manual for Theory and Practice of Group Counseling*, Seventh Edition, useful. So that this book can be improved in a future edition, would you take the time to complete this sheet and return it? Thank you.

School and address:_____

Department:_____

Instructor's name:_____

1.  What I like most about this book is:_____

_____

_____

2.  What I like least about this book is:

_____

_____

3.  My general reaction to this book is:

_____

_____

4.  The name of the course in which I used this book is:

_____

5.  Were all of the chapters of the book assigned for you to read?_____

    If not, which ones weren't?_____

6.  In the space below, or on a separate sheet of paper, please write specific suggestions for improving this book and anything else you'd care to share about your experience in using this book.

_____

_____

_____

_____

_____

_____

DO NOT STAPLE. PLEASE SEAL WITH

FOLD HERE

## BUSINESS REPLY MAIL
FIRST-CLASS MAIL        PERMIT NO. 34        BELMONT CA

POSTAGE WILL BE PAID BY ADDRESSEE

NO POSTAGE
NECESSARY
IF MAILED
IN THE
UNITED STATES

Attn:  Marquita Flemming, Counseling

BrooksCole/Thomson Learning
10 Davis Drive
Belmont, CA        94002-9801

FOLD HERE

OPTIONAL:

Your name:_____ Date: _____

May we quote you, either in promotion for the *Student Manual for Theory and Practice of Group Counseling*, Seventh Edition, or in future publishing ventures?

Yes: _____        No: _____

Sincerely yours,

*Gerald Corey*

TO THE OWNER OF THIS BOOK:

I hope that you have found the *Student Manual for Theory and Practice of Group Counseling*, Seventh Edition, useful. So that this book can be improved in a future edition, would you take the time to complete this sheet and return it? Thank you.

School and address:_____

Department:_____

Instructor's name:_____

1. What I like most about this book is:_____

_____

_____

2. What I like least about this book is:

_____

_____

3. My general reaction to this book is:

_____

_____

4. The name of the course in which I used this book is:

_____

5. Were all of the chapters of the book assigned for you to read?_____

   If not, which ones weren't?_____

6. In the space below, or on a separate sheet of paper, please write specific suggestions for improving this book and anything else you'd care to share about your experience in using this book.

_____

_____

_____

_____

_____

_____

DO NOT STAPLE. PLEASE SEAL WITH TAPE.

FOLD HERE

**THOMSON** ™

**BROOKS/COLE**

NO POSTAGE
NECESSARY
IF MAILED
IN THE
UNITED STATES

## BUSINESS REPLY MAIL
FIRST-CLASS MAIL     PERMIT NO. 34     BELMONT CA

POSTAGE WILL BE PAID BY ADDRESSEE

Attn: Marquita Flemming, Counseling

BrooksCole/Thomson Learning
10 Davis Drive
Belmont, CA     94002-9801

IIIι..ι.ιιΙΙΙ..ιΙΙ...ιΙΙΙ.ι.ι.ι.ΙΙ.....ιΙΙι.ιΙ

FOLD HERE

OPTIONAL:

Your name:_____ Date: _____

May we quote you, either in promotion for the *Student Manual for Theory and Practice of Group Counseling*, Seventh Edition, or in future publishing ventures?

Yes: _____    No: _____

Sincerely yours,

*Gerald Corey*